The RISE OF THE LATTER-DAY SAINTS

THE RISE OF THE LATTER-DAY SAINTS

The Journals and Histories of
Newel Knight

Edited by
Michael Hubbard MacKay & William G. Hartley

With the assistance of
Nathan Astel, Dallin Wright, and Thomas Sorensen

Published by the Religious Studies Center, Brigham Young University, Provo, Utah, in cooperation with Deseret Book Company, Salt Lake City.
Visit us at rsc.byu.edu.

© 2019 by Brigham Young University. All rights reserved.

Printed in the United States of America by Sheridan Books, Inc.

Deseret Book is a registered trademark of Deseret Book Company.
Visit us at DeseretBook.com.

Any uses of this material beyond those allowed by the exemptions in US copyright law, such as section 107, "Fair Use," and section 108, "Library Copying," require the written permission of the publisher, Religious Studies Center, 185 HGB, Brigham Young University, Provo, Utah 84602. The views expressed herein are the responsibility of the authors and do not necessarily represent the position of Brigham Young University or the Religious Studies Center.

Cover and interior design by Emily V. Strong.

ISBN 978-1-9443-9483-7

Library of Congress Control Number: 2019937559

Dedicated to the Newel Knight family
and the late William Hartley

CONTENTS

Acknowledgments	ix
Introduction	xi

PART 1
New York, Ohio, and Missouri, 1800–1834   1

PART 2
Kirtland, 1834–36   73

PART 3
Missouri, 1836–39   95

PART 4
Nauvoo, 1839–45   119

PART 5
The Nauvoo Exodus and
the "Mountain Expedition," 1845–46   161

Bibliography	211
Index	221
About the Editors	231

ACKNOWLEDGMENTS

This project would never have come to fruition without funding from the Religious Studies Center, the Department of Church History and Doctrine, and the Joseph Fielding Smith Institute for Church History at Brigham Young University, including research by Alan Taylor Farnes. We further express appreciation to the Religious Studies Center team for their assistance: publications directors Thomas A. Wayment and Scott C. Esplin; publications coordinator Joany O. Pinegar; editors R. Devan Jensen and Emily Cook; production supervisor Brent R. Nordgren; and designer Emily V. Strong. Thanks to R. Devan Jensen and W. Randall Dixon for locating the C. C. A. Christensen scenes from the Charles Brent Hancock Panorama at the Church History Library.

INTRODUCTION

The journals of Newel Knight are one of a handful of essential manuscript sources that every historian of The Church of Jesus Christ of Latter-day Saints relies upon to understand its early history. The Joseph Smith Papers Project has recently transcribed and made available many official histories or assigned histories from the early Church in print and on the Web.[1] They have also included other important documents, like the early history of Parley P. Pratt and Lucy Mack Smith. Left out of this massive project is a transcription of Newel Knight's journals. He was one of the very earliest Latter-day Saint converts and maintained a lifelong friendship and close association with Joseph Smith. He was one of a few early members of the Church to write about the earliest events in Latter-day Saint history with direct experience with some of the most foundational events. Knight died in January 1847, north of Winter Quarters, at the young age of forty-six. During the last five years of his life, he wrote a personal history composed of two elements,

---

1. See the introductions for *JSP*, H1, and H2.

Introduction

an autobiography and a journal, which form this valuable historical record. Though extremely important, it has always been a difficult source because it is only found in its full rendition in several different manuscripts. It is frequently cited but not always understood. This publication of his history pieces together his manuscripts and offers a way to cite and use his history more precisely.

Knight first penned a lengthy autobiography that told his life story up through the early 1840s. As he wrote, he was aware of and interacted with the official Church histories being written and compiled at the same time. Knowing that Joseph Smith's history up to 1834 was being published serially in Nauvoo's *Times and Seasons*, Knight decided to copy from and link his experiences to it. Therefore, Knight's recollections up to the year 1834 borrow extensively from Joseph Smith's published history, while including his own insights. Knight's autobiography also narrates his personal, family, and community experiences that did not involve Joseph Smith, making it a rich source of early Church history.

His writing was done in phases. Around 1844, having caught up with the Church's history and his own life story, he began a second phase of writing. He started a journal, a diary-type record with dated entries, that contains his own observations and scrawls about what was happening in in the Church after Joseph Smith's death. This material records invaluable 1846–47 details about the exodus from Nauvoo and Knight's leadership role in the large advance company that created Camp Ponca far northwest of Winter Quarters.

Found in both the autobiography and journal sections are rich source materials for understanding the Church's foundational years and the lives and circumstances of the early believers. The heart of Knight's voluminous writings, which he designed for his posterity, concerns his association with Joseph Smith, his deeply felt commitment to the Church, and his personal religious experiences. Knight wrote:

> To know that I have seen and witnessed these important events with my natural eyes, and also to know of a surety that the heavens have been opened to my view, that I have beheld the majesty on high and heard the voic[e] of my Redeemer which has spoken words of comfort and instruction to me, fills my whole being with gratitude

Introduction

to my heavenly father while I write these things which are verrily true. And I write them that my posterity and future generations may know of them and that I may leave a faithful testimony of the things which I do know to be verrily true.

For the foundational years of the Church, first-person records are not numerous, and extensive accounts like Knight's are rare. His writings therefore merit publication, circulation, consultation, and study.

Newel's widow, Lydia Goldthwaite Bailey Knight, preserved his records and brought them west with her to Utah in 1850. The autobiography and journal holographs are now a valuable collection in The Church of Jesus Christ of Latter-day Saints's Church History Library in Salt Lake City. They are catalogued as MS 767, "Newel Knight Autobiography and Journal."[2]

NEWEL KNIGHT, A BRIEF BIOGRAPHY

Newel Knight (1800–1847) was a close and loyal friend of Joseph Smith Jr. from 1826,[3] when Joseph became a hired hand for the Knight family, until Joseph's death in 1844.[4] Born at Marlboro, Vermont, on September 13, 1800, Newel Knight was the son of Joseph Knight Sr. and Polly Peck.[5] When Newel was about eight years old, his family moved to the Colesville, New York, area. He married Sally Colburn on June 7, 1825. When Joseph Smith became one of Joseph Knight's hired hands late in 1826, he told some of the Knights about his encounters with the divine. The Knights provided him with material assistance during his Book of

---

2. Working as a Brigham Young University history professor and research historian with BYU's Joseph Fielding Smith Institute for Church History, William Hartley, coeditor of this volume, wrote and published *Stand by My Servant Joseph: The Story of the Joseph Knight Family and the Restoration*. For that history, the Newel Knight records proved foundational. Knowing their value, Michael MacKay obtained permission from the Church History Department and from the Smith Institute to edit them for this publication.
3. See *JSP*, D1:50–58, 345–52.
4. "Death of Newel Knight," *Deseret Evening News*, May 25, 1907, 6; "Knight, Newel," in Jenson, *Biographical Encyclopedia*, 2:775.
5. See Jenson, *Biographical Encyclopedia*, 775.

INTRODUCTION

Bird's Eye View of Home of Joseph Smith, "The Mormon Prophet," Near Susquehanna, PA., 1907. George Edward Anderson Collection, L. Tom Perry Special Collections, Brigham Young University.

Mormon translation work—paper, food, money, and more—and helped him court Emma Hale.

Joseph Smith organized the Church in April 1830. In May 1830, Newel Knight was the first of the extended Knight family network to be baptized. Before this, Joseph Smith cast out an evil spirit from Knight. That moment has often been lauded as the first miracle performed in Latter-day Saint history, thanks to Joseph Smith's resounding interest in the event, which he described in detail in his history.[6] Upon regaining himself, Knight experienced a vision of heaven and other revelations, according to his own history. With the baptism of Knight's parents, siblings, aunts, uncles, and cousins, the Colesville Branch of the Church was organized. Hyrum Smith, the Prophet's brother, presided briefly, and then Newel succeeded him as the branch's president. By the end of 1830, some sixty Knight relatives had embraced the Church. Newel Knight continued to preside over this branch throughout its relocations in 1831, first to upper Ohio and then to Jackson County, Missouri.[7]

After local residents drove the Saints out of Jackson County in the fall and winter of 1833, Newel and his wife Sally found temporary

---

6. Smith, History, 1838–1856, vol. A-1, 40–53.
7. *JSP*, D1:172, 264, 268; *JSP*, D2:3–4, 12, 22, 31.

INTRODUCTION

quarters in Clay County.⁸ When the Church's second high council was organized in Missouri in 1834, Knight was appointed to it. He would serve on three more high councils.⁹ In September 1834, Sally died. Knight went to Kirtland, Ohio, to help with temple construction and to be "endowed with power from on high" (Doctrine and Covenants 38:32). While there, he married Lydia Goldthwaite Bailey on November 24, 1835. Theirs was the first marriage Joseph Smith performed by priesthood authority.¹⁰ As he attested in his history, he and Lydia participated in the Kirtland Temple dedication events.

One day in Nauvoo, Joseph Smith, in his private journal, paid tribute to Knight for being one of his loyal friends from the beginnings of the Restoration.¹¹ Not long after that, Knight, heartbroken when mobs stormed Carthage Jail and killed Joseph and Hyrum Smith, his longtime friends, accepted the Twelve Apostles as the successors. Newel, Lydia, and their family left Nauvoo during the 1846 spring wave of refugees. Later that year, assigned as Brigham Young's representative and head of a high council, Knight gave spiritual leadership to those at George Miller's Ponca Encampment above Winter Quarters, in what today is northern Nebraska. Knight died there on January 11, 1847, a mile west of today's town of Niobrara.

Lydia Knight's headstone at Saint George City Cemetery.

His widow, Lydia, and their children went west to Utah in 1850, taking Newel's journals and diaries with them. Among Newel and Lydia's

---

8. *JSP*, D2:147–56.
9   *JSP*, D4:90, 94, 594.
10. Joseph Smith, Journal, November 24, 1835; Jenson, *Biographical Encyclopedia*, 774–75.
11. *JSP*, J2:115–19.

Introduction

Newel Knight's obelisk monument at Niobrara, Nebraska, erected by his son Jesse Knight.

nine children was Jesse Knight, born in Nauvoo, who became one of Utah's earliest wealthy businessmen. In 1908 Jesse Knight directed the erection of an obelisk monument at the Ponca site that honors Newel Knight and others who died there.

PRESENTING KNIGHT'S WRITING IN FIVE PARTS

In this volume, we present Newel Knight's journals in five parts in mostly chronological periods. Each part begins with a brief biographical summary about Knight and the corresponding period of Latter-day Saint history.

Part 1 covers the period from Knight's birth in 1800 up to June of 1834. This period is a cohesive unit due to Knight's heavy borrowing from the *Times and Seasons* installments of Joseph Smith's "History of the Church"; that history extended only to 1834, from which point Newel continued writing independently.

Part 2, 1834 to 1836, primarily deals with Knight's departure from Clay County and his experiences for about a year in Kirtland. He draws

INTRODUCTION

from no outside record but from his own recollections and notes that he jotted down.

Part 3 contains Knight's autobiographical writings over three years, from May 1836 until May 1839. It covers Knight's struggles in Clay and then Caldwell Counties to make a living as a miller and coexist with fellow Saints.

Part 4 covers the six-year period from when the Knight family crossed the Mississippi River in May 1839, to the Church conference in the Nauvoo Temple in October 1845, when plans for the mass exodus from Nauvoo were announced. Most of what Knight wrote about leaving Missouri and his years in Nauvoo is original, his own recollections.

Part 5 documents the 1845 to 1847 period. By 1845 Knight and his pen had brought his life narrative up to the current time. The journal part of his record ended, and he then started writing about his life as it progressed, keeping a regular diary (as a set of more incremental, snapshot-like, autobiographical writings) up until his death.

NEWEL KNIGHT'S ORIGINAL JOURNALS

As early as 1830, Knight wrote history on scraps of paper. It appears that in 1839 he became interested in autobiography when he participated in compiling Joseph Smith's history. Joseph Smith's diary records on July 4, and 5, 1839, "Assisted by Br. Newel Knight dictating History."[12] They apparently reminisced about the night when Joseph cast a devil out of him, nearly ten years earlier, in 1830. After recording that experience, Joseph Smith's history then describes Knight's visions of eternity, which he alone experienced.[13] "He afterwards related his experience as follows," the history explained. Probably the "afterwards" was while Knight assisted Joseph Smith with the history in July 1839.

Joseph Smith's history was published serially in Nauvoo's *Times and Seasons* between March 1, 1842, and February 15, 1846. Knight read each installment closely, which seemed to inspire him to write his own experiences, complimentary to the official history. He did his journal

---

12. *JSP*, J1.345.
13. Smith, History, 1838–1856, vol. A-1, 48.

writing, at least the best and final version, while in Nauvoo. He began by writing his own recollections, some from memory, some copied from pages he had written previously. His wife, Lydia, explained that "Considerable of the author's [Newel's] journal was kept on detached pieces of paper, and no doubt many interesting & valuable portions are lost."[14]

For the 1830 to 1834 period, Knight extracted a good deal of information from Joseph Smith's history, painstakingly copying sections that related directly to his own experiences. Interested in supporting the official history of the Church, he sometimes altered Joseph Smith's first-person account to read as though it were Knight's own first-person account. Because the copying of large blocks of Joseph Smith's history verbatim was tedious work, Knight's narrative often notes material he intended to copy over when he had time, but he never did so.

Our featured text, which we call version 1, is the material found in folder 1 in the MS 767 manuscript file in the Church History Library titled "Newel Knight Autobiography and Journal." The version 1 journal and diary materials are in Newel's handwriting, primarily written in brown, or occasionally blue, ink and mostly on lined paper. Given the grammatical errors and the edits made during the writing process—such as cross-outs, inserted words, blank spaces, and poem lines and stanzas crossed out and rewritten (as if being changed at the time)—the manuscript seems to be the original and not a later copy by Lydia or others. Newel is most likely the redactor. Based on the flow of the narrative and the handwriting, we suspect, but cannot prove, that Newel copied this version 1 from some of his scrap paper notes and a probable set of marked up and crossed out trial drafts long since discarded. Therefore, version 1 is a compiled edition of his history.

Version 1 consists of six different groupings or sets of pages using different types of paper. It is clearly a compilation. Some is written on folded pages with string through the spine holding the folds together, as though it were used as an individual record at some point. An archivist gave each grouping in version 1 an identification, such as item 1, item 2, and so on. One set has some serious water damage in the midspine

---

14. Lydia Knight, handwritten statement, Santa Clara, Utah, February 14, 1873.

region. Another has several pages with small pieces of the outside edges chipped away, removing pieces of the original text.

His history is written from a retrospective position, combining in-moment narration with reflective personal insights. Once his history reaches May 1845, he appears to be writing journal entries with dated entries, but only occasionally.[15] These diary entries continue, though not contiguously, until he dies in January 1847. After Newel's death, his widow, Lydia, became the caretaker of his papers. She had promised him she would be sure his children had and read his record. She took his writings with her to Utah when she emigrated there in 1850 and worked on them to ready them for publication (see version 5 below).

In Brigham Young University's L. Tom Perry Special Collections are scraps of paper, part of Lydia Knight's papers, that inform us about Newel's records. These papers are important because their authors were eyewitnesses to the events and they often used earlier manuscripts that are no longer extant. Though they have the potential to introduce tradition into the record, they also have the potential to offer a historical understanding of the events included in Newel's records. We have added these into the footnotes and transcripts of the autobiography so that researchers can reference them accurately and use them carefully to interpret Newel's records.

VERSIONS 1–3

Version 1, Newel Knight's original, incomplete draft, is our featured text. However, the Church History Library has two other drafts termed "Newel Knight's Autobiography and Journal." Both differ from our version 1 and offer interesting insights into the manuscript. Unfortunately, these versions are in two different hands and their handwriting has not been identified. Each is a shortened, cleaner iteration of the version 1 text. Clearly, they are attempts to create a narration short enough to be easily read and understood. It is likely someone produced these intending to publish Newel's journal, which was done in 1883. Nonetheless, all three versions are important in the development of the

---

15. For example, his first entries are on May 24, June 14, and July 1, 13, 27, and 31.

Introduction

Newel Knight history. At some point, Lydia Knight or someone in the Knight family donated versions 1, 2, and 3 to the Church History Department, The Church of Jesus Christ of Latter-day Saints.

VERSION 4: THE TIN BOX, BUNDLED PAGES VERSION

At some point before 1871, possibly spearheaded by Lydia, Newel's version 1 was copied, embellished, and extensively reworked. Version 4 consists of 2,347 small pages tied with string into small bundles, all normally kept in a tin box. Records show that Lydia Knight loaned the boxed version 4 bundles to the Church Historian's Office. On November 9, 1871, the "Historian's Office Journal" recorded, "RLC [Robert L. Campbell] read first 100 pages of Newel Knight's history, find it good and very similar to Joseph Smith's history." Six months later, a notation for April 9, 1872, reads, "Sister Knight received her tin box containing history of Newel Knight."

Version 4 is an edited, corrected rendition of version 1, attempting to ready it for publication. It cleans up the narration by changing Newel's words and sentences. Here, for example, is a comparison between one of Newel's statements in version 1 and its version 4 analogue:

> **Folder 1**: Haveng settled my affairs to the best advantage I could I again comanced business yet not with out considerable loss which with the Sickness we had suffered the loss of health ^and other expenses attending^ I was reduced in my pecuniary affairs considerabley. Yet not discoraged for all I did seemed to prosper in my hands. I was happy in the Society not only in the society of my Fathers imediate family but my noble aunts and Cousins lived in the vicinity so that I felt allwa cheered by the Society of my kindred
>
> **Version 4**: In settling up my business affairs, I suffered a heavy loss (7) and this, with the expenses incurred by our sickness considerably reduced my pecuniary affairs. But I was not discouraged, for all my labor prospered in my hands, and I again entered into business. . . . so that I was happy, not only in the society of my father's immediate family but also of my uncles aunts and cousins ^of many relatives^ who lived in the same vicinity. (8) Peace, prosperity and plenty

Introduction

seemed to crown our labors, and indeed we were a happy family, and my father rejoiced in having his children around him.

Version 4 is significantly longer than version 1 for three reasons:

1. It includes materials Newel wrote, some on small scraps of paper, which he failed to include in his version 1. To present version 1 properly, we have inserted into it and clearly identified those new additions made by version 4 in the footnotes and the text. Three salient additions are a Joseph Smith letter of August 20, 1830; another of December 2, 1830; and an 1833 Colesville Branch list of pledges for building a temple in Jackson County, none of which are recorded anywhere else.
2. The version 4 editor(s) added in extensive materials that Newel marked in version 1 to include later in his account, but apparently he never returned to the manuscript to finish his intended changes. We chose not to include those additions, but we do explain in footnotes what those materials consist of.
3. Version 4 contains historical materials and explanations not present in version 1 that the version 4 editor(s) created or inserted where they felt Knight's narrative needed them to convey his message. We exclude those embellishments as later historical interpretation, not written or intended by Knight. The version 4 revisers sometimes explain their willingness to introduce information not in Newel's accounts: "From the reading of Bro. Knight's Journal it would appear, as though he had taken no notice of the commandment given to him by revelation [Doctrine and Covenants 52], at the time he was ordained to the High Priesthood, at the June Conference. and So I will here introduce the facts as nearly as I am able to glean them."[16]

We have labeled version 4 the Allen version because Knight descendant Robert Allen in Salem, Utah, had the tin box and bundles in his private possession. This version had been shown only to a few privileged scholars and family members until it was copied and used in 2004 as part of the Joseph Smith Papers Project research. According to

---

16. Allen version, "Newel Knight autobiography circa 1871," 310.

INTRODUCTION

Mr. Allen, the box and bundles came into his possession through grandparents Robert E. Allen and Inez Knight, daughter of Jesse Knight and granddaughter of Newel and Lydia Knight. During the Great Depression, the Jesse Knight mansion in Provo was sold to the Berg Mortuary, and Robert and Inez Allen moved from there into the top floor of the Knight Building, located in the Knight Block northeast of the intersection of Center Street and University Avenue. Robert Allen ran a business selling cameras. An employee named Don Harvey did darkroom work for him in the basement of the Knight Building, which also served as family storage. One day Harvey brought up from the basement a tin box containing bundles of small note pages, each tied in string, and gave it to Robert. Since then he has kept the bundles in his home, still with the original string and the tin box. In the early 1980s and a second time in the 1990s, Robert and his wife, Lucette, transcribed the bundled pages electronically with a word processor. In 2004 one of the Allen sons was designated to be the next caretaker of the bundles. The Church History Department has digitized the bundles (MS 19156) and the most recent Allen version (MS 17147).

VERSION 5: THE 1883 PUBLISHED VERSION

In 1883 the *Juvenile Instructor* Office in Salt Lake City published "Newel Knight's Journal." It was part 3 in a book called *Scraps of Biography*, the tenth volume in the "Faith Promoting Series" that was designed to appeal to young readers. Ten years earlier, Lydia wrote about her efforts to revise Newel's journals for publication as a small book and expressed regret she could not do a better job:

> In presenting this little volume to the public I feel a great delicacy as I am aware of my incompetence to do justice to it but it being the dying request of my kind and faithful husband, I have done the best I could, and hope its readers will realize the true spirit and intent which prompts me to do so. Considerable of the author's journal was kept on detached pieces of paper, and no doubt many interesting & valuable portions are lost, yet I trust enough is left to be a faithful testimony to the present, & future generations, that the author did know of a surety that God lives, and that He has spoken

INTRODUCTION

to men from the heavens, in this generation and that He requires all men everywhere to repent, and be baptized for the remission of their Sins & have hands laid upon them for the reception of the Holy Ghost, by His servants who have been commissioned with authority from Him to act, and officiate in His name. Yet I am aware it is far short of that interest it would have contained, if he had lived to compile the work. Having done the best I could, I trust it will be acceptable to the dead and prove a blessing to the living. Which is the prayer of a humbled, and bereaved one.[17]

Comparisons show that "Newel Knight's Journal" in *Scraps of Biography* is taken from the Allen version and varies very little from it.

In 1883 the office started a similar book series that featured life stories of Latter-day Saint women. The first volume was *Lydia Knight's History*. For both of their life stories, Newel's and Lydia's, the source material was Newel's journals, the revised and polished version 4. Lydia assisted in the writing of *Lydia Knight's History*, but the author of her life story is "Homespun," a pen name for Susa Young Gates. This version selectively enhances and extrapolates upon the Lydia narrative. That Newel and Lydia's lives appeared in print at almost the same time strongly suggests that both Lydia and Susa Gates had a hand in polishing up Newel's account for publication.

NOTES ON EDITORIAL METHOD

Knight's autobiography and journals are not easy to use. The various versions are not sufficiently self-evident for simple reading and research. As part of this project, we have made careful transcriptions of each of the versions listed above, producing parallel comparisons of all the texts. After careful textual analyses of the different journal versions and of Joseph Smith's history installments, we provide here a usable, reliable transcription of the autobiography and journals. Because Knight often failed to indicate materials he copied from other sources, our transcription provides needed editorial remarks to show what is Knight's own and what he borrowed. We provide informative footnotes but do not

---

17. Lydia Knight, handwritten statement, Santa Clara, Utah, February 14, 1873.

try to be completely comprehensive. We attempt to offer some firsthand sources, especially through the printed work of *The Joseph Smith Papers*, but we also simply try to point readers to some exemplary secondary literature describing a particular event. To be helpful to researchers and readers, we include short biographical introductions to each section of the journals.

We present the text of Knight's journal as fully and accurately as possible, retaining original spelling and punctuation unless clarification seems critical. We insert within square brackets [ ] our clarifications, which include correcting the spelling of especially garbled words, correcting misrecorded dates, identifying crossings-out and illegible words, and explaining where pages or parts of pages have been lost. We also use brackets to identify versions and other manuscripts that are used throughout. For clarity, we provide most dates in full, using a standardized form in square brackets. We divide Knight's narration into paragraphs where needed. In footnotes, we identify the people, places, and events mentioned.

PART 1

NEW YORK, OHIO, AND MISSOURI, 1800–1834

INTRODUCTION

This first portion of Newel Knight's autobiography covers his life from his birth in 1800 until late 1834. It was compiled by Newel in 1846 and consists of lined folio paper grouped together into three items in narrative format.[1] In his autobiography, he is aware of other major journals covering the same period and consciously makes unique contributions instead of covering the same material. Valuing the other sources, his narration sometimes incorporates passages taken from other sources. After a short introduction to his life, Newel quickly takes up his history with Joseph Smith, starting in 1826, and his early association with the development of the Church. Because he participated in events that Joseph Smith's history relates, he copied Joseph's version of those events, at times adding his own observations. Composing his journal retrospectively in Nauvoo, he had access to and generously borrowed

---

1. This includes file MS 767, folder 1, items 1, 2, and 3. The manuscripts have nine pages missing.

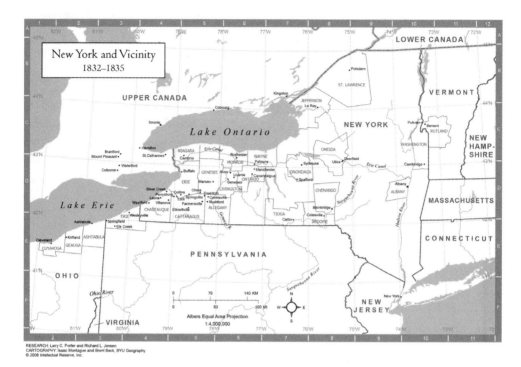

New York and Vicinity, 1832–1835. Courtesy of the Joseph Smith Papers Project.

from Joseph Smith's "History of the Church," published serially in the *Times and Seasons* between March 1, 1842, and February 15, 1846. The last *Times and Seasons* installment of the Smith "History" concluded with August 1834 events.[2] Newel's autobiographical flow leaves behind Joseph Smith's story at this point and concentrates on Newel's personal experiences. Part 1 concludes there.

In part 1, Newel borrows from two other sources published in the *Times and Seasons*. When telling about the 1833 expulsion of the Saints from Jackson County, he copied generously from "A History, of the Persecution, of the Church of Jesus Christ, of Latter Day Saints in Missouri," published in installments in the *Times and Seasons* from 1839 to 1840. And, for the 1834 Zion's Camp arrival narration, he borrowed from Heber C. Kimball's diary, published in the *Times and Seasons* during 1845.[3]

---

2. See *JSP*, H1:xxxv–xxxix.
3. It is noteworthy that Newel did not insert text from the lengthy summary of Missouri depredations that he, Parley P. Pratt, and John Corrill wrote on De-

Part 1 contains Newel's useful and original observations and recollections, particularly about the Church branch in Colesville, over which he presided in the earliest days of the Church. He adds details about Joseph Smith that are not in the Prophet's history. Newel also includes three unique documents: a Joseph Smith letter, August 20, 1830; a second Joseph Smith letter, December, 2, 1830; and the September 1833 pledge to contribute to the Jackson County temple, signed by six men in Newel's branch.[4]

---

cember 13, 1833. This long document was published in *The Evening and Morning Star, Extra*, in Kirtland in February 1834. It is possible he lacked access to that account, or perhaps he preferred copying from the recent "History, of the Persecution" installments in the *Times and Seasons*.

4. See *JSP*, D1:172–77, 214–19.

The Rise of the Latter-day Saints

VERSION 1[5]

[1] I Newel Knight was born Sept 13th 1800 at Marlborough, Windham County Vermont.[6] My Fathers name was Joseph Knight born ──.[7] Mother's Maiden name was Polly Peck, born April 16th 1774. My Father moved into the State of New York when I was nine years of age and settled on the Susquhanah River near the bend in Chenango County, Town of Bainbridge. Stayed there two years. Then moved ^down^ the river ~~nine~~ ^six^ miles into Broom County town of Coalsville and there remaind nineteen years.

My Father owned a farm, a gristmill, and Carding machine.[8] He was not rich yet possessed enough of this worlds ~~doods~~ ^goods^ to secure to him Self and family the necessaries and Comforts of life. His family consisted of himself, my Mother, three sons, and four Daughters, Viz

Naaum born
Esther
Newel
Anna
Josep
Polly
and Betsey[9]

He raised his family in a genteel and respectable manner. He only gave them a common Shool education.

My Father was a Sober, honest man, generally beloved and respected by his neighbors and acquaintances.

I do not know that any thing special occured more than is common to all families ^in general^ during our Child hood with our parents. My

---

5. MS 767, folder 1, item 1.
6. "Death of Newel Knight," *Deseret Evening News*, May 25, 1907, 6.
7. Joseph Knight Sr. was born on November 31, 1772, though Newel never adds it here. Hartley, *Stand by My Servant Joseph*, 16.
8. Often used for wool, carding is a mechanical process that disentangles, cleans, and intermixes fibers to produce a continuous web or sliver suitable for subsequent processing.
9. The birth years for the Knight children are Nahum, 1796; Esther, 1798; Newel, 1800; Anna, 1804; Joseph Jr., 1808; Polly, 1811; and Elizabeth, 1817.

Modern-day Joseph Knight farmhouse and Susquehanna River in Nineveh (Colesville), New York.
Courtesy of Knight family.

Father did not blong to any Sect but was a believer in the Universaian doctrine.[10]

Oweing to the business my Father was engaged in he often had hired help. Among the many he from time to time hired was a young man by the name of Joseph Smith Junior.[11] To him I was particularly attached: his noble deportment, his faithfulness, his kind address, could not fail to [2] gain the esteem of those who had the pleasure of his acquantance. One thing in particular I will mention seemed to be peculiar Characteristic with him. In all his boyish sports or amusements. I never knew any one to gain advantage over him, and yet he was allways kind and kept the good will of his playmates.

I continued to live with my Father until I was twenty five years of age or nearly so. June 7th 1825 I married a respectable young lady by

---

10. See Lum, *Damned Nation*; Walker, *The Decline of Hell*; Almond, *Heaven and Hell in Enlightenment England*.
11. See *JSP*, D1:345–52.

Joseph Knight Sr.'s renovated ancestral home, Ninevah (Colesville), New York. Courtesy of Knight family.

the name of Sally Coburn, ^born 1804^. Her health was rather delicate. She had long held an honorable position in the Choir of one of the most respectable Churches in that vicinity. Her Father was a great musician, Spent much of his time traveling ^home^ tuneing peanoes &c, which throwed a heavy burthen upon her Mother in raiseing her family, which She bore with much patience.[12]

On leaving my Father I went a few miles distant and put in operation a Carding machine, which I sold and after wards engaged in a grist mill. During this time Sally, my wife, gave birth to a child which did not live. Her sufferings were verry great. I found my health was gradually declineing. I was advised to leave the mill as it did not agree wit my Constitution to work in it. I had no taste for farmeing so I persisted in the mill business untill the physician told me I was in a consumption and he thought my Case doubtful.[13] I applied to a Skillful Indian doctor. With him I found relief but was obliged to chan change my business. I moved back to Coalsville near my Father's.

---

12. Hartley, *Stand by My Servant Joseph*, 18–19.
13. Consumption is tuberculosis.

My oldest Brother Naaum [Nahum] was married and lived near by, allso my Sisters Esther and Anna ^with^ their husbands William Stringham and Freeborn Demill.¹⁴

Peace, prosperity, and plenty now seemed to crown our labors; indeed we were a happy family and my Father rejoiced in his family circle.

But to return to my young friend Joseph Smith Jun. It is evident great things are about to transpire [3] that the Lord is a bout to do a marvellous work and a wonder that Joseph is to become ^an^ instrument in his hands to bring about this great and mighty work of the last days.

I will here coppy from the private journal of the above mentioned Joseph Smith Jun as it will give the reader a correct knowelege of the Comencement of the Restoration of the true and everlasting gospel to man ^in^ these last days.

Joseph Smith's and Joseph Knight Jr.'s bedroom at the Knight renovated ancestral home in Ninevah, New York. Courtesy of Knight family.

---

14. Nahum's wife's first name was Thankful, but her last name is unknown.

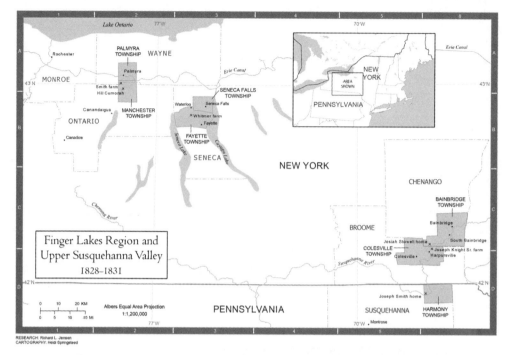

Finger Lakes Region and Upper Susquehanna Valley, 1828–1831. Courtesy of the Joseph Smith Papers Project.

JOSEPH SMITH HISTORY[15]

I was born in the year of ^our^ Lord one thousand eight hundred and five on the twenty third day of December in the town of Sharon Windsor County Vermont. My Father left the State of Vermont, and moved ^to^ Palmyra Ontario (now Wane) County in the State of New York when I was in my tenth year. In about four years after my father's arrival at Palmyra, he moved with his family into Manchester, in the same county of Ontario.

VERSION 1

Haveng settled my affairs to the best advantage I could, I again comanced business, yet not with out considerable loss which With the Sickness we had suffered, the loss of health ^and other expenses attending^, I was reduced in my pecuniary affairs considerabley. Yet not discoraged, for all I did seemed to prosper in my hands. I was happy in the Society not only in the society of my Fathers imediate family but my

---

15. The published edition available to Knight is found in *Times and Seasons* 3 (March 15, 1842): 727; Smith, History, 1838–1856, vol. A-1, 1.

noble aunts and Cousins lived in the vicinity so that I felt allwa cheered by the Society of my kindred.[16]

During this time we were occasionly visited by our young friend Joseph and heard him relate the things he has above written. And so honest and plain was he in all his statements that there was no room for any missgiveings with me on the subject. In fact there was no place for any. Besides, I found by reading and searching the bible that there would be a great falling away from the gospel as preached and established by Jesus and the his apostles, that [4] [in] the last days God would set his hand again to restore that which was lost. Then why should any ^one^ persecute this boy. I could not. Yet to my certain knowledge many did, those who professed to be preachers of the gospel were often his vileest

The Sacred Grove, Palmyra, New York, 1907. Anderson Collection, Church History Library.

---

16. Here, the Allen version includes a big block of text that was largely drawn from the Smith history. No doubt, Newel wanted that information included and intended to add it in later, so the Allen version editors inserted it here. "My oldest brother, Nahum, was married and lived close at hand, also my sisters Esther and Anna with their husbands, William Stringham and Freeborn Demill, so that I was happy, not only in the society of my father's immediate family but also of many relatives who lived in the same vicinity. Peace, prosperity and plenty seemed to crown our labors, and indeed we were a happy family and my father rejoiced in having his children around him."

Hill Cumorah, New York, 1907. Anderson Collection, L. Tom Perry Special Collections, Brigham Young University. © 2007, Utah State Historical Society. All rights reserved.

persecuters.[17] And not with standing they all professed to doubt the reality of his haveing the plates of which he has spoken, yet so eager were they to get them from him that it was only by the Lord or a kind angel warning ^to^ him from time to time of the pursuit of of his enemies that he was enabld to preserve those sacred records.[18] In fact it seems verry like as it was with Joseph and Mary the mother of Jesus being warnd of God they fled from place to place to save the youg child. So has Joseph Smith been warned and many times barely escaped his pursuers.[19] Of this I can bear faithful testimony and could relate many particulars but for brevitiy will for bear.

During this time time my wife gave birth to another child, yet not a living one. Her sufferings were verry extreme, here life b[e]ing nearly dispaired of by the most skillful physician who said it would not be possible for her to ever give birth to a liveing Child.

Joseph percevered and the Lord raised up freinds who aided him in the great work of translateing and printing the reccord which those Sacred plates containd, or a part of them for a part was sealed to Come forth in a future time. The title of this book is the Book of Mormon.[20]

On the Sixth day of April one thousand eight hundred and thirty by revelation and Comandment from God a Church was organiced

---

17. See Porter, *A Study of the Origins of the Church*, 19–20; Porter, "Reverend George Lane," 321–40.
18. See Ashurst-McGee, "Moroni: Angel or Treasure Guardian?," 39–75.
19. See MacKay and Dirkmaat, *From Darkness unto Light*; Hedges, "'All My Endeavors to Preserve Them,'" 14–23.
20. See MacKay and Dirkmaat, *From Darkness unto Light*; MacKay and Frederick, *Joseph Smith's Seer Stones*.

Called the Church of Jesus Christ of latter day Saints.[21] it was organized with Six members.[22]

Persecution now raged. Every Craft felt that they were in danger and resorted to everry Stratagem possible to stop the progress of the work of God.

That my children and future generations may know what we had to meet, I will again Copy from [missing pages][23]

JOSEPH SMITH HISTORY[24]

[7] . . . man for whom Joseph formerly worked) he was examined as follows: Q Did not the prisoner Joseph Smith have a horse of you. Ans Yes. Q Did not he go to you and tell you that an angel had appeared unto him to get the horse from you. Ans. No, he told me no such story thing. Q Well; how did he [get] the horse of you Ans. He bought him of me as another man would do. Q. Have you had your pay? Ans That is not your buisness. The question being put again the witness replied, I hold his note for the price of the horse which I consider as good, as for I am well acquainted with Joseph Smith Jr and know him him to be an

---

21. *JSP*, D1:116–30; MacKay, *Sacred Space*.
22. Smith, History, 1838–1856, vol. A-1, 37–38. On April 6, 1830, as many as sixty people may have crowded into the two rooms of Father Peter Whitmer's log home at Fayette for a meeting to formally organize what they then called the Church of Christ. One-third of the congregation, or about twenty people, were from the Colesville Branch, and almost all were Knight and Peck relatives. Fifteen attenders came from the Manchester area, where the Smiths lived. Twenty were from the Fayette area, where the Whitmers lived. For a list of seventy-three members who could have attended the organizing meeting, see Porter, "Organizational Origins of the Church," 149–64.
23. Newel's pages 5–6 are missing. On these missing pages, Newel quoted more from Joseph Smith's history, as shown by the fact that when the surviving text resumes, it is quoting Joseph Smith's history. *Times and Seasons* 4 (December 15, 1842): 40–41 is about the Colesville trial, with Newel being cross-examined at length. What Newel certainly copied into the missing pages is Joseph Smith's history account of Joseph casting a devil out of Newel, in *Times and Seasons* 4 (November 15, 1842): 12–13, and of Newel's "visions of eternity," in *Times and Seasons* 4 (December 1, 1842): 22–23.
24. MS 767, folder 1, item 2.

Smith Farm in 1907, with the Sacred Grove in the Background.
Anderson Collection, Church History Library.

honest, and if he wishes I am ready to let him have another horse on the same terms.

Mr Jonathan Thompson was next called up and examined. Q Has not the prisoner Joseph Smith Jr had a yoke of oxen of you? Ans. yes Q Did he not obtain them from you by telling you that he had a revelation to the effect that he was to have them? No, he did not mention ~~any such thing~~ a word of the kind concerning the oxen. He purchased them the same as another man would. After Several mor similar attempts, the Court was detain for a time in order that two youg women ladies (Daughters of Joseah Stowel) with whom ~~I~~ Joseph had at times kept Company: might be sent for. in order if possible to elicit something from them which might be made a pretext against ~~me~~ Josep. The young ladies arrived and were severrally examined touching ~~my~~ his Character and conduct in general, but in particular as to ~~my~~ behaviour to wards them both in public and in private, when they both bore such testimony in ~~my~~ [8] Joseph's favor as left ~~my~~ his enemies without a pretext ~~again~~ on their account. Several attempts were made to prove something against ~~me~~ Joseph and even circumstances which were alleged to have taken place in Broom county were brought forward. But these ~~my~~ Josephs lawyer would not here admit of against ~~me~~ him, in consequence of which his persecutors managed to detain the Court, until they had ~~managed to~~ succeeded in obtaining a warrant from Broom county. Which warrant they served upon ~~me~~ him at the verry moment in which ~~I~~ he had been acquitted by this Court.

The ~~second~~ Constable who served this second warrant upon ~~him~~ me had no sooner arrested him than he began to abuse and insult ~~me~~ him. And so unfeeling was he that although ~~I~~ Joseph had been kept all day in Court without any thing to eat since the morning, that he hurried me off to Broom County a distance of a bout fifteen miles, before allowing me him any thing to eat whatever. The Constable took me him to a tavern where gathered in a number of men who ~~use~~ used everry means [to]abuse ridicule and insult him They spit upon me him, pointed their fingers at me him saying prophesy, p^ro^phesy: and thus did they imitate ~~rose~~ [those] who cucified the Savior of mankind, not knowing what they did. This tavern was but a short distance from my Josephs own house; he wished to spend the night with his wife, at home, offering any wished for security for my appearrance. But this was denied me, offering to give any bail wished for for his apparance, but this was denied him. ~~I~~ He applied for some thing to eat—The Constable ordered ~~me~~ him some crusts of bread and water, which was the only fare ~~I~~ he that night received. At length ~~we~~ he retired to bed; the ~~con~~ Constable made ~~me~~ him lie next to the wall: He then laid [9] ~~in Joseph favor as left his enemies without a pretext on their account.~~ him self down by me, and put his arm around ~~me~~ him fast fearing that ~~I~~ he intended to escape from him and in this (not verry agreeable) mamer was ~~I~~ he compelled to spend the night.

Next day ~~I~~ he was brought before the ~~Court~~ Magestrates Court, of ~~Broom~~ Colesville. Broom County. and put upon ~~my~~ his trial. His former friends and lawyers were again at ~~my~~ his side; ~~my~~ his former persecutors were ~~allso~~ arrayed against him with the fury and rage of demons stamped upon their Countenances, and in their actions. Many witnesses were again called forward and examined, some of whom Swore to the most palpabl falsehoods and like to the false witness, which had ppeared against ~~me~~ him the day preivious. They contradicted themselves so plainly that the Court would not admit their testimony. Others were called who showed by their zeal that they were willing enough to prove something against me; but all they could do was to tell some things which somebody else had told them, [that] they had heard some body else say about him.

In this frivulous and vexatious manner did they proceed for a conciderabl time, when finaluly ~~Newel Knight~~ I was called upon and examined, by lawyer Seymo,^u^r who had been especially sent for on this occasion. One lawyer Burch allso was on the side of the prosecution; but Mr Seymour seemed to be a more zealous Presbyterian and appeared verry anxious and determined that people should not be deluded. [He was] one professing the power of Godliness and ~~not denying~~ the denying the power thereof.

So soon as Mr. Knight soon as I had been sworn, Mr Seymour proceeded to interrogate ~~him~~ me as follows: Q Did the prisoner Joseph [10] Smith Junior Cast the devil out of you. Ans. ~~yes sir~~, no Sir. Q Why have not you had the devil Cast out of you. Ans Yes Sir. Q And had not Joseph Smith some hand in its being done? A yes sir. Q And did not he Cast him out of you? No Sir: it was done by the power of God, and Joseph Smith was the instrument in the hands of God on this occasion. He Commanded him out of me in the name of Jesus Christ. Q And are you sure ^that^ it was the devil A Yes, Sir. Q Did you see him after he was Cast out of you. A yes sir I saw him. Q Pray what did he look like?

(Here one of ~~my~~ the lawyers informed the witness that he need not answer the question on the part of the defendant told me that I need not answer that question. The witness replied I replied I believe I need not answer your last question but I will do [so] provided I be allowed it, if I be allowed to ask you one question first and you answer it viz. Do you Mr Seymour understand the things of the Spirit? No (answered Mr Seymour) I do not pretend to such big things. Well then replied Mr. Knight I replied, it will be of no use to tell you what the devil looked like, for it was a Spiritual sight, and Spiritually discerned; and of course you would not understand it, were I to tell you of it. The lawer dropped his head, whilst the loud laugh of the audience proclaimed his discomfieture. Mr Seymour now addressed the Court and in a long and violent harangue endeavored to blacken my character the Character ^of Joseph^ and being ~~me~~ ~~him~~ in guilty of the charges which had been brought against ~~me~~ him. Mr Davidson an Mr Reed followed on ~~my~~ Joseph behalf. they held forth in true colors, the na[25]

---

25. Here Newel's autobiography resumes after the missing page segment. He is quoting from Joseph Smith's "History of the Church," *Times and Seasons* 4 (December 15, 1842): 40–41. Newel sometimes makes mistakes in his effort to shift Joseph Smith's account from first person to make it sound like Newel is the narrator, such as his writing "before allowing ~~me~~ him any thing to eat." Smith, History, 1838–1856, vol. A-1, 44–48.

[pages 11–18 are missing]

VERSION 1[26]

[19]... the everlasting gospel of the Son of God. The following is a correct coppy of a revelation given to Joseph Smith Jr, Oliver Cowdry and John Whitmer, given through Joseph Smith Jr at Harmony Penn 1830

JOSEPH SMITH HISTORY[27]

Behold I say unto you, that you shall let your time be devoted to the Study^ing^, of the Scriptures, and to preaching and to confirming the Church at Coalsville; and to performing your labors on the land, Such as is required, until after you shall go to the west, to hold the next Conference; and then it shall be made known what you shall do. and all things shall be done by common consent ~~and prayer~~ in the Church, by much prayer and faith; for all things you shall receive by faith Amen

VERSION 1

To read the above was a great consolation to the little band of Brethern and Sisters in Coalesville after haveing been abandoned from time to time by the Servants of God in consequence of the wicked who were constantly seeking to destroy the work of God from the earth.[28] It showed us that the Lord took cognisence of us and allso that he knew of the acts of the wicked. So we resolved to continue steadfast in the faith and were diligent in our prayers and in assembling ourselves to gather, waiting with patience until we should have the pleasure of again seeing Brother Joseph and others of the Servants of the Lord who had become near to us by the ties of the gospel, and of being confirmed members of the Church of Jesus Christ ^of latter day Saints^[29] by the

---

26. MS 767, folder 1, item 3.
27. Smith, History 1838–1856, vol. A-1, 50; The following is taken from *Times and Seasons* 4 (February 15, 1843): 108 and now is Doctrine and Covenants 26; *JSP*, D1:160.
28. *JSP*, D1:156–72.
29. In 1830 the Church was originally called "The Church of Christ." Then on May 3, 1834, the name changed to "The Church of the Latter Day Saints." "Communicated," *The Evening and the Morning Star*, May 1834, 160. Then on April 26, 1838, it was changed to "The Church of Jesus Christ of Latter Day Saints."

laying on of hand of the Apostles according to the pattern which had been given to us.[30]

In the forepart of the month of Aug, I in Company with my wife went to make a visit to Brother Joseph Smiths, who then resided at Harmony Penn. I found him and his wif well and in good Spirits. We had a happy meeting. It truely gave me joy to again behold his face.[31]

JOSEPH SMITH HISTORY[32]

As neither Sister Emma Smith ^the wife of Joseph Smith^ nor my wife had been confirmed, we concluded to attend to Confirming them at this time, and allso to partake of the Sacrament [20] before we should leave for home.

VERSION 1

In order to prepare for this Brother Joseph Set out to go to procure some wine for the occasion but he had gone only a short distance, when he was met by a heavenly messenger, and received the following revelation. The first paragraph of which was written at this time and the remainder in the Sept following

JOSEPH SMITH HISTORY[33]

Revelation given at Harmony Penn Aug 1830

In obedience to the above we prepared some wine of our own make and held our meeting consisting of only five persons viz

Myself and wife. John Whitmer my self and wife.[34]

We partook of the Sacrament, after which we confirmed these two sisters into the Church, and spent the evening in glorious maner. The Spirit of the Lord was poured out upon us. We praised the God of Israel, and rejoiced exceedingly. About this time a spirit of persecution began

---

30. Newel here uses the term *apostles* like others in 1830 did, in the sense of ones commissioned or sent forth to preach, not ones who were ordained to a specific office. See *JSP*, D1:143–44.
31. *JSP*, D1:164–76.
32. Smith, History, 1838–1856, vol. A-1, 51.
33. *Times and Seasons* 4 (March 1, 1843): 117; Smith, History, 1838–1856, vol. A-1, 52–53.
34. One of the two couples here is Newel and Sally Knight, the other is Joseph and Emma Smith. Newel has simply confused his pronouns again while copying text directly from Joseph's account.

to be manifest against us in th^e^~~is place~~ neighborhood where Joseph now lived, which was commenced by a man of the Methodist pursuasion who professed to be a minister of God and whose name was

VERSION 1

And so crafty was he that he s[u]cceeded in turning Mr Hale, Father in law to Joseph, that he no longer woul give protection to him although he had promised to do so.[35]

ALLEN VERSION

Harmony Aug 20, 1830

Dearly beloved in the Lord,

We are under necessity to disappoint you this time for reasons which I shall mention hereafter, but trusting that your meeting may not be an unprofitable one, may you all realize the necessity of getting together often to pray and supplicate at the Throne of Grace that the spirit of the Lord may always rest upon you. Remember that without asking we can receive nothing, therefore ask in faith, and ye shall receive such blessings as God sees fit to bestow upon you. Pray not with covetous hearts that ye may consume it upon your lusts, but pray earnestly for the best gifts—fight the good fight of faith that ye may gain the crown which is laid up for those that endure faithful unto the end of their probation. Therefore hold fast that which ye have received so liberally from the hands of God so that when the time of refreshing shall come ye may not have labored in vain, but that ye may rest from all your labors and have fulness of joy in the Kingdom of God.

---

35. See Hartley, *Stand by My Servant Joseph*, 183. Here, the Allen version inserts a very important item not in Newel's version 1, or in Joseph Smith's history. This Allen insertion clearly indicates that Newel's papers included writings he hadn't yet incorporated into version 1, but which Lydia had retained. The Allen version first gives readers a paragraph of explanation, written by whomever was creating the Allen version, and then gives the text of a very important letter found in no other records of that period. The Allen version states: "Bro Joseph intended visiting the Saints at Coal^e^sville on Saturday the 21 Aug, and on my return, arrangements were made for the brethren and sisters to meet on that day, if possible, without letting our enemies know anything about it. But Bro Joseph was prevented from keeping his engagement on this occasion, as the following ^but wrote a^ letter."

"Dearly beloved brethren we are not ignorant of your tribulations, owing that ye are placed among raveing wolves, therefore we have the more earnest desire to come to see you, but our friends from the west have not yet come, and we can get no horse and wagon, and we are not able to come afoot so far, therefore we cannot come this Saturday, but we look for our friends from the west every day and with safety we can promise to come next Saturday, if the Lord will; therefore our desire is that ye should assemble yourselves together next Saturday so that all things will be in order, when we come.

Be careful that the enemy of all righteousness will not get the advantage over you in getting the news abroad. Were it not for the prayers of you few, the Almighty would have thundered down his wrath upon the inhabitants of that place; but be not faint, th[e] day of your deliverance is not far distant, for the Judgements of the Lord are already abroad in the earth and the cold hand of death will soon pass through your neighborhood, and sweep away some of your most bitter enemies, for you need not suppose that God will be mocked at, and his commandments be trampled under their feet in such a manner as your enemies do, without visiting them in his wrath when they are fully ripe, and behold the angel cries, thrust in your sickle for the harvest is fully ripe; and the earth will soon be reaped–that is, the wicked must soon be destroyed from off the face of the earth, for the Lord hath spoken it, and who can stay the hand of the Lord, or who is there that can measure arms with the Almighty, for at his commands the heavens and the earth must pass away, for the day is fast hastening on when the restoration of all things shall be fulfilled which all the Holy Prophets have prophesied of even into the gathering of the House of Israel. Then shall come to pass that the lion shall lie down with the lamb &c.

But brethren be not discouraged when we tell you of perilous times, for they must shortly come, for the sword, famine, and pestilence ^are^ approaching, for there shall be great destructions upon the face of this land, for ye need not suppose that one jot or tittle of the prophecies of all the Holy Prophets shall fail, and there are many that remain to be fulfilled yet, and the Lord hath said that a short work will he make of it, and the righteous shall be saved if it be as by fire.

"May the grace of God the Father, Son and Holy Ghost be and abide with you from henceforth and forever, Amen.

    John Whitmer

    Joseph Smith

Newel Knight,

    P. S. waited until Saturday morning and our friends have not yet arrived. Please send Polly's Letter and also the Priest's with William, and oblige

VERSION 1

Towards the last of Aug Brother's Joseph Smith Jr in company with his Brother Hyrum, John and David Whitmor, came to our place to visit us and to hold meeting and Confirm thos who had been baptized in June previous. The following is a statement given by thos Brethren at the time they were at my house,

JOSEPH SMITH HISTORY[36]

That as they well knew the hostilities of our enemies in this quarter and allso knowing it was the duty to visit us, they called upon their heavenly Father in mighty prayer that he would grant them an opportunity of meeting with us, that he would blind the eyes of their enemies and that they might on this occasion return unmolested. Their prayers were not [21] in vain, on this occasion a little distance before reaching my place they encountered a large Company of men at work upon a public road, amongst whom were some of our most bitter enemies. They looked earnestly at them, but not knowing them, they passed on unmolested.

    That evening the Saints assembled togather and and were confirmed and partook of the Sacrament and had a happy meeting, haveing much reason to rejoice in the God of our Salvation and sing hosanna to his holy name.

    Next morning they set out on their return home and although their enemies had offred a reward to any one who would who would give information of their arrival at our place, yet did they get clear out of the neighborhood without the least annoyance, and arrived at home in safety.

---

36. *Times and* Seasons 4 (March 1, 1843): 118; Smith, History, 1838–1856, vol. A-1, 53.

The Rise of the Latter-day Saints

VERSION 1

However it was not long after the Brethren had left us when the rumor got out that they had been here, when the mob

JOSEPH SMITH HISTORY

began to collect to gather and threaten and abuse us in a most shameful and disgusting manner dureing the remainder of the day

VERSION 1

Soon after this I took my team and waggon and went to Harmony Penn to move Joseph and family out to Fayette N Y.

JOSEPH SMITH HISTORY

Mr Whitmer haveing heard of the persecutions which had been got up against Joseph in Harmony Penn. had invited him to go and live with him. About the last of Aug Joseph arrived at Fayette amidst the joy and congratulations of friends and brethren.[37]

VERSION 1

I returned home to my family. Found them well and rejoiceing in in the new and everlasting gospel commited again to man on the earth. Mean time the elders had been faithful in traveling and preaching the gospel and ma[n]y had believed and embraced the truth. The book of Mormon was a powerful weapon in the hands of the Saints. Quite a number had embraced the gospell who bid fair to become verry useful in promelgating the great work of the Lord.

I will here Copy a letter received from Joseph Smith Jr and John Whitmer[38]

> Harmony Aug 28. 1830
> Dearly beloved in the Lord
> We are under the necessity

[22] The letters mentioned in the above [in the P.S. of the August 20 letter] were on this occasion one of the greatest preists of the day began a tyrade of abuse which resulted in a correspondence betwen him and

---

37. The letter and all italicized quotes are taken from *JSP*, D1:172–76.
38. This letter, not in our version 1, is the one already presented above, where the Allen version positioned it.

my sister Polly, in which he got so used up that he was glad to give up and back ut completely whipt[39] ~~out~~

As to the things which pertained to our buisness affairs, we had been enabled to manage so that we had suffered no material loss. We were still able to live and aid the work of the lord when necessary.

After arrangeing my affairs at home I again set out for Fayette to attend our Second Conference, Which was to be held at Father Whitmers, where Joseph Smith J now lived. After my arrival I found Brother Joseph in great trouble ~~about~~ of mind on the account of Hyrum Page who had managed to bring some dissension of feeling among some of the brethren by pretending to revelation ^which he had got through a stone^, which were in contradction to [t]he new testament and allso to the revelations of God to us in these last days.[40]

However, after much labor and prayer they were convinced of their error and confessed the same and renounced it being it was not of God, but that Satan had conspired to overthrow their belief in the true plan of Salvation.

---

39. The Allen version adds this, which seems to be Newel's own words, "The letters mentioned above are two which had been written on the occasion of a t[i]rade which had been commenced, by an eminent priest of the day, against Mormonism, and he had chosen my Sister Polly as a mark for his abuse, this resulted in a correspondence between them, in which the priest was so decidedly used up, that he was glad to give it up, and back out completely whipped. I am sorry that I have not copies of these letters by me, so that my children may see how a weak woman, inspired by the Lord, was enabled to confound and put to confusion the learned of the day."

40. Smith, History, 1838–1856, vol. A-1, 54–55, 58, 60. The Allen version includes here the following text that seems written by Newel, but which is not in Newel's version 1: "Here was a chance for Satan to work amongst the little flock, and he sought by this means to accomplish what persecution failed to do. Joseph was perplexed, and scarcely knew how to meet this new exigency. That night I occupied the same room that he did and the greater part of the night was spent in prayer and supplication, and."

In consequence of these things Brother Joseph enquired of the Lord before our Conference commenced and receved the following: Revelation to Oliver Cowdry given at Fayette NY September. 1830.[41]

The same date the following was received Times and Seasons page 130.[42]

The time haveing arrived, Conference assembled [September 26, 1830].[43] The subject of the Stone in connection with Hyrum Page[44] was brought up and

JOSEPH SMITH HISTORY[45]

discussed and after considerable investigation Bother Page as well as well as the whole Church who were present renounced the Said Stone and all things connected with it, much to our satisfaction and happiness.

We now partook of the Sacrament Confirmed and ordaned a goodly number and attended to areat [23] variety of business on that and the following day during which time we had much of the power of God manifest among us

VERSION 1

and it was wonderful to witness the wisdom that Joseph manifested on this occasion for truely God did give unto him great wisdom and power[46]

---

41. Here Newel intends to insert the text of a revelation but does not. The revelation was in *Times and Seasons* 4 (March 1, 1843): 119. The Revelation is Doctrine and Covenants section 28, dated September 1830, which says Satan gave Page false revelations, and that Joseph Smith was the revelator for the Church. *JSP*, D1:183–86.
42. Newel did not copy in the revelation. His notation refers to *Times and Seasons* 4 (March 15, 1843): 130. The September revelation is now Doctrine and Covenants section 29, which deals with last-day events that will usher in the Millennium. *JSP*, D1:177–82.
43. *JSP*, D1:190–92.
44. *JSP*, D1:183–86. See MacKay and Dirkmaat, "Conclusion," in *From Darkness unto Light*, 225–28; Bushman, *Joseph Smith: Rough Stone Rolling*, 121.
45. Smith, History, 1838–1856, vol. A-1, 58.
46. *Times and Seasons* 4 (April 1, 1843): 146. The Allen version includes the following, which seems like Newel's writing and not something added by the editors, none of whom were present when this situation occurred: "and it seems to me, even now, that none who saw him administer righteousness to all, under such

JOSEPH SMITH HISTORY

On this occasion and the holy ghost came upon us and filled us with joy unspeakable; and and & faith & hope & Charity abounded in our midst.[47]

VERSION I

Before we separated the following revelation was given:[48]

Revelation David Whitmer: Peter Whitmer and John Whitmer given Sept 1830. Allso Revelation Thomas B Marsh on the same occasion,

JOSEPH SMITH HISTORY[49]

The conference lasted three days during which time great harmony prevailed and the Saints present all manifested a determination to go forward and do all in their power for the spread of the great and glorious principles of truth which had been revealed by our heavenly Father A number were baptized during the Conference and the work of the Lord spread and prevailed

VERSION I

Conference was dismissed with the benediction and blessing of Joseph Smith Jr upon the Saints.[50]

Soon after this Conference Brother Hyrum Smith and family came to Colesville to ~~labor and~~ live with me for a time. The most of his time as well as my own was spent in traveling and preaching the gospel in the regions round about, where all we could find any who would listen to it either in public or in private. I will mention one by the name of Emer Harris, Brother to Martin Harris, as he was the first man I ever baptized & who proved to be a useful laborer in the vineyard.[51] ~~many~~ ^A few^ believed and were baptized in this region of Country, while many raged and continued to persecute us an to do all in their power

---

      trying circumstances, could doubt that the Lord was with him, as he acted not with the wisdom of man, but with the wisdom of a god."

47. *Times and Seasons* 4 (April 1, 1843): 146; Smith, History, 1838–1856, vol. A-1, 58.
48. *JSP*, D1:187–89, 193. Newel next cites two revelations he wants to add in but does not. Both are in the *Times and Seasons* 4 (April 1, 1843): 146. The first is now Doctrine and Covenants section 30, and the second is section 31.
49. *Times and Seasons* 4 (April 15, 1843): 172; Smith, History, 1838–1856, vol. A-1, 60.
50. Hartley, *Stand by My Servant Joseph*, 88–90.
51. Emer Harris was born May 29, 1781. He was baptized on February 10, 1831, while living near Windham, Luzerne County, Pennsylvania.

to stop the spread of the gospel as revealed to us through Joseph Smith the prophet.[52] ~~in~~

On the fourth of Oct Brother Hyrum Smith held prayer meeting at Brother Aron Culver's and the promise of the Lord was truly verified to us in so much that we did rejoice in his blessings to us.[53] On the Sixth day of the same month we [he]ld meeting at the same place [24] and partook of the Sacrament. On the tenth day of the same month held another meeting at the same place, when two persons came forward and offred themselves for baptism. We attended to the baptism of these after meeting, and in the evening held meeting for confirming them whom we had baptized. We had a good time. On the fourteenth we held meeting at My uncls Hezekiah Pecks.[54] Brother Hyrum had great liberty of speech at this meeting and the Spirit of the Lord was poured out upon us in miraculous manner. There was [m]uch good instructions given and exhortations, which were calculated to encourage and Strengthen the Saints in this their infantile State. At this meeting four persons came forward and manifested their desires to forsake all and serve God in humility and to obey the requirements of the Gospel.

After meeting closed, Brother Hyrum and myself had intended to go and spend the night with one of the Brethren who lived a short distance off. As we were about to start the Spirit whispered to me that I should tarry here all night. I did so. We retired to bed. where ~~I sle~~ rested until about twelve oclock when my uncle Cam in to the room where I was and desired me to get up, telling me he feared his wife was about to die.[55] This surprised me as She had been well when I went to bed. After dressing and asking my heavenly Father to give me wisdom and power to rebuke the destroyer from that habitation, I went in to the room where my aunt lay, in a most fearful Condition. Her eyes were closed and She had verry appearance of one in the last agonies of death. She

---

52. See Porter, "The Colesville Branch and the Coming Forth of the Book of Mormon," 365–85.
53. Aaron Culver was the husband of Esther Peck, the sister of Newel's mother, Polly Peck Knight—hence Newel's uncle by marriage.
54. Hezekiah Peck was the brother of Polly Peck, Joseph Knight's wife—hence Newel's uncle. Hezekiah was married to Martha (Polly) Long.
55. Martha Polly Long Peck (distinct from her sister-in-law, Polly Peck Knight).

finally opened her eyes and bade her husband and Children farewell, telling then she must die for the redemption of this generation as Jesus Christ had died for the generation in his day. Her whole frame shook and She seemed to be racked with the most exquisite torment. Her hands and feet were cold, the blood settled in her fingers and feet; while her husband and Children stood wepping around her bed

This was a scene new to me and I felt that she was suffring under the power of Satan, that it was that same Spirit that had bound me and overpowered [25] me at the time Joseph cast him out of me, as I have before mentioned.[56] I now cried unto the Lord for strengh and wisdom that we might prevail over this wicked sp power with which my aunt was bound. Just at this time my uncle cryed a loud to me saying, O Brother Newel, cannot some thing be done? I felt the Holy Spirit of the Lord rest upon me as he said this, and I immediately steped forward and took her by the hand and commanded Satan, in the name of the Lord Jesus Christ, to depart. I told my aunt she should not die, but that she should live to se her children grow up; That Satan had deceived her and put a lying Spirit in her mouth; That Christ had made the only and last atonement for all that would believe on his name; and that there should be no more sheding of blood for sin. And she believed, and streched forth her hand, and bec[k]ond unto me; and Satan departed frome her.[57]

Ater laboring Somtime in this vicinity we returned to my place, found our wives well and in the enjoyment of the Spirit of the Lord. After spending a few days and comforting the Saints here at Coalsville, we went to See another of my uncls, Ezekiel Peck, Brother to Hezekiah Peck above mentioned.[58] These were my Mothers Brothers. We preached the gospel to them. Both my uncl and his wife Electa embraced the Gospel and were baptized, but few embraced the faith which we preached in that neighborhood. After spending a few day and laboring until we flt we had done all we could, or all that the people would receive, we bade

---

56. Joseph Smith's account of casting the devil out of Knight is in Smith, History, 1838–1856, vol. A-1, 40–41.
57. Hartley, *Stand by My Servant Joseph*, 92–93.
58. Newel's uncle Ezekiel Peck, born in 1785, was the brother of Newel's mother. He married Electa Buck.

to the few that had beleived farewell, and left our blessing with them and again returned home, where we found all well. On our return we found a letter from Brother Joseph Smith Jr and John Whitmer, which I will copy, also one from Oliver Cowdry, which gave us much joy.

ALLEN VERSION[59]

Fayette Dec. 2nd 1830.

Dearly beloved in the Lord.

According to your prayers, the Lord hath called, chosen, ordained, sanctified and sent unto you, another servant and Apostle separated unto his gospel through Jesus Christ ~~his~~ our Redeemer, to whom be all honor & praise henceforth and forever—even our beloved brother Orson Pratt, the bearer of these lines, whom I recommend unto you as a faithful Servant in the Lord, through Jesus Christ our Redeemer, Amen.

To the Church in Coal^e^sville.

Having many things to write to you, but being assured that ye are not ignorant of all that I can write to you, finally I would inform you that Zion is prospering here, there are many serious inquirers in this place, who are seeking the Lord. It gave us much joy to hear from you, to hear that God is softening the hearts of the children of men in that place, it being the seat of Satan. But blessed be the name of God, it also hath become the abode of our Savior, and may you all be faithful and wait for the time of our Lord, for his appearing is nigh at hand.

But the time, and the season, Brethren, ye have no need that I write unto you, for ye yourselves perfectly know that the day of the Lord so cometh as a thief in the night; for when they shall say peace and safety, then sudden destruction cometh upon them, as travail upon a woman, but they shall not escape. But ye, brethren, are not in darkness, therefore let us not sleep as do others, but let us watch and be sober, for they that sleep, sleep in the night, and they that be drunken are drunken in the night, but let us who be of the day, be sober, putting on the breastplate of faith and law, and for a helmet, the hope of salvation.

---

59. Newel intended to copy the letter, which he had in his possession, into his autobiography but never did. Editors of the Allen version include the text. This is a rare letter for which there are no copies other than what the Allen version provides. Because of its intended use and its size, it is included in the primary text.

For God hath not appointed us to ~~into~~ wrath; but to obtain salvation through our Lord Jesus Christ. Wherefore comfort one another, even as ye also do; for perilous times are at hand, for behold the dethronement and deposition of the kings in the eastern continent, the whirlwinds in the West India Islands, it has destroyed a number of vessels, uproo[t]ed [orig. uprooded] buildings and strewed them in the air; the fields of spices have been destroyed, and the inhabitants have barely escaped with their lives, and many have been buried under the ruins. In Columbia, South America, they are at war, and peace is taken from the earth in part, and it will soon be in whole, yea destructions are at our doors, and they soon will be in the houses of the wicked, and they that know not God. Yea lift up your heads and rejoice for your redemption draweth nigh.

We are the most favored people that ever have been from the foundation of the world, if we remain faithful in keeping the commandments of our God. Yea, even Enoch, the seventh from Adam beheld our day and rejoiced, and the prophets from that day forth have prophesied of the second coming of our Lord and Savior Jesus Christ, and rejoiced at the day of rest of the Saints, Yea, and the Apostles of our Savior also did rejoice in his appearance in a cloud with the host of Heaven to dwell with man on the earth a thousand years. Therefore we have reason to rejoice. Behold the prophecies of the Book of Mormon are fulfilling as fast as time can bring it about.

The Spirit of the Living God is upon me therefore who will say that I shall not prophecy. The time is soon at hand that we shall have to flee whithersoever the Lord will, for safety. Fear not those who are making you an offender for a word but be faithful in witnessing unto a crooked and a perverse generation, that the day of the coming of our Lord and Savior is at hand. Yea, prepare ye the way of the Lord, make strait his path. Who will shrink because of offences, for offences must come, but woe to them by whom they come, for the rock must fall on them and grind them to powder, for the fulness of the Gentiles is come in, and woe will be unto them if they do not repent and be baptized in the name of our Lord and Savior Jesus Christ for the remission of their sins, and come in at the strait gate and be numbered with the House of Israel, for God will not always be mocked, and not pour out his wrath upon those that blaspheme his holy name, for the sword, famines and destruction will soon overtake them in their wild career, for God will avenge, and pour out his phials of wrath, and save his elect.

And all those who will obey his commandments are his elect, and he will soon gather them from the four winds of heaven, from one quarter of the earth to the other, to a place whithersoever he will, therefore in your patience possess ye your souls, Amen.

    Joseph Smith Jun.

    John Whitmer.

Brother Hyrum, beware of the Freemasons. McIntyre heard that you were in Manchester and he got out a warrant and went to your father's to distress the family, but Harrison overheard their talk and they said that they cared not for the debt, if they only could obtain your <u>body</u>. They were there with carriages. Therefore beware of the Freemasons, This from yours &c.[60]

VERSION 1

The work of the Lord seems to be prevailing and gaining ground in various parts, for which we feel grateful.

I will mention one instance of a miraculous instance of the power of the Lord made manifest in the healing of a little child belonging to my Sister [27] Anna, Son of Freeborn and Anna Demill. The boys name was Oliver. He lay verry sick of fever so that his life was dispaired of by all who saw him. It so happened that I went to see them ju[s]t at this time. My Sister beged me to lay my hands upon her little son. I did so and rebuked the fever and the destroyer in the name of Jesus Christ of Nazareth, and commanded the Child to be made whol by virtue of that ~~power~~ portion of the holy preisthood vested in me. And it was done, for from that verry hour the Chiild was made whole.[61]

~~Oct 30~~ Oct 18[3]0 The following Revelation was given to Parley P Pratt and Ziba Peterson, Times and Seasons page 179

---

60. Hyrum Smith was a Freemason in Palmyra and owed a small debt to Alexander McIntyre, also a lodge member, and several men were challenging if the debt had been paid.
61. Oliver DeMille, son of Freeborn and Anna Knight DeMille, was born in 1830.

JOSEPH SMITH HISTORY[62]

Immediately on receveing this Revelation preparations wer made for the journey of the Brethren therein designed to the borders of the laamanites. Brother Joseph gave a copy of the above revelation to these Brethren, giving them a charge to be faithful and to lift up their voices in every place wher they could get the people to listen to them. That they should bear a faithful testimony to the things which they knew and confidently believed. All things haveing been made ready, these Brethren bade adieu to their friends and Brethren and Started on their journey preaching by the way and lifting up their voices. Leaving a Sealing testimony in the various villiges through which they passsd, they continued their journey until they arrived at Kirtland Ohio there they found a large opening. Many belived and came forward and were baptized Among the number was Sidney Rigdon.[63]

VERSION I

who came to see Brother Joseph in Dec to enquire of the Lord what he should do, and with him Edward Partridge. He was a pattern of piety[64] and a man who had been baptized by our Brethren on their journey to the Laamanites. Shortly after the arrival of these two Brethren the Lord gave the following Revelation to Joseph Smith Jr and Sidney Rigdon.:

---

62. Newel is citing *Times and Seasons* 4 (May 1, 1843). The revelation is now Doctrine and Covenants section 32, dated October 1830. The revelation calls Pratt and Peterson to accompany Oliver Cowdery and Peter Whitmer Jr. on a mission to the Lamanites. Newel does not include the revelation's text and resumes his autobiography by borrowing again from Joseph Smith's history, *Times and Seasons* 4 (April 15, 1843): 172 but writes as if he, Newel, were composing the material. *JSP*, D1: 200–201.
63. Smith, History, 1838–1856, vol. A-1, 60–61. At this point the *Times and Seasons* stopped publishing installments of Joseph Smith's history and, instead, ran installments giving a biography of Sidney Rigdon.
64. As the *Times and Seasons* stopped publishing Joseph Smith's history, they began publishing bibliographic articles about the life of Sidney Rigdon. This phrase seems to borrow from those articles, but Newel did not continue to copy portions of the Rigdon biographies, as he had with Joseph's history.

Dec 1830 Times and Seasons 320ith page, allso Revelation Edward Partridge same date page 321.⁶⁵

[27] It may be well to observe here that the Lord greatly encouraged strengthened the few who had come out from the world and had not f[e]ared to take upon them his name, in the mist an the scoffs and persecutions of the enemies of truth as revealed to us through the Prophet in these days and in the Book of Mormon [and] by giveing some more extracted information upon the Scriptures, a translation of which had been allready commenced. The Sa[i]nts often enquired among themselves what had become of all the Books refered to both

JOSEPH SMITH HISTORY⁶⁶

in the old and new testament which wer now no where to be found. The only answer was they are lost. It is evident the apostles had at least some of these writeings as Jude quotes the prophecy of Enoch the Seventh from Adam. Greatly to the joy of the Saints which in all ~~numbered~~ from Colesville to Canandaigua. N.Y numbered about seventy souls did the Lord reveal the following doings of olden times, from the prophecy of Enoch.

VERSION 1

Extract from the prophecy of Enoch, Times and Seasons page 336⁶⁷

Soon after the words of Enoch were given, which was to us a great satisfaction, the Lord gave the following Commandment: Revelation given to Joseph Smith Jr and Sidney Rigdon given Dec 1830, Times and Seasons 356.⁶⁸

---

65. Newel did not copy these revelations, which were published in *Times and Seasons* 4 (September 15, 1843), and they are now Doctrine and Covenants sections 35 and 36, both dated December 1830. The first instructs Sidney Rigdon regarding his duties, including to write for Joseph Smith, who then was revising the Bible, and the second calls Edward Partridge to preach. This next paragraph is a paraphrase of Joseph Smith. *JSP*, D1:219–23, 224–25.
66. "History of Joseph Smith," *Times and Seasons* 4 (October 1, 1843): 336; Smith, History, 1838–1856, vol. A-1, 80–81.
67. Newel did not copy into his narration the Enoch excerpts. They were published in the *Times and Seasons* 4 (October 1, 1843).
68. Newel wrote the wrong page number. The revelation is in *Times and Seasons* 4 (October 15, 1843): 352. He did not copy it into his account. The revelation is

The year 1830 is about Closeing upon us. Great things have transpired, too great for pen to paint. To reflect that the closeing year has been one to which all future ages will date the rise or organization of the Church and kingdom of God upon the earth, no more to be thrown down, and to know that I have seen and witnessed these important events with my natural eyes, and allso to know of a surety that the heavens have been opened to my view, that I have beheld the majesty on high and heard the voic of my Redeemer which has spoken words of comfort and instruction to me, fills my whole being with gratitude to my heavenly father while I write these things which are verrily true. And I write them that my posterity and future generations [28] may know of them and that I may leave a faithful testimony of the things which I do know to be verrily true. And may the Lord bless me with a wise and an understanding heart that I may ever do his will and help to establish his great purposes on the earth is the greatest desire I have.

Jan 1ˢᵗ 1831. A new year is now opening upon us. Who can tell the results of the present year. Tomorrow comences the third year Conference held by the Church of Jesus christ in this dispensation.

Jany 2ⁿᵈ 1831.[69] Conference being assembled at Fayette N Y, it was opened by Singing and prayer, after which much good instruction was given and the Saints manifested an unshaken confidence in the great work in which we were engaged. Much buisness was transacted for the Church and there appears to be a Great and glorious prospect for the kingdom of God. In addition to the following buisness of the Conference the following revelation was given to Joseph Smith and Sidney Rigdon Jan 1831.[70]

---

now Doctrine and Covenants 37. It contains the first commandment concerning a gathering in this dispensation. It calls on the church to "assemble together at the Ohio." *JSP*, D1:226–27.

69. *JSP*, D1:229–30.

70. The January 2, 1831, revelation, now Doctrine and Covenants section 38, was published in Joseph Smith's history in the *Times and Seasons* 4 (October 15, 1843): 352–53. *JSP*, D1:229–32.

Jan 1831. Haveing returned from Conference, in obedience to the commandment which had been given, I togather with the Coalesville branch began to make preparations to go to Ohio.[71]

JOSEPH SMITH HISTORY[72]

Towards the latter part of January Brother Joseph Smith Jr ^and wife^ in Company with Sidney Rigdon ^&^ Edward Partridge started for Kirtland Ohio

VERSION I

As might be expected we wer obliged to make great sacrifices of our property. The most of my time was occupied visiting the Brethren and helping to arrange our affairs so that we might be ready to go in one Company and journey to gether from here to Ohio. I need not say that we greatly missd the Society of Brother ~~of~~ Hyrum and his verry amiabl wife when they left us to prepare for ther journey to the west. Father Joseph Smith and family started a little before the Coalesville branch did.[73]

Haveing made the best arrangements we could for the Journey, we bade adieu to all we had [h]eld dear on this earth, except the few who had embraced the gospel of the new and everlasting ~~gospel as~~ covenant as revealed through Joseph [29] Smith Jr, togather with the little of our earthly substance which we could take with us. We Started the forepart of April for Ohio. We had proceeded a few days on our journey when I was Supeoned as a witness and taken back to Coalesvill. On arriveing there it was verry evident that this plan had been adopted by our enemies to add a little more to the persecutions all ready heaped upon ^us^. The Lord reward us all according to our works.[74]

The whol Company declined traveling until I should return. Soon after I left the company, My aunt Electa Peck fell and broke her shoulder in a most shocking manner.[75] A Surgeon was called who did all he could to relieve her sufferings which was verry great. My aunt dreamed

---

71. Porter, "The Colesville Branch in Kaw Township, Jackson County," 281–311.
72. *Times and Seasons* 4 (November 1, 1843): 368; Smith, History, 1838–1856, vol. A-1, 92.
73. Porter, "A Study of the Origins," 119–22.
74. Hartley, *Stand by My Servant Joseph*, 109.
75. Electa was the wife of Newel's uncle Ezekiel Peck.

that I returned and laid my hands upon her and prayed for her and she was made whole and pursued on her journey with the Company. This dream she related to the Surgeon who replied if you are able to travel in many weeks it will be a mericl, & he would be a mormon too. I arrived at the place where this Company had stoped, late in the night. On learning of the accident which had hapened to my aunt I went to see her. Immediately on seing ^me^ entering the room She said, O Brother Newel if you will lay your hands upon me I shall be well and able to go on the journey with you. I s[t]eped up to the bed and in the name of the Lord Jesus Christ rebuked the pain with which she was suffering and Commanded her to be made whole. And it was done, for the next morning She arose, dressed her self, and pursued the journey with us.

We arrived at Buffalo without any further trouble. Here we was to take passage on board a Sloop for fairport, Ohio. The winds blew so that the harbor filled with Ice so that we were detained near two weeks.[76] When we Set Sail on lake Erie the winds continued boisterous So that it rendered our voyage on the lake verry disagreeable. Nearly all the Company being Seasick. However we arrived in Safety at our place of destinatination.

On our arrival it was advised that the Coalesville Branch remain togather and go to [30] a neighboring town Called Thompson, as a man by the name Copley owned a considerable tract of land there, which he offered to let the Brethren occupy on termes agreed upon by both parties. And we comenced work in all good faith, thinking to obtain a living by the sweat of the brow. We had not labored long before the above named Copley broke the engagement which he mad with us.[77] At this time I went to Kirtland to see Brother Joseph and to attend a

---

76. The Colesville Branch and Thomas Marsh's group of about thirty Waterloo Saints, which included Lucy Mack Smith, were blocked by Lake Erie ice. Lucy had her party pray for clear water, and it opened just long enough for them to slip out of the harbor. The Colesville Saints left three days later. A third New York group, based in Palmyra and led by Martin Harris, followed shortly thereafter.
77. Leman Copley, a Shaker, was baptized into the Latter-day Saint faith in 1831. He allowed Saints to settle on his land under the law of consecration but then rescinded his agreement.

Ohio, 1831–1838. Courtesy of the Joseph Smith Papers Project.

Conference which had been appointed to commence on the Sixth of June 1831.[78]

JOSEPH SMITH HISTORY[79]

Conference Convened the elders from various parts of the Country where they had been laboring Came in and the power of the Lord was displayed in a manner that could not be mistaken. The authority of the Melchesidec Preisthood was manifested, and confered ^for the first time^ upon the elders.[80] ~~for the first time~~ It was evident that the Lord gave his people power in proportion to the work which was to be done, and grace ~~which~~ and help as our needs required. Great harmony prevailed; several were ordained: faith was strengthened, and humility, so necessary ~~to strengthen~~ for the blessing of God to follow prayer, Characterized the Saints. The next day as a kind continuation of this great work of the last days Joseph Smith Jr recived the following revelation given June 1831.

VERSION I

Times and Seasons page 416 [Vol. 5, February 1, 1844]

As the branch in Thompson did not know what to do on the account of the covenant which had been made haveing been broken, We sent some of us elders to get Brother Joseph Smith to enquire of the Lord what we should do, and receieved the following Revelation to Newel Knight given June 1831, Times and Seasons page 432[81]

---

78. *JSP*, D1:334–35; John Whitmer, History, 29, in *JSP*, H2:41–42; Held in Kirtland on June 3–4, 1831, this was the Church's fourth general conference. Gathered in a schoolhouse near Isaac Morley's home were forty-three elders, nine priests, and ten teachers. During the conference, the first recorded ordinations to the high priesthood occurred.
79. Smith, History, 1838–1856, vol. A-1, 118.
80. See *JSP*, D1:317–27.
81. The revelation in *Times and Seasons* 5 (February, 15 1844): 432 is now Doctrine and Covenants 54. It instructs Newel to "stand fast" in his appointed office, that his brethren needed to repent, and that they now must "flee the land" and journey, with Newel as leader, to Missouri. There, rather than trying consecration, they were to seek to make their livings "like unto men, until I prepare a place for you." *JSP*, D1:334–36.

JOSEPH SMITH HISTORY[82]

The elders soon began to take their journey two by two as they had been commanded by the word of the Lord

Brother P P Pratt who had returned from last falls expedition had given us inteligence respecting that mission. And the elders who had not returned gave inteligence by writeing. I will here Copy one letter from Brother Oliver Cowdry as it Seems to be a subject of Considerable interest to us at the present time.

VERSION I

Times and Seasons page 432

On receiveing the above, we who had Constituted the Coles-[ville Saints] [31] set immedately to prepare for the journey. And on the third day of July Took passage with the Coalsville Company at Wellsville Ohio, and [ar]rived at St Lewis Mo on the thirteenth. And on the eighteenth tok passage on the Steamer Chieftan for Independence.

My Mothers health was verry poor and had been for a Considerable length of time. Yet She would not consent to stop traveling. Her only, or her greatest desire, was to Set her feet upon the land of Zion, and to have her body intered in that land. I went on Shore and bought lumber to make a coffin in her in case she should die before we arrived at our place of destination, so fast did she fail. But the Lord gave her the desire of her heart, for she lived to stand upon that land where we arrived on the twenty fifth of July 1831.[83]

This was the first branch of the Church which had emigrated to the land of Zion. I had found it required all the wisdom I had to lead this Company through So long a journey in the midst of enemies; yet so great were the mercies and blessings of God to us that not one of us were harmed, and we made our journey in safety.

---

82. Smith, History, 1838–1856, vol. A-1, 122.
83. Newel said elsewhere that the *Chieftain*'s captain was named Shalcross and that the Colesville group, numbering about sixty men, women, and children, landed at Independence Landing on July 26, 1831. Pratt, Knight, and Corrill, "'The Mormons' So Called," December 12, 1833, in *The Evening and Morning Star, Extra*, February 1834, reprinted in *BYU Studies* 14 (Summer 1974): 505–15.

Brother Joseph Smith Jr, Sidney Rigdon, Martin Harris, Edward Partridge, W. W. Phelps. Joseph Coe, A S Gilbert and his wife, had started for missourie on the 19 of June and had arrived at Independence about the middle of July. On our arrival we were glad to find these Brethren who preceeded us well an ^d in^ good health and Spirits. It truely seemed good for Brethren to meet to gather in unity.[84]

Unknown artist, *A Pioneer Home*, engraving, 1881. *History of Jackson County*, Missouri (1881), 25.

But our reflections can be better imagined than told. Haveing Come from a highly Cultivated State of Society in the east, we could not but feel deeply the contrast as we now Stood upon the western limits of the U S A and wer oblged to mingle ~~with~~ and Associate with those who had known nothing but a frontier life until they were but a littl above the natives in point of Education and Refinement. And were full of bigotry, superstition, and prejudice, the natural result of ignorance. All this to gather with the Laamanites before us caused us to exclaim with the prophets of old

JOSEPH SMITH HISTORY[85]

When will [33] the willderness blossom as the rose? When will Zion be built up in her glory, and where will thy te^m^plel stand unto which all nations shall flow come in these last days

VERSION I

Our anxiety was soon relieved by receiveing the following Revelation given in Zion July 1831, Times and Seasons 434.

---

84. Hartley, *Stand by My Servant Joseph*, 121.
85. Smith, History, 1838–1856, vol. A-1, 127.

The Rise of the Latter-day Saints

JOSEPH SMITH HISTORY[86]

We were no longer at a loss to know the exsact Spot for the temple and the City of Zion to be built. We immediately set about building and on the second day of august Brother Joseph Smith Jr the prophet of God assisted the Coalesville branch to lay the first log as a foundation for Zion in Kaw township, twelve miles west of Independance. The log was carried by twelve men in honor of the twelve tribes of Israel. At the same time, through prayer, the land of Zion was Consecrated and dedicated for the gathering of the Saints, by Elder Sidney Rigdon. Tis wa[s] truely a season of joy and rejoiceing to all the Sants wh witnessed it.[87]

VERSION I

As Elder Sidney Rigdon [has] been appointed to write a description of the land of Zion and has taken everry possible means to gather information and I believe he has done justice to the subject, I will copy from him Times and Seasons page 450[88]

JOSEPH SMITH HISTORY[89]

On the third day of August the Spot for the Temple a little west of of Independance was dedicated in presence of eight men by Joseph Smith Jr., Sidney Rigdon. Edward Partridge, W W Phelps, Oliver Cowdry, Martin Harris, Joseph Coe, and my self. The eighty seventh p,^sa^lm was sang read and the scene was solemn and impressive. On the fourth I attended the first Conference held in the land of Zion It was held at the house of Brother Joshua Lewis in Kaw township in the presence of the

VERSION I

Coalsville branch of were present and and much buisness was done and much good instructions given to the Saints. And we felt ^to^ give thanks to that God who had brought us out from the land of our nativity and planted us in the Land of Zion.

---

86. This is in *Times and Seasons* 5 (February 15, 1844). It is now Doctrine and Covenants 57, dated July 1831. It states that Independence, Missouri, is the place for the city of Zion, that Saints are to purchase lands and receive inheritances, and that William Phelps is to be the Church's printer. *JSP*, D2:5–11.
87. *Times and Seasons* 5 (March 1, 1844): 450; Smith, History, 1838–1856, vol. A-1, 137.
88. *Times and Seasons* 5 (March 1, 1844) includes the description, a half page long, but Newel did not include it in his manuscript.
89. Smith, History, 1838–1856, vol. A-1, 139.

On the ~~twenty 6~~th Sixth my Mother died. She qietly fell asleep in death rejoiceing in the new and everlasting Covenant of the gospel and praiseing God that she had lived to see the land of Zion, and that her body would rest in peace after Suffering as She [34] had done from the persecution of the wicked, and journeying to this place.[90] On the Seventh Brother Joseph Smith attended the funeral of my Mother and addressed us in verry able and consoleing manner.

JOSEPH SMITH HISTORY

This was the first death in the Church in this land and I can Say a worthy member Sleeps in ~~death~~ Jesus till the Resurection.[91]

VERSION I

Brother Joseph recived the following Revelation given August in Zion 1831, Times and Seasons page 450[92]

JOSEPH SMITH HISTORY

On the [August] 9 in Company with several Elders Brother Joseph Smith left Independence landing they started down the River in Canoues.[93]

The time now passed in our Common labors in building houses, plowing, and sowing grain. and ~~ob~~ we were obliged ^to^ labor with all diligence to s[e]cure food and prepare ~~food~~ for the comeing winter. As

---

90. Hartley, *Stand by My Servant Joseph*, 135.
91. After Polly's death, Father Knight chose to maintain his own living quarters. Apparently, three of his children still lived with him: Joseph Jr., twenty-three; Polly, twenty; and Elizabeth, fourteen. Before 1831 ended, death claimed two more Knight relatives. Newel's sister Esther, married to William Stringham, died at age thirty-three and left three children. Death next claimed Aaron Culver, leaving Esther Peck Culver, the oldest sister of the deceased Polly, a widow in need of care, so her nephew Newel and his wife Sally took her into their home.
92. The page is in *Times and Seasons* 5 (March 1, 1844): 450, and the revelation is now Doctrine and Covenants 59. It says, among other things, "blessed are they whose feet stand upon the land of Zion who have obeyed my Gospel." *JSP*, D2:30–35.
93. The Colesville Branch, with Newel presiding, settled in Kaw Township, twelve miles southwest of Independence. Smith, History, 1838–1856, vol. A-1, 142. The Colesville settlement was on an elevated plain about four miles southwest of the main crossing of the Big Blue River. The Colesville settlement was in Kaw Township (R33W and T19N). Joshua Lewis's property was in section 21 of that same township. See Romig, *Early Jackson County, Missouri*, 2.

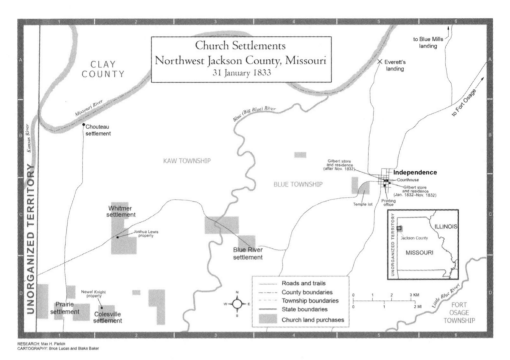

Church Settlements in Northwest Jackson County, Missouri, 31 January 1833.
Courtesy of the Joseph Smith Papers Project.

I had been appointed to preside over the Coalsville branch in this land I felt to humble my Slf and pray to my Father in heaven to give me wisdom to do it acceptable unto him.[94]

---

94. Religious investigator William E. McLellin showed up in August 1831, wanting to talk to Saints, attend their meetings, and see what kind of religion they professed. "Saw love, Peace, Harmony and Humility abounding among them," he said. On August 20 he felt some private doubts about the Church. Newel discerned them. "The time for evening prayer came, and I was glad," McLellin said. "I told my brethren that I felt bad and they prayed for me. Bro. N. Knight after arising from prayer came and by the Spirit of God was enabled to tell me the very secrets of my heart and in a degree to chase darkness from my mind." McLellin accepted baptism, became a vigorous preacher of the Church, and then, briefly, served as one of the twelve apostles. Shipps and Welch, *The Journals of William E. McLellin*, 33–34.

We passed the winter in a tolerable Comfortable maner although, as might be expected, without many of the comonveniencies of life to which we had been accustomed. But we did not murmur for we were welling ^to^ make every Sacrifice which was necessary for ^the^ kingdom of heavens Sake.[95]

On the twenty fourth ^day^ of April eighteen hundred and thirty two Brother Joseph Smith Jr landed at Independence, much to the joy of the Saints in this land.

On the twenty Sixth of April eighteen hundred and twenty two Brother Joseph Smith Jr called a general Council of the Church by which he

JOSEPH SMITH HISTORY[96]

was acknowledged th president of the high preisthood according to a preivious ordination at a Conference of high preists Elders and members held at Amherst Ohio on the twenty fifth of January 1832. The right hand of fellowship wa given to him by the Bishop Edward Partrige in behalf of the Church. The scene was solemn, impressive, and delightful. During the intermission a difficulty which had existed betwen Bishop Partrig^d^ e and Sidney Rigdon was amicably settled and when Conference convened in the after noon all hearts seemed to rejoice

VERSION I

To gether. Besides the business of the Conference, much good instruction was given By Brother [35] Joseph. Allso the following Revelation was g^i^ven Aril 1832 showing the order ~~of Enoch~~ given to Enoch and the Church in his day. Times and Seasons page 624.[97]

---

95. Parley Pratt said that, despite the "dreary winter," he enjoyed "many happy seasons" in the branch's prayer and worship meetings, "and [that] the Spirit of the Lord was poured out upon [them], and even on the little children, insomuch that many of eight, ten or twelve years of age spake, and prayed, and prophecied in [their] meetings, and in [their] family worship." He felt "a spirit of peace and union, and love and good will manifested in this little Church in the wilderness." Pratt, *Autobiography of Parley Parker Pratt*, 72.

96. *Times and Seasons* 5 (September 2, 1844): 624; Smith, History, 1838–1856, vol. A-1, 210.

97. The Enoch material, now Doctrine and Covenants 82, is in *Times and Seasons* 5 (September 2, 1844): 624. It is included in the "History of Joseph Smith" and

JOSEPH SMITH HISTORY[98]

On the twenty Seventh [April 1832] was transacted Considerabl business for the benefit and Salvation of the Saints who were Settling among a frocious set of mobbers like lambs among wolves. Brother Joseph endeavored to so organize the Church hat the Brethren might eventually be independent of everry incumbrance beneath th Celestial kingdom, by bonds and Covenants ~~beneath~~ of mutual friendship, and mutual love

On the twenty eighth and ninth Brother Joseph visited the Brethren above big Blue River in Kaw township, twelve miles west of Independence, and received a hearty welcome only known by Brethren and Sisters united in the same faith and by the same baptism and supported by the same Lord. The Coalsville branch in particular

VERSION I

(I suppose on account of their early acquaintance with him and also the vile persecution he endured for the establishment of the great work of Salvation to the human family or to all who will embrace the gopel as reveeled through him in these last days) were greatly rejoiced to meet with the prophet Joseph to bhold his face and shake hand with him and eat and drink with him again.

JOSEPH SMITH HISTORY

It is good to rejoice with the pople of God. On the thirtieth Brother Joseph returned to Independence, and again Sat in council with the Brethren and received the following Revelation given April 1832.[99]

Council was continued on the firsts of May Arangements were made for printing, and Considerabl business done for the benefit of the Sa[i]nts in this land. Arrangements were allso made for supplying the Saints with Stores which was generally hailed with joy by the Brethren.

---

is captioned "Revelation given April, 1832, showing the order given to Enoch, and the church in his day." *JSP*, D2:233.

98. *Times and Seasons* 5 (September 2, 1844): 625; Smith, History, 1838–1856, vol. A-1, 212–13.

99. The above Joseph Smith text is from Joseph Smith's history in *Times and Seasons* 5 (September 2, 1844): 625. The revelation, dated April 30, 1832, is now Doctrine and Covenants section 83, which deals with women's claims on husbands and children's claims on their parents for for their maintenance. Smith, History, 1838–1856, vol. A-1, 213; *JSP*, D2:240–43.

Elder Rigdon preached two verry powerful discourses before he left which appeared to give satisfaction to the people[100]

VERSION 1

On th sixth of May Brothers Joseph Smith Jr, Sidney, and Newel K Whitney took leave of us and started for their home in Kirtland In July [June 1832] the first number of the even[36]ing and morning Star was Issued by W W Phelps.[101] This paper was hailed with joy by the Sants, as it conta^i^ned much useful matter for them. It was allso a source of joy to know that in so short a time we had ben enabld to do so much and that our prospects were so good. The following are extracts from the evening and Morning Star, Times and Seasons, 626.[102]

The prospect for Crops is tolerable good and the Brethren continue to gather from various parts. The gospel seemes to be gaining ground among the People where it is preached. "On Writing letters" is so rich I copy from the evening and morning Star September 1832, On letter writeing.[103]

On the 14 of Oct 1832 my wif bor to me a son. As I have before stated, her health was poor and she had never before given birth to a liveng Child, and the Doctors who had attended her had said it would not be possible for her to give birth to a liveing Child. But Brother Joseph had blest her and told her she should have the desire of her heart. She never doubted the prophets words, and as soon as her son was born she desired him to be called Samuel, for she said she had asked him from

---

100. Smith, History, 1838–1856, vol. A-1, 214.
101. *The Evening and the Morning Star* was the first Latter-day Saint newspaper. It was initially published in the printing office of William Wines Phelps in Independence, Missouri. The first issue was printed in June 1832. Printing continued until the office was destroyed by a mob on July 20, 1833. In late 1833, printing of *The Evening and the Morning Star* temporarily resumed in Kirtland, Ohio.
102. Newel did not copy the material, which is in Joseph Smith's history installment in *Times and Seasons* 5 (September 2, 1844): 626. It deals with the start of *The Evening and Morning Star*.
103. Newel meant to copy the September 1832 *The Evening and the Morning Star* excerpt of "Writing Letters," but he never did (republished in Joseph Smith's history in *Times and Seasons* 5 [October 15, 1844]: 672).

the Lord. My wif soon recoverd from her sickness and both herself and Child are doing well.[104]

Brother Joseph from time to time sent Copies of Revelations to me for the benefit of the branch over which I presided, in common with all the Saints in Zion. On reading one of these revelations to the branch over which I presided, my aunt of which I have made mention in the fore part of this work,[105] arose and contradcted the revelation, saying It must be taken in a Spiritual light. She went to such a length that I felt constrained to rebuke her by the authority of the preisthood in which [I] was Called to act. At this she was angry, and from that time sought to influence all who would listen her. The result was a division of feeling in the branch. Her husband partook of her Spirit until he became so enthusiastic he went from branch to branch Crying hosanna Glory to God, Zion is redeemed, and blessed is he that bringeth good tidings to the people

Sister Peck at length began to feel the weight of what she had done, but she could not recall [undo] it. She seemed racked with great torment. Her mind found no rest until a burning fever brought her to a sick [37] bed. She sent for several of the Elders to administer to her. Yet She did not find the desired relief. She at last sent for P P Pratt, Lyman Wight and my Self. We all layd our hands upon her and administered to her after which She looked up in dispair and said she had hoped that I would deliver her from the awful State she was in, but now all hope was lost, hell was her portion for ever. Hr whole frame was racked with the most exquisite anguish, while hr mind seemed allmost in dispair.

Brother Parley [Pratt] [said] to me, Brother Newel you must do something for her. My Soul was drawn out in pity for her yet I knew not what to do. I felt impressed to Call the Branch to gather that evening. Whe we had assembled our meting b[e]ing opened by Singing and prayer, I arose, not knowing what to do or what to say. After requesting the prayrs and united faith of all present, the Spirit of the Lord came upon me so that I wa enabld to sho the make plain to the

---

104. Hartley, *Stand by My Servant Joseph*, 154.
105. Apparently, this aunt was Martha Polly Long Peck, wife of Hezekiah Peck.

understanding of all present the cause of Sister Pecks present situation. That She ~~an~~ ^had^ risen up in opposition to the priesthood which had been placed over that branch of the Church and ~~in~~ contradcted the Revelations of God, and that being the ~~sm~~ sympathies shown her, a division of feling had gained advantage over them until Sister Peck had fallen completely into the power of Satan and Could not extricate herself from that power.

I told the Brethren and Sisters if they would repent of what they had done and renew their Covenants one with another and with the Lord, to uphold the authorities placed over them and allso the Revelations which the Lord had given unto us, I [it] would be all right with Sister Peck for this [would] break the bands of Satan [and] make us all freen. I had no sooner Closed my remarks than with one unted voice all came forward and agreed to do so. I then went to Sister Peck and ~~and~~ ^in the name of Jesus Christ and by virtue of the Pr[iesthood]^ Commanded the evil powers to depart from her, and blessed her with peace and Strength both of body and mind. I then dismissed the meeting and told the family to go to bed and rest as usual and all would well.

Early the next morning I called to See Sister Peck. She streched forth her hand as Soon as She saw me and said, [38] O brother Newel, forgive me, I did not believe one word you Said last night, but when I awoke this morning I found I was not in hell.[106] He[r] rejoicings were verry great, and union again prevailed with us and we all flt that we had learned a lesson that would be of lasting benefit to us.[107]

---

106. Hartley, *Stand by My Servant Joseph*, 154–55.
107. In the fall of 1832, bickering among Newel's relatives tested his patience, and he partially failed that test. Church records say that on October 21, elders met at Newel and Sally's house "to search out & examine into the nature of grievances as set forth by sister Emily Colburn & Elizabeth Gilbert respecting the teaching & Spirit which had actuated br. Newel Knight for a length of time past." Eight council members listened to testimony, including "considerable" from Newel. The men voted by lots regarding "the Spirit which br. Newel was actuated by this evening." The vote was unanimous against him, although two men abstained. But when Newel protested the decision, the two abstainers added their votes against him. The council also reproved the two sisters for unspecified "out of the way" doings. When Newel asked what he should do, and what would

The following beautiful instruction given by Joseph Smith is worthy [of] a place in everry mans journal and should be Constantly in the heart and habitation of everry Saint. Times and Seasons 600.[108]

In May the second number of the Star was issued. The following is an extract Times and Seasons page 640,[109]

The same number of the Star contains the following Times and Seasons page 656, allso the following on letter writeing, Times and Seasons page 672 Sept No. The following is a Copy from Joseph Smith Junior to W W Phelps, allso Orson ^Hyde^ and Hyrum Smiths Epistle to the Saints in Zion.[110]

---

become of him, the council advised "that he should not officiate as an Elder until he ~~should~~ could see with the other Elders & be able to discover that he had a bad spirit." Unlike several early elders who disaffected because they were chastised by church officers, Newel humbled himself and repented. Soon he received back his presidency. *JSP*, D2:231–32.

108. Newel's citation, page 600, is an error—that page has nothing Newel would want to copy. The editors of the Allen version, however, insert an article called "Common Schools" without any citation. That article is probably what Newel meant to refer to.

109. This citation to *Times and Seasons* 5 (September 15, 1844): 640 is to "The Elders in the Land of Zion, to the Church of Christ Scattered Abroad," published in the second issue of *The Evening and Morning Star*. It gives general information about the state of the Church in Zion in 1832. Preceding that item is the "Common Schools" discussion, which the Allen version copies into Newel's account, published in that issue of the *Star*. Next, Newel mentions three items he wanted to copy from the *Times and Seasons*.

110. Newel's first reference here is to *Times and Seasons* 5 (October 1, 1844): he notes page 656, which probably meant 657–58, containing the "On Priesthood" revelation that is now Doctrine and Covenants 84 and dated September 22–23, 1832. The second reference, page 672, contains the "Writing Letters" article. The third reference is to two letters. Newel gives no citations, but the Joseph Smith letter to W. W. Phelps and the Orson Hyde and Hyrum Smith letter to the Saints in Zion are in the "History of Joseph Smith" installment in *Times and Seasons* 5 (December 1, 1844): 720–23. The letter to Phelps is dated January 11, 1833. It was sent to pacify Phelps and the "inhabitants of Zion." "Repent is the voice of God to Zion." Enclosed with the letter was the revelation termed the "Olive Leaf," now Doctrine and Covenants 88. The Orson Hyde and Hyrum Smith letter to the bishop, council, and inhabitants of Zion criticizes rebellious attitudes in Zion. *JSP*, D2: 334–47.

Jan first 1833. Great are the events that have transpired the past year. A catalogue [of] disasters never before heard of have been recorded during the past year. Yet the honest in heart stand firm and unshaken in the gospel of salvation and rejoice that they are counted worty to be numbered with the people of God. The following is Copy of a Revelation sent to me from Brother Joseph from Kirtland Ohio.[111]

On the 6 of April 1833 the Inhabitants of Zion for the first time celebrated the birthday of the Church Times Seasons pag 752[112]

Soon after this meeting the following letter come to hand from Brother Joseph Smith, Times and Seasons page 753.[113]

In the latter part of April the first regular mob rushe[d] to gather, in Independence, (Zion) to council upon a plan. This as might be expected caused considrabl uneasiness among the Saints and required great wisdom and care on our part in ord[er] to keep all as quiet and as diligent in all our duties as the circumstances required. However, we kept on with our farming operations, building, and so forth. In the mien time the Lord had given a Revelation [to] the inhabitants of Zion instructing them to build a temple to his holy name.[114]

The following is an explanation of the plot of ^the city^ Zion Sent to the brethren in Zion the twenty fifth of June 1833.[115]

---

111. Newel says the revelation, which he did not insert, was "sent to me." It is not clear which revelation this is. At least five revelations came during January–April 1833 (sections 88, 89, 90, 91, and 92). He is probably referring to the Word of Wisdom revelation received on February 27, 1833, now Doctrine and Covenants 89, which is addressed to, among others, the Saints in Zion. Or perhaps the revelation in question is the March 19, 1833, revelation, now Doctrine and Covenants 91, concerning the Apocrypha. *JSP,* D3:11–23, 32–34.
112. Two paragraphs describing the celebration, held at the Big Blue ferry, are in "History of Joseph Smith," in *Times and Seasons* 5 (January 1, 1845): 752.
113. The letter, Joseph Smith to "Dear Brethren in Zion," dated March 21, 1833, was published in *Times and Seasons* 5 (January 1, 1845): 753. It responds to an epistle from Zion that contained confessions of their disloyalty.
114. This is the June 1, 1833 revelation, now Doctrine and Covenants 95. In it, the Lord says he chastises those whom he loves, and the Zion Saints are chastised for their failure to build the house of the Lord. *JSP,* D3:104–8.
115. Newel intended to include the explanation that is in the "History of Joseph Smith" installment published in *Times and Seasons* 6 (February 1, 1846): 786–87.

The same [day] was written a letter to W Phelps and others from Kirtland as follows Times and Seasons page 780[116]

[39] July 29 1833, hostile feelings seem to be increaseing towards the Saints in this Region and our glorious Indepence which once dwned upo a peaceful and happy people will now have to blush at the savage barbarity and mobocracy of Missouri. Most of the Clergy acting as missionaries to the Indians, or to the frontier inhabitants, were among the most prominent Characters who rose up and rushed on to destroy the rights of the Church as well as the lives of her members. One Pixley who had been sent by the missionary Society to civilize and Christianize the heathen of the West, was a black rod in the hands of Satan as well as a poisoned shaft in the power of our foes, to spread lies and falsehoods.

He followed writeing horible accounts to the religious papers in the east, to sour the public mind, Besides useing his influence among Indians and whites to overthrow the Church. On the first of July he wrote a slanderous article entitled "beware of false prophets" which he actually carried from house to house, to ~~increase~~ cense the inhabitants against the Church to mob them and drive them away.

This is a letter that describes the one-square-mile plot, tells how the lots are to be laid off, calls for twenty-four public buildings in the middle of the city (including a temple), and says the city would be for fifteen thousand to twenty thousand people. It also includes a description of the temple. See *JSP*, D3:131–46.

116. Newel listed the wrong page number. The letter is in the "History of Joseph Smith" installment in *Times and Seasons* 6 (February 15, 1845): 800–801. Addressed to Phelps and others in Zion, the letter discusses consecration, the lost books of the Bible, and instructions regarding high priests. Enclosed with it is a draft of the city of Zion with explanations. The letter also praises how *The Evening and Morning Star* is being handled. See *JSP*, D3:147–56.

117. *Times and Seasons* 6 (March 1, 1845): 816; Smith, History, 1838–1856, vol. A-1, 319–20.

New York, Ohio, and Missouri, 1800–1834

C. C. A. Christensen, *Mobbers Raiding Printing Property & Store at Independence, Mo., July 20, 1883* (ca. 1882–84), photograph of panorama. Courtesy of Church History Library.

VERSION 1

Copy from *Times and Seasons* page 816.

The ^July N of^ evening & morning Star pursued a mild and pacific course. The evening & morning Star extra, times & seasons 818.[118]

On the 2 inst [August] the Same day of publication of the mob in the moniter [*Western Monitor*] ^times and seasons 1833^ the following Revelation was given, times & seasons page 848[119]

---

118. Newel refers here to an *Evening and Morning Star, Extra* item, dated July 16, 1833, included in the "History of Joseph Smith" installment in *Times and Seasons* 6 (March 1, 1845): 818–19. The big excerpt is from the *Star*'s article "'The Mormons' So Called,'" which Newel wrote along with Parley P. Pratt and John Corrill. It deals with the initial mobbings the Saints suffered in Jackson County. See *JSP*, D3:165–75.

119. Now Doctrine and Covenants 97, the revelation is included in the "History of Joseph Smith" installment in *Times and Seasons* 6 (April 1, 1845): 848. It deals with the upset affairs of the Saints in Jackson County and contains "my will concerning your brethren in the Land Zion." *JSP*, D3:198–202.

JOSEPH SMITH HISTORY[120]

A[t] a Council of high preists in Zion, Elder Christian Whitmer was ordained to the high preisthood. And on the 28 [August] the Council resolved that no high preist ^shall ordain any^ Elder or preist shall ordain any high preist, Elder, or preist in the land of Zion without the consent of a Councilnce of high preists.

VERSION 1

In the mien time Oliver Cowdry had been sent to Kirtland, whereupo[n] Orson Hyde and John Gould were despached to us as soon as possible. As soon as necessary preparations could be made, Elders W W Phelps and O hide were dispached to the governor of Missouri resideing at Jefferson City, with the following petition, times and Seasons page 851.[121]

[40] Oweing ^to^ great scarsity of mills in the Country, I had been induced to build one. I had succeeded, and not only the Sants but allso the old settlers found themselves greatly benefited by it. We now found it necesssary to keep a guard at the mill both day and night. While engaged in guarding, Brother P P Pratt was struck over the head by one of the mob with a gun and severely injured.[122]

---

120. *Times and Seasons* 6 (April 1, 1845): 850. Newel attended both of these meetings, the first on August 21, 1833, and the second on August 28. Cannon and Cook, *Far West Record*, 62–64.
121. Elders W. W. Phelps and Orson Hyde delivered the petition to Governor Daniel Dunklin. It detailed at length the course of anti–Latter-day Saint activities through July 1833 at least. The petition is part of the "History of Joseph Smith" installment in the *Times and Seasons* 6 (1 April 1845): 851–54.
122. Hartley, *Stand by My Servant Joseph*, 174. For context, see Givens and Grow, *Parley P. Pratt*, 43–53.

On receiveing the the Revelation to build a house to the name of the Lord in Zion,[123] the following paper was circulated in Coalesville branch, when the following Subscriptions were made for the same:[124]

We the undersigned subscribers feeling desirous to assist in building a house for the use of the Church of Christ as a house of worship, but more ~~especially~~ particularly designed to accommodate the officers or ordaned members of Said Church to meet in, to attend to all business that may be necessary for them to transact; Said house to be built of brick or stone on the S E qr of Sec 3. Township 49 and Range 32. We therefore agree to pay the several sums annexed to our names, to the order of Bishop Edward Partridge any time after the first day of January next. If in money or grain to be delivered at the Store of Gilbert and Whitney, and if in materials for building on or near the spot designed for said building, and if in labor when called for by said order. In testimony where ~~unto~~ we have here unto set our nanes with the sum annexed:

Jackson Co Sept 1833

Caleb Baldwin	in labor	$20.00	Benjamin Slade	in labor	20.00
Ezekiel Peck	"	30.00	Ira J Willis	"	30.00
Joseph Knight Jr	"	20.00	Joseph Knight Sen	"	100.00
Clark Slade	"	50.00	Newel Knight	"	100.00

---

123. The June 1, 1833 revelation that is now Doctrine and Covenants 95. An August 2, 1833, revelation (Doctrine and Covenants 97) urged in verses 11 and 12 that "it is my will that an house should be built unto me in the Land of Zion, like unto the pattern which I have given you yea, let it be built speedily." *JSP*, D3:104–7.

124. The following document is significant for two reasons: it is found in no other source, and it shows that as of September 1833, the Jackson County Saints did not believe they would be expelled from the county. All of the signers were members of the Colesville Branch.

The Rise of the Latter-day Saints

Notwithstanding the persecution of our enemies, many of the Saints manifested by their works [41] a determination to Carry out the council of those who were placed to manage and preside in Zion. In fact we could not believe that the government was so far from granting us that protection guaranteed to us by our parent goverment, which had been won by the blood of our Fathers, as to suffer us to be expeled by a lawless mob, which the sequel will show really was the case.

As yet the Sa[i]nts had made no resistance but had continued to petition the civil authorities for protection. their ^Our^ petition to the Governor of the State seemed to enrage the mob and to urge on their hellish designs.

JOSEPH SMITH HISTORY

They began by stoning houses, breaking windows and doors, and committing other outrages. But nothing verry serious was done until the last of Oct. On thursday night the thirty first a mob of forty or fifty collected and proceeded to armed to a branch of the Church who lived eight or ten miles South west of Independence. There they unroofed ten houses and partly threw down the bodies of some of them; they caught three or four of the men and, notwithstanding the Cries and entreaties of their wives and Children, they whipt and beat them in a barbarious maner. Others evaded a beating by flight. [T]hey were taken by surprise by the mob, consequently wer not collected to gether or in a situation to defend themselves against so large a body, therefore the made no resistance. The mob, after threatening to visit them again in a rougher manner, dispersed.

The news of this outrage soon spread through the different settlements of the Saints and produced feelings more easily felt than described. For they verry well knew by the threatenings of the mob and their breaking the treaty of agreement which was made only a few days before as it were that there was trouble a head. The Sants were in a scattered condition and what to do for safety they knew not and did not know what to do. . . . A consultation was held, near Independence, by some of the principal men of the church to see what was best to be done; it was concluded to get peace warrants, if possible. . . .

Some of the principle men of the Church held a consultation and desided to try to get peace warrants against some of the principle leaders of the mob. Accordingly they went to a magistrate and applied for a warrant but he would not grant one.

The governors letter directing them to proceed in that way was then read to him, upon which he replied he did not care any thing about it. At that time the Streets were filled with [42] mobbers in every direction passing and repassing, threidening the Saints in different directions with destruction. To be deprived of the benefit [of] law at so critical a moment was calculated to make the Saints feel solemn and to mourn over the depravity of man. But we had not much time for reflection, for we had much to do to prepare for the night which was just at hand in the which we expected the mob would be upon us. Up to this time the persons of women and children had been considered Safe as they had seldom been abused. Therefore the men ran togather for the night, leaveing their families at home.

At Independence the men met half a mile from the Court house. Night came on and a party of the mob who had staid in the village were heard brick batting the houses; Spies were sent to discover their movements, who returned with information that they were tearing down a brick house belonging to Gilbert and Whitney, and allso breaking open their store. Upon hearing that news, those who were collected to gather formed them selves in to two small companies and marched up to the public Square where they found a number of men in the act of Stoneing the Store of Gilbert and Whitney (which was broken open and some of the goods thrown into the street). They all fled, but one Richard McCarty who was taken. Gilbert and one or two others went to Esq Westons and demanded a warrant for him, but he refused to give him one; consequently McCarty was Set at liberty. Next morning it was ascertaind that windows were broken open where there where none but women and Children were alone. One house in particular which had window shutters, and they were shut, had a rail thrust through in to the room where there were none but women and children. Seeing that neither Sex nor age were safe, the women and Children were all moved out of the village that day.

That same night the other party of the mob collected ten or twelve miles from Independence near a body of the Saints. Two of their company went [to] discover the situation of the Brethren. They came near the guard, when P. P. Pratt, discovering them, went up to them, when one of them struck him over the head with a gun which cut a large hole in his head and nearly knocked him down; but he recovered himself, called to his men, who were near. They took the spies and disarmed them of two rifles and three pistols [and] kept them in custody till morning, then gave them their arms and let them go without injureing them. The rest of their company were heard at a distance but they dispersed without doing [43] any harm.[125]

Saturday Nov Second, it was concluded to try again for a peace warrant. Accordingly application was made to magistrate by the name of Silvers who resided some distance from town and who had not as yet openly joined the mob. But he refused to grant a warrant, saying if he did he feared his life would be in danger.

The next day four men started to the C^ircuit^ [Ct.] Judge forty miles distance. After considerable delay by the Judge, they obtained a warrant against a number of individuals. When the warrants arrived it was too late to do any thing with them for the whole Country was getting up in arms, and it was all the Saints could do to take care of them slves to save their lives as they best could for. On Saturday night a party of the mob went to a Settlement liveing on ^the^ big blue river about six miles west of town. They first tore the roof from a house, and injured the furniture within; the[y] then divided their company into two parties. One went to pulling the roof from another dwelling house, while another party went to another and broke it open. They found the owner D Bennet in bed, whom they took and beat unmercifully; one of the Company drew a pistol and swore that he would blow out his brains. But the ball laid bare his skull with out fractureing it, thus narrowly he escaped wih his life. A party of the Saints were collected near by who, hearing the disturbance, went to the place. The mob ~~went to the place~~ began to fire upon them and they returned the compliments. A few guns were discharged from both parties, but the fire was not gen-

---

125. Newel continues here by copying from the next installment of the Robinson and Smith, "History, of the Persecutions," published in the *Times and Seasons* 1 (January 1840): 33–36.

eral. At length a young man was shot in the thy, (but by which party it is unknown) and soon after the mob dispersed for that night.

Sunday Nov 3rd Many threatinings were heard from the mobbers. They were greatly enraged, and were exerting themselves to strengthen their party; for as yet some of the inhabitants manifested friendship for the Brethren. Such told them that they expected they would all be destroyed massacreed, for the enemy were about get a six pounder, and come openly against them the next day.

Monday Nov 4 A large mob collected at Wilsons Store about a mile west of big Blue, took the ferry boat, and threatend [44] some lives. But for some unknown cause, perhaps to take some more whiskey, they left the blue and returned to Wilsons Store again.

Whilest they were at the Blue threatening the Saints, word was sent to a body of the Brethren about five or six miles distant to the Southwest that a large mob was collected, and they expected that they should need help. Whereupon, nineteen brethren started to go and assist them. But before they reached Wilsons store, they learned that the mob had returned there. Upon hearing this they proceeded no farther, but returned back. The mob by some means feared that they were on the way road west of them, when from fifty to seventy of the mob took their rifles, mounted their horses, and went in pursuit of them. After traveling about two miles they came in sight of them, when they all fled into the cornfields and woods. Some went immediately to the body, and informed their brethren, of what they had seen. About thirty of the saints (mostly those who had lived in the Settlement where the mob then was, some of whom had had their houses unroofed but a short time before) took their arms, and started as soon as possible, to meet the mob.

Mean time the mob turned their horses into cornfields of the Saints, and then hunted for them who had fled. They went to Christian Whitmers, a lame brother who had not left home, and pointed their guns at him and threatened his life if he did not tell them where his brethren had fled to. They allso threatened women and Children In this maner for a bout an hour, when about sundown a company of a bout thirty brethren marched up. As soon as they came near enough, the mob fired upon them and they immediately fired back. After a round or two, the mob retreated and left the ground They were followed a short distance but not far.

Two of the mob ^were killed^ and a number of horses were killed, and some five or six wounded. The mob were so frightend that they left their dead on the ground over night. The Saints had four or five wounded, one by the name of [45] barber a young man, mortally who died the next day This young man was the first who had fallen a martyr in this dispensation. Philo Dibble was allso wounded ^in the bowels^ by the first gun fired he[126]

VERSION I

was examined by a Surgeon of great experience and practice, he haveing served a Srgeon in the Blackhawk war. He said he ^seen he^ had never known a man to live wounded as Brother Dibble was. Alanson Cleaveland was another who was wounded in his shoulder but not mortally.[127]

The next day I went to see brother Dibble. I found the house where he laid surrounded with the mob. I managed to get into the house when two of the mob Seated them Selves in the door. I went up to the bed wher he lay in extreme agony. As I looked upon him, not dareing to utter a word of prayer, I laid one hand upon his head while wih the other I drawed the bed curtain to hide us a little from the mob, and lifted my desires to the Lord in behalf of Brother Dibble, after which I arose and went away. As I left him I saw tears fast streaming from his eyes, yet no word passed, but I felt that I had done my errand and felt to trust the event to the Lord. As I to well knew the design of the mob who had been stationed there, the I did not feel to give my self in to their power at that time.

The next day I had buisness about ten miles [dis]tant, where to my great joy I found Brother Dibble to all appearance perfectly well. He

---

126. Robinson and Smith, "History, of the Persecution," 33–34. Here Newel stops copying and tells his own remarkable involvements with the wounded Philo Dibble. Dibble's own statement about Newel's healing him is in Christensen, "Before and After Mt. Pisgah," 79.
127. Alanson, family genealogy records show, was either newly married to or about to marry Newel's first cousin Anna Slade.

told me that at the time I laid my hand upon his head he felt the Spirit of the Lord rest upon him and pass gently through his body, and before it pass all pain and soreness so that he felt perfectly easy. In a few minutes he discharged about a gallon of putrid blood allso the balls that had entered his body and peices of his clotheing. He rested that night and the nex day made his escape and was nearly out of the County when I met with him. O how did our hearts rejoice and give thanks to that God who had heard and answered the petitions although offered up secret in behalf of this his Servant while surround with feinds [46] in humane form.[128]

But to[129] return to the day of battle

JOSEPH SMITH HISTORY

The same [day] at Independence. As Gilbert, I Morley, J Corril, and Wm E McLellin were taken for assault in and battery, and false imprisonment by McCarty. whom they had taken the friday night before, and although they could not get a warrant for him, for breaking open the store, yet he had obtained one for them for catching him at it.[130]

[p. 898] On the nights of the 5 & 6 of Nov, Tuesday & Wednesday, Women & Children were fleeing in every direction before the merciless mob. One party of a bout one hundred & fifty women & children fled to the prairies where they wandered several days under the broad canopy of haven with about Six men to protect them. The prairie had recently been burnt. and the Children being barefooted their feet were so cut and worn that it was easy to track them by the blood left up on the earth & stubs. Other parties fled to the Missouri river & took lodgeings for the night where they could find it. One Mr Bennet opened his houses for a nights shelter, to a wandering party of distressed women &

---

128. Hartley, *Stand by My Servant Joseph*, 175–77.
129. Smith, History, 1838–1856, vol. A-1, 375–76.
130. Robinson and Smith, "History, of the Persecution," *Times and Seasons* 1 (January, 1840): 34. Here Newel resumes quoting, with but slight word modifications, from the "History of Joseph Smith" installment in *Times and Seasons* 6 (May 15, 1845): 896–900. As a refugee, on December 12, 1833, Newel coauthored with Parley P. Pratt and John Corrill a circular, "'The Mormons' So Called," offering facts about the Saints' expulsion from Jackson County. It was published the next April. But he does not quote from it in this autobiography.

Children who were fleeing to the Missouri river. During this dispersion of the women & Children, parties of the mob were hunting the men, fireing upon some, tying up & whipping others, and some they pursued upon horseback for several miles.

On the 5 [of November] Elders Gilbert Phelps and McClellan went to Clay CO and made affidavit to similar to the foregoing sketch, & forwarded the same to the Governor by express; & the [g]overnor immediately upon the recepton there of ordered a Court of inquiry to be held in Clay county, for the purpose of investigating the whole affair & meeting out justice to all; but alas corruption wickedness & power have

Left the wretches unwhipt of justice

And innocence mourns in tears unwipt

Thursday Nov 7. The Shore began to be lined on both sides of the ferry with men women & Children, goods, waggons boxes, Chests, provisions &c. while the ferry [47] men were busily employed in crossing them over. And when night again closed upon the Saints, the wilderness had more the appearance of a Camp meeting. Hundreds of people were seen in every direction, some in tents, and some in the open air, around their fires, while the rain decended in torrents. Husbands were enquireing for their wives & wives for their husbands; parents for children and children for parents. Some had the good fortune to escape with their families, house hold good, and some provisions, while others knew not the fate of their freinds and knew not the fate of their goods. The scene was indiscribable, and would have melted the hearts of any people upon earth, except the blind oppresser, and prejudiced and ignorant bigot. Next day the Company increased, and they were Cheifly engaged in felling trees, and erecting them into temporary Cabins, so that when night again Closed upon us we had the appearance of a village of wigwams. The rain had passed, by the night was Clear, and we began to enjoy a little degree of comfort, and we did not forget to lift our voices to God ^in gratitude^ for the blessings we did enjoy, and allso to ask for his protecting care to be over us. And for wisdom to direct all of our movements ~~and~~ and that he would soften the hearts of the people

C. C. A. Christensen, *[Solomon] Hancock & Company's Exit from Jackson Co. Mo. Nov. 1833* (ca. 1882–84), photograph of panorama. Courtesy of Church History Library.

among whom we had fled, that we might obtain where with to sustain our selves.[131]

[p. 898] Lieutenant Governor Boogs presented a curious external appearance; yet he was evidently the head and front of the mob, for, as what may be easily seen by what follows, no important move was made without his sanction. He certainly was the cecret spring of the 22 & 23 of July & as will appear in the sequel. By his authority the mob were molded into militia, to effect by stratagem, what he knew as well as his hellish host could not be done by civil force. As Lieut Governor he had only to wink and, the mob went from maltreatment to murder. The horrid Calculations of this Second Nero were often developed in a way that could not be mistaken. Early on the morning of the 5, say at one oclock A M, he come to Phelps, Gilbert & Partridge and told them to flee for their lives. Now unless he had given the orders so to do, no one

---

131. Smith, History, 1838–1856, vol. A-1, 374–75. Regarding the Saints' expulsion from Jackson County, see Jennings, "Zion Is Fled"; Hartley, "Mobbed from Jackson County, Missouri," 21–45.

would have attempted to murder after the Church [48] had agreed to go away. His conscience vassilated on its rocky mooring, and gave the secret alarm to these men.

The saints who fled took refuge in the neighboring Counties, mostly in Clay CO which received them with some degree of kindness. Those who fled to the County of Vanburen were again driven and compelled to flee, & those who fled to Fayette CO were soon expelled, or the most of them, and had to move where ever they could find protection.[132]

The Governor D Dunklin was disposed to bring the mobbers to justice.[133] Consequently, ten or twelve witnesses were subpoened to attend the February term of the Circuit Court. Capt. Atchison was ordered to guard them over to Jackson, and back with his Company of [Liberty] Blues. The attorney Gen. was also ordered, or requested to by the Gov., to attend the Court to assist the Circuit attorny in the investigation. The witnesses were guarded over to Independence, and after haveing been there a short time, they were visiti^e^de by the circuit attorney, ~~in the investigation.~~ accompanied by the attorney General. They informed the witnesses that such was the excitement prevailing there that it was ~~doub~~ doubtful whether any thing could be done to bring the mobbers to justice. That if they should be convicted, they would only be fined in some trifleing sum not to exceed $5 at most, just enough to answer the law. And they advised the witnesses not to go before the Grand Jury, intimateing at the same time that they might be in danger.

---

132. Smith, History, 1838–1856, vol. A-1, 375–76. Newel fails to record that shortly after midnight on November 13, the Saints encamped along the river bottoms saw the heavens "enveloped in splendid fireworks" and "thousands of bright meteors" as thick as snowflakes shoot in every direction for several hours. People went from tent to tent, waking up sleeping Saints to see the heavenly show. Even Joseph Smith witnessed the display, the Leonid Meteor shower, which was seen from the Rocky Mountains to New York City. Some Saints saw it as a sign that God would soon open the way for them to return to Jackson County; others beleived that Christ's Second Coming was near at hand. Pratt, *Autobiography*, 97, 103; "History of Joseph Smith," in *Times and Seasons* 6 (May 15, 1845): 898. Several descriptions of the meteor shower by the homeless Saints are in Parkin, "History of Latter-day Saints in Clay County," 44–47.
133. Newel now resumes quoting from Robinson and Smith "History, of the Persecution," *Times and Seasons* 1 (February 1839): 49.

Unknown artist, *The Falling of the Stars, Jackson County, Missouri, November 13, 1833* (ca. 1882–84), photograph of panorama. Courtesy of Church History Library.

The witnesses replied that they had been ordered there by the Court, and they supposed they were still subject to the Court, or to them the attorneys. As to the danger in going before the Grand ^Jury^ they feared it not. They were ready and willing to go and testify to the truth.

The attorneys left them, and in a short time after they were informed by Capt Atchison that the judge, Mr Ryland, had sent him word that the witnesses and guard were not wanted there any longer. Capt Atchison paraded his men as soon and as well as he could for the crowd, and immediately marched off, the witnesses following [49] him. All hopes were now given up of ever bringing that hope to justice. Their hatred towards the Saints appeared to be unabateing. They had frequently sent over word to Clay CO, that they were comeing over to drive the Saints from that place. They even went so far as to Circulate a paper in Clay Co., the object of which was to get volunteers there to assist them in driveing the Saints away. In Clay CO, however, they had but few friends (for some time) and could not obtain many signers.

A wealthy farmer by the name of Arthur, liveing in Clay CO. who was then friendly to the Saints, and who was in the the habit of sending flour & whiskey into Jackson to sell, (it generally being higher there than in Clay Co. in consequence of the Indian trade), sent over one of his negroes and team with a load. They were stopped on the road by some of the people of Jackson, who mounted the load, & with axes cut the barrels to peices, and wasted the flour & whiskey upon the ground[134]

VERSION 1

The following letter written Brother Joseph Smith Jun was received with great satisfaction by the Saints, Times and Seasons page 928[135]

---

134. Robinson and Smith "History, of the Persecution," *Times and Seasons*, vol. 1, no. 4, February, 1840, 49. The letter, which Newel did not copy, is dated December 10, 1833, and is addressed to six elders in Missouri (he is not one of them) and to "all the saints whom it may concern." It is found in the "History of Joseph Smith" installment in *Times and Seasons* 6 (June 15, 1845): 928. It is a response to a November 19 letter from Zion regarding the Saints' flight from Jackson County.

135. *JSP*, D3:375–81.

The following letter written by W W Phelps in behalf of the Saints to the Prophet Joseph, Times page 944[136]

On the same page Revelation Sent to the Saints is given.[137]

The Saints generally, ^although^ ~~felt that~~ the hand of persecution was heavily upon them, felt firm and unshaken in the faith of the gospel which they had embraced. And allthough they had strong inducements held out to them by the most influential of the mob, but verry few seemed to be in the least degree moved by them; for all that was required of any one of the Saints in order to be acknowledged a good citizen of Jackson CO. was to deny the faith of the gospel as revealed to us in this dispensation through Joseph Smith Jun. This I think speaks well for the brethren.

The Coalesville branch with a few more families remained near to gather near the Missouri river [in Clay County].[138]

[50] On the first day of January 1834 was held a Conference. Bishop Edward Partridge presided. After transacting much ~~buis~~ business in relation to comforting and strengthening & comforting the Saints in their present sorrowful condition, it was resolved that Lyman Wight & Parley P Pratt be sent as ^special^ messengers to represent the situation of the scattered brethren in Missouri to the presidency & Church in Kirtland & to ask their advice &c.[139]

On the 9 of Jan Bro A S Gilbert wrote as follows to Governor D Dunklin of Missouri.[140]

---

136. *JSP*, D3:382–86. Phelps's letter is written to Joseph Smith, dated December 15, 1833, and is included in the "History of Joseph Smith" installment in *Times and Seasons* 6 (July 1, 1845): 944. It says the Saints are scattered, their situation dubious, and their prospects looked gloomy.

137. *JSP*, D3:386–97. Newel refers here to a revelation dated December 16, 1833, which is now Doctrine and Covenants section 101. It says the Saints in Missouri are chastened and afflicted because of their transgressions. They are to importune for redress of their grievances.

138. Regarding the Saints in Clay County, see Parkin, "History of Latter-day Saints in Clay County."

139. Newel here paraphrases from "History of Joseph Smith," *Times and Seasons* 6 (July 15, 1845): 961.

140. Newel did not insert this item, which is included in the "History of Joseph Smith" installment in *Times and Seasons* 6 (July 15, 1845): 962–63. In the letter,

On the 4 of Feb Governor wrote to the brethren as follows, Times and Seasons page 977[141]

Times and Seasons page 992:[142]

Also page 1022 & 3 & 4 allso 1041[143]

Gov Dunklin wrote as follows. Times & Seasons 1056 7 & 8, also 1059[144] ~~On the 20 of Feb~~

I will here insert an affidavit by Abigail Leonard, Times & Seasons. 1033 [1023][145]

A young man by the name of Ira T Wellis, who had lived for a long time with me & who was a verry worthy and exemplary young man, went over in to Jackson County to hunt for a cow. The mob on seeing

---

Algernon Sidney Gilbert proposes that Saints "purchase out" the possessions of the most violent leaders of the Latter-day Saint antagonists.

141. *Times and Seasons* 6 (August 21, 1845): 977–78. Newel did not include this item. It is a letter from Governor Dunklin to the Missouri brethren, dated February 4, 1834, saying the law does not allow him to raise a military to help Saints regain their lost homes in Jackson County. The pages contain a petition and letters to the governor.

142. This document is a letter from Algernon Sidney Gilbert to A. Leonard; it is undated but is from February 1834 and deals with Missouri negotiations. It is published in the "History of Joseph Smith" installment in *Times and Seasons* 6 (August 15, 1845): 992–93.

143. Page 1022 is a February 19, 1834, letter to Judge John F. Ryland from Partridge, Phelps, Gilbert, Corrill, and Whitmer regarding an upcoming court of inquiry. Page 1023 is a deposition by Abigail Leonard regarding a mobbing incident. Page 1024 has no relevance. Page 1041 contains a petition to the president of the United States, dated April 10, 1834.

144. This is a repeat of the governor's February 4, 1834, letter noted above that is addressed to "the brethren," and it includes an undated letter to the president of the United States from Gilbert, Phelps, and Partridge that mentions an accompanying petition signed by 114 Saints seeking his intervention in their behalf. *Times and Seasons* 6 (December 15, 1845): 1056–57. Also, page 1058 has an April 10, 1834, letter to the Missouri governor, asking him to write a letter to the president in support of the Latter-day Saint petition, and pages 1058–59 have a letter to the Missouri senate and Governor Dunklin's reply to the April 10 letter, saying he would not write to the president because the president had no legal right to intervene.

145. In this short statement, Mrs. Leonard describes how fifty or sixty men came to her cabin and beat and whipped her husband.

him pursued and caught him & whipt & beat him until it was with difficulty that he got back. Another brother by the name of Lewis Abbot went over into Jackson to ask ^a^ man for some thing which he owed him he was abused and beaten so badly that I do not think that he will ever fully recover from it. In fact no age nor circumstance is regarded by that ruthless mob & ^no saints^ ~~ones~~ life is safe under any circumstances to set their feet upon the soil within the limits of Jackson CO, not even to visit the graves of their dead.

Brother Phelps wrote the following letter Tim se[146]

The brethren again wrote the Governor as follows Tms [*Times and Seasons*] 1072 to 9 also 1088 & 9 [and] 1090. 1 & 2 [1091 and 1092].[147]

The colesville Branch continued to live togather untill spring when it bcame necessary to place ourselves in a condition to provide for the comeing season. Som went one way and som another, where ever a chance for renting land ^or get labor^ could be found [51] in order that we might provide for the wants of our families. With the opening of Spring many of us were taken sick and it would be impossible to discribe the sufferings of the Saints driven from our homes, Stript of all our comforts & even the necessaries of life, exposed, hunger, nakedness & privations of all most every kind. We had but little strength left ^to^ resist disease.[148]

My Father had married again after my Mothers death, a widow Peck, my Mothers Brothers widow, with four small children.[149] He was now getting old & it seemed a hard struggl for him to get along.

---

146. *JSP*, D3:468–72. Newel did not include the letter, which was written by Phelps to "dear brethren," dated February 27, 1834. It is published in the "History of Joseph Smith" installment in the *Times and Seasons* 6 (November 15, 1845): 1025. The letter tells of Phelps and others going to Jackson County to give testimony. Phelps noted that the mob had stopped its whippings and now used clubs.
147. The items, which he didn't copy, are in *Times and Seasons* 6 (January 1, and 15, 1846). They include statements and letters containing updates from Clay County written from April through June 1834 and one response from Missouri officials.
148. Hartley, *Stand by My Servant Joseph*, 188.
149. Phoebe Crosby Peck, widow of Polly Knight's brother, Benjamin Peck.

I went back from the river a bout a half a mile on a beautiful little stream of water & commenced building a mill. My brother Joseph lived near by & worked with me some of the time.[150]

We were expecting a large company of our Brethren from the east [Zion's Camp] to arrive here. According to the advice which had been given us by some of the leading men in Missouri to assist us in gitting reinstate again in Jackson, great excitemen prevailed among the mobbers. And it really seemed that if the Lord did not interfere in a mirraculous manner his Saints would be overcome & destroyed.

The Jackson CO people went over into Clay Co. & called a meeting and stired up all the feelings ^there^ they possibly could against the Saints. The anger of the people ^of^ Jackson Co rose to a great height. They had furnished themselves with a number of Cannons. And their neighbors of the adjoining Counties, on the south side of the Missouri River, volunteered by hundreds to assist them, provided that the Governor should attempt to set the saints back upon their lands in Jackson CO, which he had said he would do as soon as enough of their brethren should arrive to guard them selves when reinstated upon their possessions in Jackson CO.

On Wednesday the 18 a large company of our brethren camped at night one mile from the town of R,^i^chmond. In this town the people had sworn that that Company should not pass alive. But the On Wednesday the [June] 18 a large company of our brethren camped at night one mile from the town. But they were on the elert & before the inhabitants were up our people had all pass through unobserved & were safely on their journey, intinding to get in to Clay CO. the next

---

150. Newel's forty acres, as recorded in Clay County Plat Book, were the SW 1/4 of the SW 1/4 of Sec. 7, Township 50N, Range 32W. A list of lands that members owned in Clay County is found in Parkin, "A History of the Latter-day Saints in Clay County," appendix G, 318–19. A number of Saints bought land in Clay County. Newel purchased a forty-acre lot from the land office in Lexington on March 29, 1834. The land is located ten miles southwest of Liberty on what is now called Rock Creek. The west half of today's tiny town of Avondale occupies land Newel once claimed. His property was ten miles southwest of Liberty, nine miles north of the Colesville Branch's location in Jackson County, and seven miles upriver from the Independence Landing.

day.[151] But one waggon broke [52] down and ~~a wheel run of another~~ the wheels run off of others & there seemed to be an overruleing providence to retard the progress of the Camp so that they only traveled fifteen miles that day.

JOSEPH SMITH HISTORY[152]

[Feb 4] They camped that night ^on an elevated spot^ betwen the two branches of the fishing river, the main branch of which is formed by seven small streams, these being two of them.

Just as we halted & were makeing preparations for the night, five men rode into ~~our~~ their camp & told them they would see hell before morning, useing ~~the~~ most horrible oaths. They said Sixty men from Ray CO. were on the way, well armed, who had sworn to destroy that camp, also seventy more from Clay would be there to assist in their destruction. They said these men were well armed & all the Country was in ~~an uproar~~ rage against the mormons & nothing but the power of God could save them from the vengeance of the mob.

At this time the weather was fine & pleasant. So[o]n after these these man left the Camp a small black Cloud wa visible coming in the west. And not more than 20 minutes passed a way before it began to rain and hail. But they had but verry little hail in their camp. All around them the hail was heavy, some of the hailstones, or rather lumps of ice were as large as ~~lumps of ice~~ hens eggs. The thunders rolled with awful majesty, the [red] lightnings flashed through the horrizon, the earth quaked and trembld allmost wihout cessation. It seemed as though the Almighty had issued forth his mandate of vengeance. The wind was terribl so that it was not possible for the tents to be kept in their place.

---

151. Because the *Times and Seasons* published "Extracts from H. C. Kimball's Journal," which told about Zion's Camp, Newel copied into his journal large chunks of Heber C. Kimball's journal, paraphrasing in several places, skipping parts, and occasionally inserting his own short comments. The parts of the Kimball journal that he includes here were published in the *Times and Seasons* 6 (February 1, and 15, 1845): 787–90, 803–5. The first segment below is from the February 1, 1845 issue, 790–91. Newel paraphrases the first three lines and then copies Kimball's words, changing them from Kimball's first-person voice to second person.

152. Newel now paraphrases and copies from the Kimball account that is in the *Times and Seasons* 6 (February 15, 1845): starting on page 800.

There being an old metng house near by, the brethren fled there to cecure themselves from the Storm. Many trees were blown down, and others twisted & wrung like a withe.

The mob come to the river two miles from the Camp, but the river had risen to such a height it was impossible for them to pass over. The hail fell so heavily upon them that it made holes in their hats & in some instances broke the stocks of their guns; their horses being frightened fled, leaveing their riders on the ground. Their powder was wet, & it was evident the Almighty fought in the defence of his Servants. That night the river rose [forty feet].

VERSION 1

[53] The next morning it was impossible to cross the river, which was overflowing its banks, although the night previous the water was no more than ancle deep. As soon as the water subsided so that it was possible, W W Phelps. S. W. Denton, John Corrill, & many more of the brethren went to see our brethren & a joyful meeting it was to us. But a short distance from ^w^here the brethren were camped

JOSEPH SMITH HISTORY

the ground was litterally covered with branches of trees which had been cut off by the hail.

VERSION 1

The Camp moved about five miles from [t]hat place [to] where they could obtain feed for their animals and provisions for themselves; and allso get in to a more secure place & be better prepared to defend them selves from the rage of their enemies. They stayed here a few days until the rage of our enemies was a little allayed.

JOSEPH SMITH HISTORY

On the 21 of Oct Colonl Searcy & two other leading men from Ray CO came to see them, desiring to know what their intentions was. For. Said he, "I see that there is an Almighty power that protects this people, for I started from Richmond Ray CO with a Company of armed men haveing a fixed determination to destroy you, but I was kept back by the Storm and was not able to reach you." When he came into Camp he was seized with such a trembling that he was obliged to sit down in order to compose himself. When he desired to know what our intentions were, Brother Joseph Smith Jun arose and began to speak & the power of God rested upon him. He gave a relation of the sufferings of our people in Jackson CO & allso of all our persecutions & what we had suffered by our enemies for our religion. And that we had come one thousand miles to assist our Brethren to bring them clothing & to reinstate them upon their own lands; that we had no intentions to molest or ~~disturb~~ ^injure^ any people, but only to administer to the wants of our afflicted brethren. And that the evil reports that were circulated about us were false, and were circulated by our enemies to get us destroyed.

[54] After he had got through, haveing spoke quite lengthy, the power of which melted them into compassion, they arose & offered him their hands, and said they would do all in their power to allay the excitement that everry where existed against us. They accordingly went forth & rode night & day to pacify the people; and they wept, because they saw we were a poor & afflicted people & our intentions were pure.

The next day the Sherrif of that Co. named Gilliam came to deliver a short address to us. We formed into Companies & marched into a grove a little distance from the Camp & there formed ourselves into a circle, & sat down upon the ground. Previous to his (Mr Gilliams) address he, ^Gilliam^ said I have heard much concerning Joseph & I have been informed he is in your Camp. If he is here I would like to see him. Brother Joseph arose and Said I am the man. This was the first time he was made known during the journey. Mr. Gilliam [gave] some instructions concerning the manners & customs of the people, their disposition &c, and what course he thought advisable to be persued in order to gain their favor & protection.

VERSION 1

It was at this place the Cholera first broke out in this Camp.

JOSEPH SMITH HISTORY

Brother Joseph called the Camp togather & told them that in consequence of disobeidience of some who had not been willing to listen to his words, but had been rebellious, God had decreed that sickness should come upon them & they should die like sheep with the rot. Said he, "I am sorry but I cannot help it." In the after noon of this day. we began to receive the revelation known as the fishing River Revelation[153]

---

153. Doctrine and Covenants 105.

VERSION I

On Monday, Council was held as held as follows:

JOSEPH SMITH HISTORY

Clay County Mo June 23 1834 A Council of high priests met according to a Revelation received the day ~~following~~ preivious, to choose some of the first Elders to receive their endowments: being appointed by the voice of the Spirit, throug^h^ Joseph Smith Jr president of the Church[154]

VERSION I

On the morning of the 24 [June 1834] the Camp Started for Clay CO. where the brethren resided who had been driven from Jackson Co,

JOSEPH SMITH HISTORY

takeing their course around the head of Fishing River [55] in consequence of high water. When they got within 5 or 6 miles of Liberty, General Atchison and Several other Gentlemen, met them desireing that they should not go to Liberty, as the feelings of the people of that place were much enraged against them. Changeing their course & bending to the left, they pursued their ~~course~~ ^way^ across a prairie; then passing through a wood until they came to brother Sidney Gilberts, where they camped on the bottom of rush Creek in a field belonging to brother Burket on the 25th.

VERSION I

This night the Cholera broke out in their Camp, as they had been warned by the Servant of God. About twelve oclock Cries & groanes were heard from those who had been taken with the Cholera & they fell before the destroyer. So violent were the attacks that in some instances those who were standing on guard fell with their guns in their hands to the ground & it was only by great exertion that we were enabled to take care of &

---

154. Newel did not copy the meeting's proceedings, which included the calling of a number of the brethren to go to Kirtland and receive endowments. See Cannon and Cook, *Far West Record*, June 23, 1834, 68–70. He then copies from the next installment of the Heber C. Kimball journal, in *Times and Seasons* 6 (March 15, 1845): 838–40.

JOSEPH SMITH HISTORY

attend to the Sick & dying, for they fell on everry hand. In the morning the Camp was divided into Several Small bands & dispersed among the brethren.[155]

A Council was held at brother Lyman Wights which I [Kimball] attended with the brethren generally belonging to the priesthood. The Churc^h^, was reorganized. A presidency & high Council Chosen ^&organized^ at which I was ~~called~~ chosen to be a member. And manyy were Chosen from them to go to Kirtland to be endowed.[156]

From that time the destroyer ^ceased^, haveing afflicted the Camp four days. Sixty eight were taken with the disease of which number fourteen died. The remainder recovered as we found out an effectual remedy for this disease which was by putting the person afflicted into Cold water or pouring it on them which had the desired effect of stopping the cramping & purgeing & vometing. Some of the brethren when they were seized with the disease & began to cramp & purge, the fever rageing upon them, desired to be put into cold water & some striped & plunged into the stream themselves & obtained immediate relief. This led us to try the experiment on others & in everry case it proved highly beneficial & effectual where it was taken in season.

VERSION I

Our brethren now began to make preparations to return [to Ohio].[157]

---

155. Knight is paraphrasing Kimball's journal; see previous footnote.
156. The high priests in Zion assembled on July 3, 1834, in accordance with Doctrine and Covenants 102 (minutes of the first high council of the Church, at Kirtland, February 17, 1834). Joseph Smith was present. They chose David Whitmer as president of the high council, with Phelps and John Whitmer assisting him. The twelve council members were, in addition to Newel: Christian Whitmer, Lyman Wight, Calvin Beebe, William E. McLellin, Solomon Hancock, Thomas B. Marsh, Simeon Carter, Parley P. Pratt, Orson Pratt, John Murdock, and Levi Jackman. Joseph Smith ordained all fifteen men. Cannon and Cook, *Far West Record*, 70–74.
157. Newel's MS 767, folder 1, item 3 journal segment ends.

PART 2

KIRTLAND, 1834–36

INTRODUCTION

Part 2 starts in late 1834 and primarily deals with Newel's departure from Clay County early in 1835 and his experiences for about a year in Kirtland. It concludes with his return to Clay County on May 6, 1836. Unlike Newel's records in part 1, where he borrowed regularly from published accounts, he sticks with his own account here. He draws from his own memory and notes, making this part of the record determinately his own material. Our featured text, version 1, has missing material between part 1 and part 2. This involves the period from August 1834 to October 1835—more than a year. Fortunately, in version 4, the Allen version, we find his missing record. Therefore, it is included here to start part 2. Also, the Allen version contains other material that clearly is part of Newel's autobiography but not included in version 1, so we insert that material where it best fits in the transcript.

In part 2 Newel provides a lengthy and insightful discussion about his personal involvements with Kirtland, Hyrum and Jerusha Smith, Joseph Smith, Ohio marriage laws, the temple construction, and the dedication experiences. He writes a detailed biography of Lydia Goldthwaite's life story as an abused wife, her loss of two children, desertion by an alcoholic husband, her recovery in Canada, her unusual conversion story when listening to Joseph Smith and Sidney Rigdon preach, her decision to move to and live in Kirtland, Newel and Lydia's love story, and the historic wedding Joseph Smith performed for them.

Newel received a valuable official certificate designating him a Church elder and authorizing him to preach the gospel. Version 1 does not contain the certificate, but it was among papers associated with the Allen version. They copied it into the final pages of their manuscript. We insert it here in part 2 when Newel's account mentions it. Newel's account also records a detail about Christ's visitation to the Kirtland Temple that is not in Joseph Smith's history.

During his return trip to Clay County, Newel describes a shocking event in St. Louis. A mob burned a black man to death, causing Newel and members with him to fear for their own safety.

Kirtland, 1834–36

ALLEN VERSION

After having spent a little time so profitably and so agreeably, and our brethren having left for their homes in the east, the brethren generally resumed their business and labors with renewed diligence, and with a full determination to keep the faith of the Gospel under all and every circumstance through which they might be called to pass. Yet we were sorrowful to reflect that so many of our brethren [Zion's Camp] had laid down their lives after performing so long and tedious a journey under such unfavorable circumstances as they had done. But I trust they sleep in peace; and that their works will follow them. "Blessed are the dead that die in the Lord" [Revelation 14:13].

The summer [1834] passed without anything special transpiring. The inhabitants generally manifested a kind feeling towards the Saints. Yet owing to the exposure of the previous winter and the hunger and privation, which the brethren had suffered, many of them were afflicted with fever and ague which is somewhat prevalent in this country and more especially on the bottoms and lowlands.

I began to make preparation to go on my appointed mission to Kirtland, but it seems as if a struggle had commenced.[1] Both my wife and myself took the fever and ague, also my aunt, Esther Culver, my mother's sister.[2] She was an aged woman whose husband had died previous to our exile from Jackson county, and whom I had taken into my family as she had no child to care for her.

On the fifteenth of September Sally, my wife, died Truly she has died a martyr to the Gospel of our Lord and Savior Jesus Christ. She was of a frail constitution and the hardships and privations she had to endure were more than she could survive. A short time previously she had given birth to a son [Eli], which had also died. She was buried. Her grave and her infant's, is in a lonely grave where they will remain undisturbed by all enemies until the wicked cease to rule, and the righteous possess the earth for ever and ever. I can truly say in her I have sustained a very great loss as a partner in life, and a mother to our little son Samuel. Yet I do not mourn as those who have no hope, for if I continue

---

1. *JSP*, D3:266.
2. Esther Peck, born in 1766, was the widow of Aaron Culver.

faithful, I am fully persuaded that in the morning of the resurrection, I shall receive both her and her offspring to my embrace no more to be separated for ever.³

My health continued poor, so that I could do but little work until the time had arrived for the Elders, who had been called to go to Kirtland to start. I made the best arrangements I could for the care of my little son ^Samuel^ and aged Aunt, and in company with a number of my brethren, got on board some canoes which we had got for the purpose, and floated down the Missouri river, committing ourselves to the care of Him who rules the universe. We traveled on the river by day, and at night camped on its shore. I was hardly able to walk when I started on this journey ^but my strength gradually increased^ of about a thousand miles, without purse and script and but poorly clad, yet we endured the inclemency of the weather and gained strength. So that [w]hen we had got far enough from those who were so bitterly prejudiced against the Gospel, that we could get a hearing, we left our canoes and parted, traveling two by two preaching the gospel to those who would listen to us.

I had an uncle by marriage, named Elisha Kirtland; he had married my mother's sister,⁴ and lived at Sidny, Shelby county, Indiana. I called on him, and he and family treated me very kindly. I spent a few days, with them, they administered to my wants, and I again started on preaching wherever an opportunity could be found.

I arrived ^safely^ in Kirtland in safety, in the Spring of 1835, my health tolerably good. After visiting a few days I went and boarded with brother Hyrum Smith. Both he and his ever kind and amiable wife Jerusha, did all they could to make me comfortable. I ^and^ commenced labor on the temple, where I continued to work until it was finished, and ready for the endowments which had been promised to the faithful servants of the Lord.

Soon after I arrived in Kirtland I was called to fill a vacancy in the High Council, which was a source of great instruction to me as the

---

3. Obituary for Sally Knight, *Messenger and Advocate* 1 (October 1834): 12.
4. Polly Peck's sister is not identified. Possibly she was Anna Peck or Bethena Peck, both of whom we lack information on.

prophet Joseph Smith often met with us, and was ever full of wisdom and instruction.[5]

My father, brothers, sisters and friends are continually mindful of me, and I constantly receive kind and affectionate correspondence from them. They are getting [missing material]

VERSION I[6]

Some time in ~~the month~~ the fore part of the month of Oct [a] woman by the name of Lydia Goldthwait came to live at Bro Hiram ~~Smit~~ Smith's where I was boarding.[7] She had not been long in the family, when I found there was a growing attachment in my bosom towards

Lydia Goldthwaite Knight was Newel's second wife. They were married while Newel was working on the Kirtland Temple. It was the first marriage performed by Joseph Smith with priesthood authority. Courtesy of Knight family.

her, which I, in vain, strove to over come. She was verry reser^v^d in her manners, while prudence and wisdom seemd to mark her course in all her move ments. Seldom did I hear her speak, unless it was to Sister Smith[8] concerning the affairs she was engaged in. Yet [I] Could now and then see by the Crimson dint upon her Cheek, as she would occasionally, as she supposed unperceivedly cast her eyes towards me, that ~~cu~~ Cupids dart had found its way to her heart. Yet it appeard she did not intend to let any one perceive it.

I do not think I had ever [ex]changed a dozen words with her until November the 18th. I came to the determination to make my feelings

---

5. Newel is listed as a Kirtland high councilor at a September 19, 1835, trial for Jared Carter. Kirtland High Council Minute Book, September 19, 1835, 113.
6. MS 767, folder 1, item 4.
7. The Mormon Historic Sites Foundation website says the traditional site for the house was just south of the temple at 9097 Chillicothe Road, on its east side. There is a small historical marker at the front of the home. Lydia Goldthwaite was baptized by Joseph Smith on October 27, 1833, at Mount Pleasant and moved to Kirtland in May 1835. "Knight, Lydia Goldthwaite," in Jenson, *Biographical Encyclopedia*, 2:776.
8. Jerusha Smith.

known to her. I did not wait long, for an oportunity util it presented in the evening I found her a lone in an uper room. I took her by the hand and after a few words with her, I told her I thought her situation, as well as mine, was rather lonely, and if it was agreeable to her perhaps we might be some company for each other. She at first made me no answer. Her heart was full the tears that streamed from her eyes bespoke the emmotion of her soul. As soon as she could suppress her tears, She replied the true feelings of my heart are known by none save the Lord. I suppose you are aware of my situation. I would rather sacrifice everry feeling of my own and even life ~~its sel~~ rather than step aside from virtue or offend my heavenly father or violate the law of God. I replied I doubt not the integrity of your heart, for I saw that virtue [small tear in page] her bosom. But, said I, when you fully understand the law of God you will know that you are free [small page tear]. I would ask nothing at your hand contrary to that law. Her heart was full, her bosom heaved the tears she could ^not^ restrain, which forbade her to reply but spoke the truth and love of her heart. She broke from my e^m^,brace & left the room.

I was now left to reflect alone. From her reserved decorum I had half supposed that a ~~a~~ proposition of this kind would be utterly rejected by her, which would set my feelings more at rest ~~for~~ in Case there was no compliance on her part. But in this, to my great satisfaction, I was wholly disappointed. I now saw the only thing wanting was let her fully understand the law of the Lord more perfectly. For three days and nights I kept all these things and pondered them with a prayerful heart, when I came to the conclusion to tell all to Brother Hiram, which I did on Monday morning the 22 [November].

He replied he knew it was all right, that the Lord never designed a virtuous inteligent female as she was should spend her life single & in her present lonely situation. For God requires all both male and female ~~to~~ to fill the measure of their Creation & to multiply upon the earth as he hath commanded. I told him I was satisfied, I believed all he said to be correct. Yet lest ^any^ might take ecceptions or speak evil of that in which there is no evil, I should be glad to have Bro Joseph decide the matter, for if the Lord gives her to me no man can say why do ye so. Bro Hiram said that was right, it was my privilige & he would go to Joseph for me. I thanked him, and lifting my ^heart^ to God with a prayer of thanksgiving & allso supplication for ~~action~~ continuation of his blessings to us. I left the Chamber & retired to my labor on the house of the Lord.

A little after noon Bro Hiram came to me. [He] said he had laid the affair before Bro Joseph, who at the time was with his Council. Broth Joseph, after pa [small tear in page] or & reflecting a little, or in other words enquiring of the Lord, Said it is all right. She is his & the sooner they married the better. Tell them no law shall hurt [them]. They need not fear either the law of God or man for [neither] shall not touch them & the Lord bless them. This is the will of the Lord concerning that matter.

I to the house where I found her alone in the room where I had first introduced the subject. I told her all that had transpired, & we lifted our hearts with gratitude to our heavenly Father for his goodness to wards us, & that we live in this momentous age & as did the ancients, so we have the privilege of ~~of~~ enquireing through the prophet & receiveing the word of the Lord concerning us. After a short interview with her I went to the dinig room & partook of food, for I had fasted & prayed three days & knights & did not desire food until after I had learned the will of the Lord, & Lydia & myself had made a Covenant to be for each other. Bro Hiram ^& his wife^ kindly offered to mak a feast & advised that we be married the following evening to which we readily consented.

In order to fulfil the gentile law it was necessary to obtain licence from the County Clerk to get married. I took a horse & rode nine miles to obtain such licence. I returened a bout three in the evening. Both myself & Lydia had desired that it might be so that the Prophet might Seal the bond of matrimony for us, but had not made our desires known to any save the Lord. As Bro Hiram was going to invite the guests, I requested him to ask Elder S. Brunson to come to marry us, not expecting Brother Joseph would attend to that ordinance as he never had married any one, he haveing no licence from the State. The State refused to give such licence to the Elders of this Church on the ground that they were not Considered by the State as preachers of the gospel, &

> Certificate to Copy of Paper on File
>
> The State of Ohio, Geauga County. Probate Court
>
> I, the undersigned, Judge and ex-officio Clerk of the Probate Court within and for said County, and in whose custody the Files, Journals and Records of said Court are required by the laws of the State of Ohio to be kept, do hereby certify that the foregoing is taken and copied from the original Marriage Record C, Page 141 now on file in said Court, that it has been compared by me with said original document, and that it is a true and correct copy thereof.
>
> IN TESTIMONY WHEREOF, I hereunto subscribe my name officially, and affix the seal of said Court, at the Court House in Chardon in said County, this 24th day of April A.D. 1964.
>
> *Frank G. Lavrich*
> Judge and ex-officio Clerk of said Probate Court
> *Ina Norton*
> Deputy Clerk
>
> This photostatic copy obtained by Lewis Phelps by his personal visit to (141) the courthouse in Chardon, Geauga Co., Ohio, 8/28/1986. Recorded in Book C, page
>
> BE it Remembered, that on the Twenty fourth day of November in the year of our Lord one thousand eight hundred and thirty five, Newell Knight and Lydia Goldthwait of the County of Geauga, were legally joined in Marriage, by competent authority, in conformity to the provisions of the Statute, signed by Joseph Smith jr. of Ohio in such cases made and provided; and a certificate of the said Marriage, signed by who solemnized the same, has been filed in the office of the Clerk of the Court of Common Pleas for said County of Geauga, this Twenty Second day of February Anno Domini, one thousand eight hundred and thirty Six
> ATTEST,
> *L. D. Aiken* Clerk.
>
> Other interesting facts he found: From 1835 to 1837 Joseph Smith performed 20 marriages in Kirtland; A title is omitted in most of the certificates, but on the entry for 17 Apr 1836 BE it Remembered, that on the *fourth* day of *December* he is called in the year of our Lord one thousand eight hundred and thirty five, Warren "Prophet of the Parrish and Martha H. Raymond of the County of Geauga, were legally Most High", on 4 June 1836 "elder of the church of the Latter Day Saints."

Newel and Lydia's marriage certificate. Courtesy of Knight family.

if any attempted to marry without such licence they would & did cause them to pay a penalty, it being according to the ^law^ of the State of O.[9]

---

9. Bradshaw, "Joseph Smith's Performance of Marriages in Ohio," 7–22. *JSP*, D5:66. (Page 66n283 gives more information about this and even quotes Lydia Knight.)

But to return to the subject, when Brother Hiram invited the Prophet & his family he observed that was going to invite Brunson to marry us. Joseph replied, Stop, I will marry them myself. This was good news to us. It seemed that the Lord had granted unto us the desires of our hearts. Suffice to say the feast was prepared the guests were ready. The Prophet & his Council were there. We received much Instruction from the Prophet Concerning matrimony & what the ancient order of God was & what it must be again concerning marriage. In the name of the Lord & by the authority of the priesthood which he held, he joined us in the bond of matrimony on Tuesday Nov 23rd [24th] 1835.[10] The evening passed of well & all felt edefied & glad of oportunity of enjoying instruction from the Lord through the beloved Prophet. Long long has the world been shrowded in gentile ignorance & superstition, but the Shackles are beginning to be blown awy lik the summer threshing floor, & light & inteligence to be given to the Children of the kingdom.

Nothing special hapened in the course of he[r] Childhood more than what is common to youth. She had an opportunity only of a common School education, but as she had a mind that was never satisfied with learning, She acquired a knowledge of many things of which many of superior advantages are ignorant. At the age of 17 she married a man by the name of Calvin Bailey. Her mind at this time was young & alltogather unacquainted with the deceitfulness & treachery of man. She had lived in innocence & peace with her parents & had never seen but little of the ills that were incident to man in life. Her Father was a temperate & moral man & more reserved in his maner & Conversation than is Common for this age. He ^was a farmer &^ had ever lived in the Country, so that his Children had never been as much exposed to scenes of Confusion & intemperance as many are who live in towns or Cities among the gentiles w[h]o practice vice in stead of virtue, which had rendered the subject of our present naritive less qualified for the change of Circumstances that awaited her

---

10. Both Newel's account and Lydia's recollections say November 23, which was a Monday. The *JSP* has the marriage occurring November 24. *JSP*, D5:66n285. See Flake, "Development of Early Latter-day Saint Marriage Rites," 77–105.

Little did she dream or expect the leaveing her Parents, Bros & Sisters for the protection of one in whom she had confided for Safety for protection & for a protector under all circums would be the beginning of sorrow to her. Although s^he^ felt a Sorrow at the Idea of leaveing her Parents who had given her birth & from whom She had derived everry advantage & instruction their circumstances would admit, & allso of leaveing her Bros & Sisters & the Scenes of her Childhood, yet the anticipation of happiness She fancied to be hers in future life with her new companion bouyed her Spirits up & she at that tender age united in the bonds of matrimony & left her Parents. For about 3 months all things went well & she [tear in page] no sorrow.

But alas, She to truely found all was not gold that shone. Judge her Sorrow when her husband returned ^home^ one evening after indulgeing too freely in the intoxicateing bowl. Her joy was turned to Sorrow of the deepest die: in a moment all her earthly anticipations vanished & she gave way to a flood of tears & raised her heart heaven in silent prayer. From this time a Silent melancholly rested upon he[r] countenance, yet no one heard a word from her. In vain did she try to conceal her greif & hide cause of her ^grief^ husband sorrow. In vain did she now & then indulge a fond hope that he husband would reform & yet be a Comfort to her & that She would yet lean upon his bosom in security. But all her hopes of happiness wer blasted like the morning dew. Intemperance stole lik a withering blast upon him, while sorrow lik a canker worm preyed upon her heart, yet a murmur was never heard to lips

In the fall of 1830 She gave birth to a Daughter. This, to use her own language, added to her greif. Not withstanding She loved her infant with all a Mothers fondness, yet the idea of bringing helpless innocence to suffer from an intemperate Father & to see & realize the sorrow that intemperrance brings & from one that ought rule & guide his house in wisdom & with Sobriety, was like dagger to her heart & caused her to mourn over her little ^one^ she so dearly loved. Oh, thought She, how Cruel that I have thus forsaken my Dear Father & Mother with the fond hope of happiness with one I so fondly loved & from whom I looked for comfort & protecion in my future life. And is my joy all blasted & am I a fond Mother to innocence that may & probably will have to feel & suffer from a Father both shame & wretchedness ~~as I~~. My own sufferings I can better bear than this, Said She.[11]

But to be breif, She partially recovered her health & her little [one] grew. yet as it would look & smile upon its Mother, the tear of Sorrow would roll from her pale Cheek & often did. She raise her heart in silent prayer to God to protect her & her little one to reclaim her husband, that she might yet delight in his Society as she had fondly anticipated when at the hymenal altar. Through intemperance & bad man^a^gement, he had all ready disposed of his farm & rendered his family measurebly destitute. He moved in to the Village of Lodi where he rented a small & uncomfortable house. His time was mostly spent at the Shop or tavern.

About a year & an half passed in this way, when Lydia gave birth to a Son.[12] Yet the infant was not long for this life, it lived but a day. Lik the Sweet flower, he was nipedt in the bud & Soon bade farewell to this world. The Mother lingered for considerable time with little prospect of health. Allready her furniture was taken by he[r] husband to pay fo the fluid that Caused him to be worthless & his family destitute & miserable. Yet She had never even told her Mother her Sorrow or even been heard to Complain of him that had made her thus miserable. Her trust was in God & to him alone did she tell he greif, although his Conduct was such that for whole nights did she weep & Sleep departed from her. He often threatened her in a Cruel manner & even abused their little Daughter.

About two weeks after the birth of her Son Mr Bailey arose one morning before light & went out with out Saying any thing. He did not come. The girl that was nursing at the time arose, made a fire & got breakfast. He did not return until about one oclock. He came in & Spoke to Lydia & Said, you must get ready to move to morrow morning to New Abion, a distance of about one hundred miles. This was a new Idea to her as she had never heard any intimacy of the kind before. She replied her health would not admit of of it as She was not able to set up a half hour. To which in a hastey manner he Said, wel if you are

---

11. Gates, *Lydia Knight's History*, 10.
12. Gates, *Lydia Knight's History*, 11.

so independan you may Stay where you are, but I shall go where you will never see me again. He ate some dinner & dressed himself in the best he had & went away.

He had been gone but a short time when a gentleman came & drove away their Cow which gave milk & was their main dependance for a liveing. Bailey had the cow [sold] to get money to go away with. He went away & was gone Considerable time, when he returned & sought to get the Child & take her life. But through the interference of kind friends She & her little Daughter were rescued from him. Soon after this her Child was taken Sick & died.

About two months after th death of her Child, a friend kindly offered to take her home to live with his family. The Gentleman was a respectable ~~farmer who of~~ merchant and had preiviou^sly^ moved from the neighborhood of her Father, into the province of upper canada. She accepted of the invitation & went with him, where She continued to live until Phrs [preachers?] [Joseph] Smith & [Sidney] Rigdon came to that place, who were hospitably entertained by the family. This gave Lydia a favorable opportunity of investigateing the the Subject of mormonism as it was termed. She had been a member of the Episcopal Methodist Church nearly seven years, but after hearing the true principles of the doctrine of Christ Set forth She embraced it with all her heart. She was baptized by the hand of Joseph Smithe on the 24 [26] of Oct 1833. She was confirmed a member of the Church of latter day Saints the same evening & began to realize the difference betwen the sectarian forms of the present age & the gift & power of the holy Ghost.[13]

On Monday the 25 two mor persons requested baptism Phs Smith stayed & administered the ordinance to them, makeing 14 persons he had baptized in that place during a Stay of a little mor than one week. Mormonism had never before beem preached in that Section. The same evening as a number were sitting in a family capacity converseing upon the things of the kingdom. One of the bo[dy] Said, [if] any one who he was acquainted & new no language but the English, would Speak in tongues he would never doubt the reality of the things hey had then

---

13. Her baptismal date appears to have been October 27, 1833. *JSP*, J1:19n50. See Hartley, *Stand by My Servant Joseph*, 212, 215.

embraced. ~~when all at onc~~ Phs Smith replied if any one will rise up in the name of the Lord they Shal Speak in tongues, when all [attenders] at once called upon Lydia to arise. She arose & as She opened her mouth the holy ghost fell upon her and She spok in tongues. The room was well lighted yet there was a cloud of light above the brightness of burning Candles Covered the room where thy were sitting & feell upon her. This light was visible to thos sitting in the room & it was a time of joy long to be remembered.

On Tuesday morning the 26 [28] Phs Smith & Rigdon took their leave of this kind family. Whil they were waiting for the Carriage to be in readiness, Brother Joseph looked Steadfastly on Lydia for some time. He at length spoke & Said, I now know the Cause of Sister Lydias former afflictions. The Lord has had his eye upon her & he hath suffered her to be afflicted that She might be brought to a knowledge of the things of Salvation. This, I have often heard her Say, has been a Strength & support to her in trials & persecutions She has had to pass through Since that time. For She says that her greatest afflictions have always been the Source of bring blessings to her in the due time of the Lord.

Lydia did not return to her Parents until the 12th of Sept following. Here she was again disappointed, for she had taken so much pleasure in the gospel she had embraced & the principles of Salvation looked so plain & so glorious to her, that She had hoped when She could See & converse with her Parents, Bros, & Sisters, they would believe allso & s[e]cure to themselves a Croun & place in the kingdom of God. But in Sted of this they appeard cold & indifferent to her. On the account of her faith they would not converse freely on the subject & tried every method [to] turn her from what they termed delusion. When they found that neither entreaties nor persuasions would do, they offered of the things & goods of this world, which proved equally ineffectual. For Said She, I had rather trust in God & continue in the faith I have embraced than to enjoy all ^th^ wealth of this world.

Her anxiety to be with the Saints increased as their Coldness dailey did towards her on the account of her religion, until at length She determined to leave all & go to Kirtland wher She Could enoy the Society of the Saints & learn more perfectly the way of life & Salvation. She fully determined to bid farewell to those She most dearly loved

& who had ever done all in their power to alleviate her sorrows, until after She had embraced the gospel or faith of the Latter day Saints. Notwithstanding She dearly loved her friends, She loved the cause of righteousness still better She bade her Fathers house farewell & Started for Kirtland about the 20th of ~~June~~ ^May^. 1835, arrived at Kirtland the latter part of May. She lived with Bishop [Vinsom] Knights family until about the time of my first acquaintance with her at Bro. Hirams.[14]

Haveing given so much of the history of my new partner for time & allso for the life to come, I shall proceed with my own journal. 24th.[15] I went to my usual labor on the house of the Lord for I consider this to be of the greatest importance at present, for it has been long since the Lord has had an house upon the earth, & the Saints are laboring & waiting with prayerful hearts to see & to finish the house so that they may receive the promised endowment from on high[16]

[Nov. 29] 28. Sabbath I attended meting. Phs Smith addressed the Congregation in a very appropriate maner. He told in public that he had married Bro Knight & that he had done ^it^ by the authority of the preisthood, which he had recd from God & not from man. And further, said he, the gentile law shall not have power to hurt me for it fo I have done as God hath required at my hand & he will bear me out & eventually bring me off conquor over all my adversaries for his kingdom shall prevail.[17]

I continued to labor on the house of the Lord & to board at Br H. Smiths as I had done heretofore. Lydia allso lived at the Same place.

Soon after this a hebrew School was opened in Kirtland for the benefit of the Elders of Irael.[18] Many attended & mad[e] unusal pro-

---

14. Hartley, *Stand by My Servant Joseph*, 218.
15. Actually November 25, 1835.
16. *JSP*, D5:189. Just a few days earlier, Joseph Smith had visited the temple to observe the finished work of the interior and was vigorously working on an early manuscript of the Book of Abraham. *JSP*, J1:107.
17. *JSP*, J1:112.
18. The Hebrew school started on January 4, 1836. Backman, *Heavens Resound*, 270; *JSP*, D5:101–2. Joshua Seixas arrived in Kirtland on January 26 and began teaching Hebrew.

Hyrum and Jerusha's home in Kirtland, Ohio, ca. 1900. This nonextant home is traditionally identified as the site of Newel and Lydia's wedding. Courtesy of Community of Christ Library and Archives, Independence, Missouri.

ficiency in acquiring the language. I did not attend the School as my labors was verry much needed on the house. Bro Joseph Said it would be better for me to labor there than to go to Shool. The Elders came from every quarter to attend School, to labor on the house, ^& to^ be instructed mor perfectly in the ways of the Lord &c. The word of the Lord grew & the Saints waxed Strong in the new & everlasting Covenant. For Some time all things seemed move well, notwithstanding our enemies had resolved that house should not be reared. They have never been suffered to hinder its progress & at this time the Lord does not suffer that they gain any power or advantage over his Saints.

From time to time we receive such instructions from Phs Smith as is calculated enlarge the mind & expand the Soul & prepare the Elders to receive knowledge of the things of Salvation, which he from time to time brought forth to us for considerable time. I do not know that any thing Special personally transpired with me. About the middle of Feb ~~Lydia~~ Lydia was taken quite sick for about 2 week. She was quite ill, when she began to regain her health & was soon able to attend to her usual employment.

ALLEN VERSION[19]

To whom it may concern.

This certifies that Newel Knight has been received into this Church of the Latter-day Saints, organized on the sixth of April, in the year of our Lord, one thousand, eight hundred and thirty, and has been ordained an elder according to the rules and regulations of said Church, and is duly authorized to preach the Gospel, agreeably to the authority of that office.

From the satisfactory evidence which we have of his good moral character, and his zeal for the cause of righteousness, and diligent desire to persuade men to forsake evil and embrace truth, we confidently recommend him to all candid and upright people, as a worthy member of society.

We, therefore, in the name and by the authority of this Church, grant unto this, our worthy brother in the Lord, this letter of recommendation as a proof of our fellowship and esteem, praying for his success and prosperity in our Redeemer's cause.

Given by the direction of a Conference of the Elders of said Church, assembled in Kirtland, Geauga County, Ohio, the third day of March, in the year of our Lord, one thousand eight hundred and thirty-six.[20]

Signed: Joseph Smith Jr., Chairman

F. G. Williams, Clerk

---

19. Here we insert a certificate found among Newel's papers, which the Allen version transcribed and positioned near the very end of its text. At a March 3, 1836, conference, Church officials decided that all licenses had to be recorded in a record book and be signed by the chairman and the clerk of the conference. Existing licenses needed to be turned in and replaced by new ones. Such ministerial certificates had validity in courts of law, showing that the bearers had authority to act as ministers for the Church. Joseph Smith's history implies only that licenses were issued to the conference attenders, but Newel's certificate proves that they were. A note with the certificate says "This certifies that the within Licence was recorded on the 30th day of March 1836 in Kirtland Ohio, in the Licence Records."

20. *JSP*, D5:186–88.

KIRTLAND, 1834–36

VERSION 1

About this time the upper rooms in Lords house were finished so that each quorum in its turn was call in to recive necessary instruction preparitory to their washing & anointing.[21] During the month of March Phs Smiths time was nearly all taken up in attending to these ordinances as well as those that were Set apart to assist in attending these Sacred ordinances. In fact he has had but verrry little leisure during the winter as there were hundreds who have Come up hither to be instructed. He has not failed on his part to give all necesssay instruction to them.[22]

Interior of Kirtland Temple with priesthood pulpits, 1907. Anderson Collection, L. Tom Perry Special Collections, Brigham Young University.

~~April 3 I went with Lydia to Father Smiths to have her receive her Patriarchal blessing from under his hand~~

March the 27th 1836. The lower room of the temple was dedicated to the Lord to day & the power of God, the ministering of Angels attended. Brother Frederick G Williams bore testimony to the whol Congregation that that during the first prayer made by Phs Smith an Angel came & Sat betwen him & Father Smith.[23] When Bro. Williams gave a discription of the Angel & his dress, Bro Joseph Said it was Christ.[24] This was to me a Satisfaction to [know] that the Lord did come in to the house we had labored so diligently to build unto his mame & that he had accepted it of his Saints. The house was filled & yete many of the

---

21. *JSP*, J1:165–71.
22. See Harper, "'A Pentecost and Endowment Indeed'"; Buerger, "The Development of the Mormon Temple Endowment Ceremony"; Petersen, "Kirtland Temple," 400–409.
23. *JSP*, D5:209.
24. *JSP*, D5:209n143 says it was Peter.

Kirtland Temple from the northwest side, 1907. Anderson Collection, Church History Library.

Saints could not get in.²⁵ Meting was appointed the following day for the accommodation of those that for want of room could not attend.

To day [March] 28. The house was again fill & the same order & Services attended as was the day preivious. In order that Same privileges might be enjoyed by all who had assisted in building the temple, another meting was appointed for the accomodation of all in the ajoining neighborhods wo might wish to attend & a polite invitation given to all who wished to attend.

[March] 29. I now began to make preperations to return to Clay Co M.O., haveing fill^ed^ the mission & recd the endowment for which I had been called ^where^ to this place for.

April 3 [Sunday] I went ^to^ the Prophets house where Father Smith resides to have Lydia receive her patriarchal blessing from under his hand The following is a Copy of her blessing then recd Recd By Joseph

A Patriarchal Blessing

By Joseph Smith Sen Kirtland Ohio Aril 3. 1836

---

25. *JSP*, D5:189: "Some of those unable to enter held a meeting in the adjacent schoolhouse while others returned home to await a second dedicatory event."

For Lydia Knight
Who was born June 9 1812 in Sutton Worcester C.O. Mass

Sister Knight, in the name of ~~The Lord~~ Jesus I lay my hands upon thy head & ask my heavenly to give me wisdom & power to pronounce such things as Shall be acording to the mind of the holy Spirit. And I ask my heavenly Father to prepare thee to receive such blessings & to pour them in to in to thy Soul, even a fullness, & to give the[e] wisdom to abide all things that shall come upon thee. And bless thee in thy in comeings & in thy out goings. & I Seal a Fathers blessing upon the[e] & for thy posterity, for thou shalt be a Mother of many Children & thou shalt teach them righteousness & have power to keep them from the power of the destroyer. And thy heart shall not be pained because of the loss of thy Children, for the Lord shall watch over them & keep them. And they Shall be raised up for ~~his~~ glory & be an ornament in the Church.

Thou hast been afflicted much in thy past life & thy heart has been pained. Many tears have fallen from thine eyes & thou hast wept much. But thou Shalt be Comforted, for thy sorrows are over. The Lord loves thee & has given the[e] a kind & loveing Companion for thy Comfort, & your Souls shall be knit to gather, & nothing shall be able to dissolve them, neither distress nor depth [death?] shall separate you. You shall ~~go safely~~ be preserved in life & go Safely & Speedily to the Land of Zion. Thou shalt have a good passage & receive an inheritance in Jackson C. O. in due time. Thou shalt allso See thy Friends [in] zion, thy Brothers & Sisters, & rejoice with with them in the glory of God.

Angels Shall minister [u]nto thee & thy heart shall be enlarged & thy Soul expanded & thou Shalt Stand to see Israel gathered from their dispersion, the ten tribes come from the land of the North Country, the heavens rend, & the Son of man Come from the Clouds of heaven with ~~power & great glory~~ all the g[l]ory of his Father. And thou shalt rise to meet ^him^ & reign with him a thousand years & thy offspring with thee. Great are thy blessings. I confirm bl^e^ssings for thee in common with thy husband, blessings of the earth & all things which thou kneedest for Comfort. Thou Shalt be a Mother in Israel & thou shalt relieve the wants of the oppressed & minister to the needy. All kneedful blessings are thine. I seal them upon thee, & I seal thee up unto Eternal life, in the name of Jesus, Amen.

Sylvester Smith, Scribe

After the above was written we had a Social interview with Phs. Smith & family, after which ~~Lyde~~ Lydia & myself went in to the house of the Lord & retired to a Secret Chamber & there for the last time in the house of the Lord offered up our prayers to God, when we retired to our lodgings. This is a Sabbath long to be remembered by me & may the Lord preserve us hence forth & the holy Spirit guide & enlighten our understanding that we may be preserved from evils of everry kind & increase in the knowlede of the things of Salvation, that we may in the end of our probation receive an inheritance with the Sanctified & be Crowned with glory, even that of a Clestial.[26]

Thursday April the 7th 1836. A[s] things now being ready, we Started fo Clay C.O. M.O. Bro H. Smith let me have his horses & waggon to go to the O. River at [East] liverpool, wher we intended to take passage on board a Steamer & by that conveyance make our place of destination. The roads were verry bad.

[April] 9th. In the after noon it rained verry hard so that we put [up] before knight. It so happened that we stayed at a Sectarian Priests who treated us with great politeness until he learnt we were Mormons, when his politeness was changed to hostility. However it rained so severe he suffered us to remain until morning.

Sunday the 10th. I arose, the rain had abated. I got my horses in readiness, paid my bill & bade this modern host good bye. We went a few miles & stoped & got breakfast. We soon after found ourselves in water so high that we were obliged Stop & tarry until the next morning. As I attempted to cross a bridge theat was covered in water about two feet in depth, the logs floated & the horses fell, so that it was with considerable dificulty I safely rescued them.

11th. The water has fallen & I again resumed our journey. We arrived safe at liver pool. I sent back the horses by Bro Hill. We had to wait a few days for a Steamer, when the Waca^u^ssta arrived & we embarked

---

26. See introduction to Doctrine and Covenants 110 in *JSP*, D5:225–28.

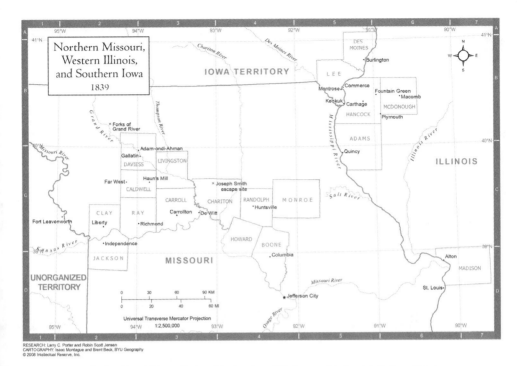

Northern Missouri, Western Illinois, and Southern Iowa, 1839. Courtesy of the Joseph Smith Papers Project.

at liverpool [on] April the 13th. We had a good passage & arrived safe lewisville [Louisville, Kentucky] on the 16th.

18th Lewisville. On board the Bob Morris Steamer, Capt Miller. Arrived at St Lewis on the morning of the 22nd. The prospect is that we shall be obliged to Stop several days for about to proceed further. A member of the Brethren who had been in Company at Kirtland during the Winter were here, I think, Eleven in all. We tried to rent a room but it was to no purpose. Emigration was so great at this time [that] everry vacant room was taken. We wer obliged to hire our board at a tavern.

While we were here, we Saw much of the wickedness & depravity of man. Wicked[ness] prevails & that too in high places. A difficulty took place betwen a Sheriff & a black man. The black was put in jail for trial. In the night a posse of men collected, in took the black man & Chained him to a Stake & burnt him a live. All this was well enough, no one spoke against it, no law tried this high handed murder. The true hearted patriot cannot but blush to see his Countries Shame. Has the liberty our fore fathers so nobly fought & bled to etablish come to this. Wickedness of everry kind is waxing bolder & bolder.

We the Brethren, namely Bishop Edward Partridge, Isaac Morley, James Emett, Peter Phitmore, [Whitmer], W. W. Phelps, Waterman Phelps, Lyman Wight, Elias Higbee & [George] Morey, considered ourselves in the midst of our enemies & daily commited ourselves to the keeping of our heavenly Father. That we might the better have an opportunity for this, we retired to a lovely grove with out the City & ther in secret united in prayer fo the preservation & safety of our Selves both in this place & allso journeying upon the waters. A Boat at length arrived to on which we embarked to ascend the M.O. river.

April 30. A little before night we left St Lewis on board Steamer [ ]. The boat was so crowded, ase our situation was rendered quite inconvenient. We had a safe passage & landed in Clay on the 6 of May.

MISSOURI, 1836–39

INTRODUCTION

This section of Newel Knight's autobiographical writings covers three years, from May 1836 until May 1839. It includes accounts from memory, dated, diary-like entries in places, and some borrowing in the form of quotes and paraphrases from available sources. For example, he was not present during much of the war in Missouri, from the summer through the fall of 1838, so he copied from three published sources that contained the details. The Allen version of this material contains no additional writing of Newel's beyond that already included. He records his efforts to make a living in Clay and Caldwell Counties, including several mill construction projects. Particularly valuable is Newel's documentation of his family's difficult winter travel during the Saints' mass exodus from Missouri in early 1839. He touches on but does not wade into ecclesiastical issues. He mentions disaffections from the faith by men who had been his close associates but does not explain the cases or express personal reactions to them. He has a unique reaction to the arrival of Joseph Smith in Far West in March 1838.

VERSION 1[1]

April 30 [1836]. A little before night we left St Lewis on board Steamer. The boat was so crowded ~~ase~~ our situation was rendered quite inconveinient. We had a safe passage & landed in Clay on the 6 of May.

We [Newel and Lydia] first went to Uncle Ezekiel Pecks. Found well. Sayed over night. Th next day went [to] Fathers. I found him in good health & in good Spirits. Went Clark ~~Slade~~ Slades[2] where I had left Samuel my little Son. I concluded to move to the place I left when I went to Kirtland & build a mill I had commenced. It was the place where my Wife Sally died. I moved here the 10 of May.

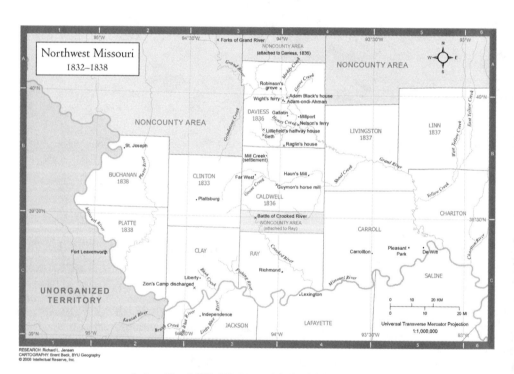

Northwest Missouri, 1832–1838. Courtesy of the Joseph Smith Papers Project.

---

1. MS 767, folder 1, item 3.
2. Clark Slade was Newel's nephew, being the son of Newel's sister Molly Knight. He was married to Emily Colburn, the sister to Newel's first wife Sally Colburn.

Aunt Es[t]her Culver, my Mothers Sister, whose husband died in Jackson C. O., came to live with us. My first buisness was to repair my house, & plough & plant a garden. As soon as this was done I commenced operations for my mill. All things ^have^ moved well for a few days.

[May] 25 I have Bought a Cow, & Contentment seems to reign in my family. Aunt Esthers health is not as good as I could wish, yet she is comfortable the most of her time.

June 1st all are well. The inhabitants of Clay begin to be more hostile. Th[e]y are holding metings for the purpose of expelling the Mormons from the County. There is at present no prospect of our wrongs being redressed by goverment, which gives our enemies boldness to Still persecute drive & plunder us at their leisure.[3]

[June] 15. Lydia has the fever & Ague, & for a bout a week I have felt quite ill. Some ague seems to be lurking in my Systom. Rumors are that the inhabitants of Clay do not intend to let the Sa[i]nts remain in the C.O. The Brethren are trying make a treaty with them so as to give the Brethren an opportunity to leave & not suffer as they did in being expeled from Jackson C.O.[4]

But few days have passed since writing the above. Lydia health is no better & I have had some severe Shakes of the Ague.

To day inteligence arrived that the Brethren would hold a Council tomorrow & try to devise some plan of a present Salvation for the Saints & requested that I should attend. Notwithstanding I have had a sever Shake of the Ague to day I have thout I should attempt to go to the Council. I have no [ho]rse & shall be obliged to walk the distance is a bout 12 mils. The next morning I arose & after commiting myself & family into the hands of Our heavenly Father, I Started, resolveing to pursue my Course as long as God should give me strength. I arrived at the Council in time & have had no Ague today.

The Brethren met in Council & the Lord blessed us light, & inteligence seemed to be given as our day demands. We agreed that if the

---

3. See Johnson, *Mormon Redress Petitions*; Rogers, "To the 'Honest and Patriotic Sons of Liberty,'" 36–67.
4. Newel testified in the Kirtland high council meeting the next day. *JSP*, D5:248–53. See Greene, *Facts Relative to the Expulsion*, 37–38.

State would Sell us the County of Calldwell, it being about 50 miles west of Clay, & uninhabited, we would use our endeavors to have [t]he Saints all gather to that County & leave Clay in the Cours of the Summer & fall.[5]

The above propositions were made to the inhabitants of Clay & Ater a little Consideration & Correspondence with the Governor, the a treaty to the above effect was entered into. The Clay inhabitants agreed to lay asid hostilities & suffer us to leave in peace. B This greatly Changed the face of affairs & the Saints began to have some hopes of being again secure from mobs for a Season.[6] We now had to devise means & regulations for Commenceing a Settlement in our new Country. Land was purchased of Goverment & the Brethren soon commenced moveing to our new location. They soon erected houses & prepared for raising Crops such as Buckwheat, turnips, sowing Buckwheat Winter wheat, & c.[7]

July 02 [1836] I have had no Ague since I attended council with the Brethren. That day, After Council Clsed I returned home & felt better than I had for several days preivious, makeing travel for the day about 24 mils. Lydias health continued bad & Aunt seemes to be declineing. I concluded to leave all & I had & move to our new settlement & began to make preparations to that effect.[8]

---

5. Cannon and Cook, *Far West Record* does not include this meeting. On June 29, 1836, Clay County residents formally asked the Saints to leave. They said they would not use force but hoped the Saints would avert a crisis by finding somewhere else to live. The Saints agreed and gained First Presidency approval to relocate. Some members already had scouted the lands in what would become Caldwell County, and by June 22 individuals and leaders had purchased about 1,600 acres. By early August 1836, the exodus from Clay County began. Gentry and Compton, *Fire and Sword*, 23–29.
6. See *JSP*, J1:215; *JSP*, D4:106; Gentry and Compton, *Fire and Sword*, 26–27. On July 25, 1836, a general assembly of Saints met and, among other business, appointed W. W. Phelps, John Whitmer, Edward Partridge, Isaac Morley, and John Corrill to be a committee "to search for lands for the Church to settle upon." Cannon and Cook, *Far West Record*, 104–5.
7. See Letter to John Thornton and others, July 25, 1836, in *JSP*, D5:258–68.
8. Starting here, Newel summarizes rather than using dated entries.

At this time I was oweing James Prindle a few dollars. He Said If I attempted to go until I paid him he would attach & take my goods from me on the road. I tried to reason with him. I told him I would pay him as Soon as I could, that my family were Sick & in an unhealthy place & I was in hopes moveing to a better place would be an advantage to their healt. But all to no purpose. He persisted, saying a man that could wear broad Cloth Should pay his debts.

My mill was not finished & I could not sell it for any thing, so I was obliged to stay & do the best I could. I continued building as I could, but was hindered much with the Sickness of my family. In Sept I resolved to go at the risk of all I had, think the life & health of my family of greater value than all I had. Beside Aunt was an aged woman & her health fast declineing. My little Son allso was Sick & my wife no better. She had the Ague every day. I had got nearly ready to move [but] Lydia was taken so ill we could not move.

The fore part of OCT Aunt was taken quite ill & die.[9] This to gather with sickness of my wife & Child prevented me from moveing. About this time a man by the name of Charles Young^er^ agreed to buy my mill. I would finish it by a Set time & give me a trifle sum for it thoug it was not near the value of the property. But as I was obliged to Stay I concluded to take up with his offer. At the time I could hire men enoug at a reasonable price & give them such pay as I should receeve for my mill when finished, But soon after the Brethren mostly emigrated to their new homes in Calldwell & it was allmost impossible to hire labor at all.

Dec 1st [1836] Lydia gave birth to a daughter.[10] After this she recovered slowly & I began to hope for her final recovery. I continued to do wat I could for the Compltion of the mill but for the last 3 months I had been able to do but little.

About the middle of Feb [1837] Lydia was taken verry Sick. She had a run of the inflamatory fever. For about a week She lay sensless. Her babe was obliged to be taken from her to be taken care of. [No]

---

9. It seems likely that Newel buried his aunt on his Clay County property, where he'd buried his wife Sally and son Eli.
10. They named their daughter Sally.

one thought She could recover. After the Doctor had done all he Could he left her. I felt that I Could not give her up & resign her to the silent grave. I now felt that there was no hopes of help but in God. I left her bed Side & retired to a lonely grove & ther I told my heavenly Father all my greif & mad my request un to him alone for in my heart I had resolved to Call upon God & to take no denial, for I had buried one Companion in that place & I felt that Could not endure to [u]nder go the trial again. I allso felt that she was worthy & might yet do much good upon the earth, & that I might Claim her life at the hand of God & not offend. I watered the ground with tears of supplication & Continued to Call upon God until I received a testimony that She Should recover.

When I returned to the house I soon saw that she began to amend. I Sat by her upon her bed when she Seemed to a wake from the stupor she had been in for some days & she looked upon me & then looked for her infant. She then asked me where is Sally. This was the first her recollection had ben visible fo a week or that she had missed her babe ~~She~~ which had been absent for a bout a week. I now felt to [t]hank God for his blessings to me. Lydia continued to gain from that time with remarkable vigor & in a few days she was able to set up & nurse he infant.

About 2 weeks after this I was taken sick & was unable to do any thing for a long time, so that I failed to get the mill done at the set time, which togather with the sickness of my family had brought me much in debt. After I recovered my health I found ther was no alternative but for me to finish the mill or loose entirely all that I had done. I had no Cow at this time. A horse & harness ^and house I had built in farwest^ was all that I Could command. my Bro Joseph had been helping me but said he could help no longer with out pay. Immediately I Settled with him & gave him my house in far west, my horse & harness, which was all that I could command. He agreed to help finish the mill which took us a bout 2 weeks longer. I delivered up the mill. On making an estimate of all expenses, I found my self about 2 hundred dollars in debt & no means to pay one dollar.

June [1837] had arrived & I knew not how to extricate my self from debt. Previous to selling my horse, I had moved my Father to Far west so that I felt no anxiety for his Safety. My Bro Joseph ~~said~~ moved a soon as the mill was finished, & I was alone with my family. About this time a man by the name of Shaver Came to give me a ~~Job~~ job of building a mill & Carding machinery. As debts at this time forbade me the privilege of gathering with the Saints, I engaged to do the job. I moved to the place where the mill was to be erected, hired two men, & commenced work. Lydias health had improved so that she was [a]ble to do all her work & some besides.

In the fall or latter part of Summer [1837] Brother Hiram Smith came to Farwest. I went to see him & attend Conference.[11] During the Summer there had been apostates telling all maner of evil about Joseph & Hiram, but as soon as I saw him & heard him speak I felt the testimony of the Spirit that truth eternal still lived in his bosom & I more sensibly than ever felt ^the^ weight of the old maxim, Truth will prevail & th righteous stand & shine ^when^ Error & false hood, with Apostates & liars, will vanish like ^dust befor the^ the summer threshing floor & the wicked go to thei own place, while the righteous Shine ~~forth &~~ forth in their Fathers Kingdom & be crowned with glories & honor that will have no end.[12]

I found it would be late in the fall before I could accomplish the job I had engaged. And as Mr Shavr gave me a good offer to stay & tend his mill during the winter [1837–1838] I concluded to accept as I could better winter my cows there & earn somting yet more by so doing. I sent butter & pork to my Father & saw him in Comfortable situation for the winter. The place where I lived was about 35 miles distant from Farwest.

I went again to in the fall to Farwest. I found my Father & family well & Comfortabl, the Brethren generally well & in good Spirits, hopeing they would now have the privilege of building & inhabitng, of

---

11. Joseph and Hyrum Smith were in Far West from about November 1 to 10. In a conference on November 7, Newel was resustained as a high councilor. See Smith, History, 1838–1856, vol. B-1, 775–77; Kirtland Camp, Journal, March 17, 1838; Smith, "To the Saints Scattered Abroad," *Times and Seasons* 1 (December 1839): 21.
12. Joseph and Hyrum's visit was also wrapped up in ecclesiastical conflicts from problematic leaders to early rumblings of polygamy. See Gentry and Compton, *Fire and Sword*, 69–84.

planting & enjoying the fruits of their labors. Great industry marked Settlement of the Saints & it appeared as if the wilderness was allready turned in to a fruitful field & the Solitary place made glad for the Saints of the most high.[13]

After enjoying the Society of my Brethren ~~a short~~ a few days, I returned to my family with my heart lifted to heaven with ardent desires that God would smile upon me & continue to bless me & my family with health & to prosper the labor of our hands, so that we may hve privelege of gathering with the Saints, fo their home shall be my [mine] & with them is my Delight.

During winter my health was tolerable good & all things seemed favorable & to prosper with me. Towards the latter part of Feb [1838] I concluded to move to farwest. I had been so far blest that I had paid for eighty Acres of land & Satisfied all demands against me so far as to satisfy my Creditors, that I was at liberty to go when & where I Choose. This seemes like a year of release or jubilee to me.

Th 24th of Feb I started with my family for Farwest & arrived there Safe on the 26th. I offerd the thanks & gratitude of my heart for the privilege of Settleing with those I love & of takeing my place with the Brethren ^of^ the high Council & again enoying instruction & blessing with them. For oft times when we have met in prayer & Conversation for the edification of each other it has seemed that wer in heavenly places.

Brother Joseph [Smith] & family & many others arrived at Farwest.[14] This was a general time of joy to the Brethren & Sisters who all felt to greet them with a hearty welcome, for we had longed for the Company & Society of our beloved Prophet.[15] And on the Sabbath his

---

13. Here and through his other mill projects, Newel participated in one of the most profitable and hopeful periods of the Saints' stay in Missouri. See Gentry and Compton, *Fire and Sword*, 47–67.
14. Joseph Smith's journal states, "On the 13th of March I with my family and some others arrived within 8 milds [miles] of Far West and put up at brother Barnerds [John Barnard's] to tarry for the night." *JSP*, J1:237; Burgess, *Labors in the Vineyard*, book 12, 68.
15. "On the next day as we ware about entering the town Many of the bretheren came out to meet us who also withe open armes welcomed us to their boosoms." *JSP*, J1:237.

words were meat & drink for us fo with wisdom & edification did he speak to us & made plain the way of life & Salvation & made the glories of the kingdom shine with a more briliant lusture than before. No wonder the A[n]cient exclaimed how beautiful are the feet of those that bring good tidings &.C.[16]

April 6, 1838 Conference. Phs Smith Presided. Business was done such as was needful for the benefit of the Church.[17] Sabbath was appointed for preaching, blessing Infants &. C. It was a profitabl time to all the Saints. The Printing Press & apparatus were fet[c]hed from Kirtland & preperations soon made for commenceing business.

[April] 15 Bro B Young Came before sunrise to my house & Said he knew of no other that would suit for the printing press so well as it would, & if it would suit me he would be glad to have me accommodate them with it. I told him he should have it. Immediately moved out & commenced to build another.

By the 24 [April] my house was up & covered & I moved into it.

[April] 29th My wife gave birth to a Son [James Philander Knight] I now had to prepare for a garden & do all I could in a few [days] for I had engaged to build for a man by the name of Brown in Clay C. O.

May 7th Sabbath. Father [Isaac] Morley came to my house to name & bless my little Son.[18]

I Started go to build the mill which I had engaged. I hired hands to help so that I made a short job of it, & in less than a month [near the start of June 1838] returned again to my family. I found them well & my garden growing finely.[19]

[Difficulties with his younger brother Joseph]

---

16. Newel next writes a few diary-type entries.
17. This was the first quarterly conference held in Far West. General and local officers were sustained, including the high council with Newel on it and three new members. Smith, History, 1838–1856, vol. B-1, 787.
18. Isaac Morley was a patriarch ordained at a council meeting held at Far West on November 7, 1837. Cannon and Cook, *Far West Record*, 124.
19. Newel returns here to writing summaries, but it's hard to tell if these are written close to the time when the matters happened or if he wrote these later in Nauvoo.

I had engaged to build another mill in Clay C. O. I stayed a short time with my family, hired Bro Demil[20] to put up hay for my Cattle &.C. Attended to my affairs and again hired hands & went to build the mil I had engaged.

About the middle of Summer [1838] ther seemed to be a Spirit of dissatisfaction growing in my brother Joseph. He made Complaints to Bishop Patridge against me, which I thought to be unjust & uncalled for. I invited him & his wife with as many of our connection as lived near to come to my house, thinking that a family interview & investigation of affairs would be the best method to Check the Course Joseph was takeing. After hearing his story & allowing him his full assc of everr thing & price he could make against me, I still owed him 14 dollars. But as I had given up my house & lived in a hired one myself & let him have every thing I Could Command at the time of his leaveing me after the sickness & misfortune I had encountered in Clay, it was decided by the family that his complaints were unjust & ought cease.

I told him as I had found labor for him during the winter at the sum of 20 dollars per month & had given up my house & my all to pay him. I thought I had done all the law of Righteousness could require, & as soon as I could I designed to pay him the uttermost farthing. And I hoped from this time forward brotherly friendship might abound betwen us, for it was not in my ~~hear~~ heart to wrong him at all. That it was for the sak[e] of salvation wee had made many sacrifises & now I did not want any thing to grow up & become a root of bitterness betwen us, for as long as the principles of Righteousness were cultivated betwen us we should find it our Salvation.

He agreed to the above & appeared to be Satisfied, both he & his wife, & we parted as I ^s^upposed with union, which I hoped would be lasting.

I was at home & attended Council occasionally during the summer yet the principal part of my labor was in Clay.

---

20. He hired Freeborn DeMille, his brother-in-law, who was married to Newel's sister Anna.

Ma^n^y of the prophet[']s ^allmost^ nearest freinds turned apostates & Caused him great trouble.²¹ But as he keeps a correct history of all & ^I^ design to be as breif as possible, I shall omit them.

During the Summer [1838] our Brethren labored with unceaseing diligence to make improvements & to till the earth, to build houses, barns & C., & truely the Lord blest their labors. Crops looked delightful & promised the laborer an abundant reward fo all his toil. But our enemies did not long behold our prosperity intil they began to covet our homes & to devise & lay plans for our destruction. But so Care ful were we of violateing any law or giveing them any advantage over us that they could get no pretext by law against us. Their only alternative was to let us alone & let us enjoy our rights as freeborn Americans or drive us in mass from the State, the latter they at length resolved to do. Some time in august the inhabitants ^of the adjoining Counties^ began to hold metings & to adopt measures for the accomplishment of this Crewel & Bloody design.²²

At this time I was engaged in building a mill in Clay fo[r] Robison. I had allso engaged to build another for the Indians 60 miles above fort Leavensworth a goverment job.²³ A bout th first of Sept I hired hands, layed in a store of provisions, procured waggon & teams &.C., & sent them to the place to make preparations for doing the job. I had a bout a weeks work to do yet on Robisons mill for my Self & men that were with me.

As I was engaged & considerable of a hurry to finish the job, I took up an axe to Cut a Sill a littl, which was in the way of putting up work. I struck the axe through my foot. It cut through the sole of the Shoe on my foot 2 inches in length.

This was an unlucky blow to me, or it look so to me for the present, had it not been for the Goverment job I should not have felt so bad. I

---

21. See full treatment of dissension and apostate leaders in Gentry and Compton, *Fire and Sword*, 69–122.
22. Gentry and Compton, *Fire and Sword*, 171–219.
23. Though Newel was not necessarily aware, Fort Leavenworth may have played into the motivations for the Missouri War. See Riggs, "Economic Impact of Fort Leavenworth," 124–33.

had paid considerable for teams provisions &. C. & sent a set of hands to the place & it was too late to give up the job. It was on my hands & must be done by the set time. For a while I knew not what to do as it Could not be accomplished without me to do or attend to the more particular parts of the machinery. We had yet about three days work to finish here. I was obliged to be present as it was the finishing & putting up the gears of the mill. After my wounds were dressed I requested a bed to be f[e]tched to the mill & placed so that I Could over see the work. And in this way the mill was completed. But the pain of the wound & the labor of mind I was obliged to labor under was great, yet the Lord gave sufficient strength to endure it.

I hav to Mr Robison I must Say I never was better treated or nursed wit more tenderness. When the job was finished he Settled & paid me honorably, making no Charge of his attention and Care which he had taken of me wholly him Self after my foot was Cut. He fixed his Carriage in the best possible manner & Sent his most trusty Slave to carry me home, th distance was about 35 miles. I rode with more ease than I could have expected. We were but one day going through.

I found my family as well a I could have expected, for Lydia & the two youngest Children had been afflicted with the inflamation in their eyes. Lydia had been quite blind & the Children verry bad. She Could find no relief, the pain she suffered from her eyes was great, until one morning after a Sleepless night she requested her nurse to go & call on Bro J. P. Green to come & administer to her.[24] He Came & while his hands were yet on her head the pain ceased & for the first time for some days she knew eace from pain. She allso opened her eyes & beheld light. For some days preivious she had not been able to discern any thing. The Children soon amended & She was now ble to wait upon me which she did with the greatest attention.

The mob were now rageing, threatening death & extermination to the Saints.[25] I now had to make the best arrangements I could to accom-

---

24. John P. Greene (1793–1844), a convert from New York in 1832, was a fellow high councilor with Newel. He was married to Brigham Young's sister Rhoda.
25. Newel here tries to find a way to record the Missouri War, in which he participated very little. He therefore simply summarizes what he heard and read

Mormon Troubles in Missouri Begin, from T. B. H. Stenhouse, *The Rocky Mountain Saints* (1887), 81.

plish the goverment job I had taken. I made a bill & draft of the work & put it into the hands of Competent workmen, & engaged them to go & do the best they could until I should be able to go.[26]

The number of Saints had increased to about [4,500][27] as there had been allmost an unceaseing tide of emigration. Calldwell was mostly Settled, & the Brethren had bought great quantities of land both in Davies C.O. & some in D^e^wit & Commenced Settlements. The mob at first comenced depredations on the more scattered Settlements, such

---

about the complicated situation. See Gentry and Compton, *Fire and Sword*, especially part 2, 171–393, for the outbreak and progression of open violence. At the time Newel describes, antagonistic groups had begun making personal threats to force out the Saints—though he did not make a legal statement, the involvement of local judge Adam Black intensified the antagonists' power; mobs had also formed for scattered attacks on Latter-day Saint people and property and once to prevent them from moving to the relative numerical safety of Far West. It is unclear whether Newel writes before or after the unarmed fight on election day, August 6, that was intended to prevent Saints from voting. Gentry and Compton, *Fire and Sword*, 174–77.

26. Both his injury and the situation's climate would have kept Newel close by. When mob threats and as-yet isolated acts of violence increased, local and statewide legal powers showed themselves less and less reliable. See Corrill, *Brief History of the Church*, chapters 22–23.

27. Newel's manuscript leaves empty space here for a population estimate but makes none. This estimate of somewhere between four and five thousand is taken from Daugh and Riggs, "'That They Might Rest Where the Ashes of the Latter-day Saints Reposed,'" 135–42.

as robbing, plundering, & burning houses &.C. They probbly thinking that by so doing they would provoke us [into] self defence & they could thereby get some pretext against us. But the Saints hav already learnt to profit by the Saviors maxim, be ye therefore wise Servants & harmless as doves[28] so that they could not justly accuse.

The Prophets life was [s]ought & hunted for by the mob with great diligence, for in Cool deliberation they had sworn to destroy him from the earth & that his lineage should be come extinct. At this time hundreds were moving from different parts of the States to this place. To prevent their getting here the roads were blockaded & kept guarded by strong parties of mob who did not hesitate to commit any depredation upon either persons or Cattl, horses, waggons, or any property belonging to the Saints.

At Dewit[29] there was a settlement of Brethren & many had been compelld to stop becauss of the mob there.[30] Th enemy surrounded the town & commited the most hostile depredations both upon persons & property. Many of the Saints were sick & suffered greatly while kept in this distressed situation. Some died for want of necessary food & could not be buried, only at the risk of the lives of those that performed this duty for them, as the ene^m^y were lurking & continually shooting at those that appeared in sight. A messenger at last managed to make his ecape & by much exertion & stratagen & by travelling in the night he arrived at Farwest & gave the information. And Compa^n^y from Farwest started. By stratagem & great exertion, our men made their [way] to

---

28. Newel is referencing Matthew 10:16, though the King James Version reads "wise as serpents and harmless as doves." He may have been influenced by the Joseph Smith Translation, which says "wise servants." Wayment, *Complete Joseph Smith Translation*, 30.
29. Jenson, "Dewitt," 603–8.
30. See De Witt Mormons to the Governor, September 22, 1838, in *Document Containing the Correspondence, Orders &c.*, 29–30. Citizens of Carroll County wrote, "You are advised by the citizens of Carroll County to leave DeWitt forthwith and all the citizens of that place who are determined not to take part with the Mormons, as a state of thing will exist there in a few days that if any of the friends of the people of Carroll should be injured would be extremely painful to them." Journal History, September 10, 1838.

Dewit, & through the Provide[nce] of him [who] hath Said th wrath of man shall praise God & the remainder I will restrain,[31] th[e]y succeeded in a Compremize so that the Brethren were permited to make their escape, all though it was at the loss of nearly all they possessed, & some died by the way & had to be intered with out a Coffin.[32]

The wound continued to heal upon my fo^o^t & th health of my family to increase, yet the Storm with out raged with great violence. T mob came upon a Company of our Brethren a hauns mill & murdered & wounded them in a most shocking manner.[33] Soon after this the mob grew bolder & commit deppredations upon the settlements in Coldwell & Daviess, So that they were obliged to flee into Farwest from all quarters to save them selves. Two families came in to my house with me, viz Freeborn Demill & Becklehammar. Ma[n]y could not get in to houses & were obliged to remain under some shelter of bed Clothes or tent as thy could. While in this situation we had a severe snow storm which rendered their sufferings verry great.

I began to walk on Crutches about the time the troops came to Farwest & to ride a little on horse back, as a Spy or picket guard[34]

Hawn's Mill, 1907. Anderson Collection, L. Tom Perry Special Collections, Brigham Young University.

---

31. See Psalm 76:10.
32. See *The History of Carroll County, Illinois: Containing a History of the County-its Cities, Towns, Etc., a Biographical Directory . . . War Record . . . Statistics, Portraits of Early Settlers and Prominent Men . . . History of the Northwest . . . Illinois . . . Miscellaneous Matters, Etc.* (United States of America: H. F. Kett & Company, 1878), 258; Gentry and Compton, *Fire and Sword*, 192–204.
33. See, among others, Pratt, *History of the Late Persecution*; Gentry and Compton, *Fire and Sword*; Moore, *Bones in the Well*; and Baugh, "Rare Account of the Haun's Mill Massacre."
34. This next narration paraphrases the June 1840 installment of Pratt, *History of the Late Persecution*, 113–16.

Rmors came to our ears that troops of great numbers wer advanceing in to our County, ^and committing great depredation.^ We thought it advisable to send a Company of a bout an hundred & fifty horsemen to ascertain the true situation of affairs. Towards evening we discovered a large armed force advancing to wards our town & not far distant. What men we had on hand immediately flew to arms & Calculated to defend themselves & there families & homes to the best advantage they could when the enemy saw our formidable line they halted.[35] A while [white] flag was sent by each army, but judge of our surprise when enquiring their design, our flag bearer was abruptly informed that they wanted three men out of our City & then they designed to massacree the remainder.[36] This was unexpected news to us this night was spent in trowing up a breast work & fortifying our City to the best advantage we Could, there being at this time a large quantity of timber for building on hand which served for that purpose. The little compay of an hundred & fifty returned just at sunset. Thy had been hemed in during the day by the mob & only exaped thm by their sperior knowledge of of the course & Country through which they made their way to our City.[37]

Notwithstanding the fatiegue thy had endured through the d^a^y they they hitched their horsees around my garden fence & quickly formed in line to strengthen our little force while our women spared no pains or lost any time in bakeing, Cooking, sending food to the weary yet brave & undaunted Soldiers who lost no time or thought their lives too dear to defend the helpless & innocent. This was a night long to be remembered by all the Saints.

T[he] next morning[38] we again sent messengers to the enemy & requested an explanation of facts or of their intentions. We were in-

---

35. Paraphrase of Pratt, *History of the Late Persecution*, 115.
36. Quoting Pratt, *History of the Late Persecution*, 115.
37. Paraphrase of Pratt, *History of the Late Persecution*, 115. See Gentry and Compton, *Fire and Sword*, 355. Newel now stops paraphrasing and relates his understanding of information he had heard or read. From the later accounts he cites, it becomes clear that he was not writing this at the time it happened but afterward in Nauvoo.
38. The morning of October 31, 1838. Most scholarship suggests that a small group comprised of the First Presidency and Latter-day Saint militia leaders

formed that they were commissioned by the Cheif executive of the State & th[e]ir Commission authorized them to exterminate or massacree the Mormons in mass.[39] Troops were on hand to the number of 13 thousand.[40] We now saw that there was no alternative with out acting in direct opposition to the ~~laws of~~ the authorities of the State, although we well knew them to be illegal & unconstitutional.

We therefore submited ourselves to the first demand of these Commissioned made, which was to surrender our arms. Our men were Called to gather and surrounded by a large number of armed force & compeled to lay down their arms. We were kept und[er] a Strong guard until towards evening when we were permited to go to our houses, which we found had been plunderd of evvery thing the mob thought worth takeing. The armed Crew had been during the day searching our houses insulting our women & committing such unheard of barrarities a would make any true born son of freedom that had a spark of patriotism blush to see his rights so trampled upon.

[Back on] the first day that the enemy entered our City they killed one of our Brethren & wounded another.[41] After our arms were given up & the enemy were satisfied with insulting & plundering, they requested an interview with Joseph & Hyrum Smith & Sidney Rigdon, the officers pledgeing there most sacred honors that as soon as a treaty

---

approached General Lucas's forces on the 31st and were taken prisoner then, but that Lucas did not march into Far West and force a surrender until the following day, November 1. See Gentry and Compton, *Fire and Sword*, 355–61. However, Newel describes these events in a different order than the traditional sequence—that the Church leaders were captured after the surrender in Far West when they handed over their weapons.

39. See Hartley, "1839: The Saints Forced Exodus from Missouri," 347–90.
40. Lucas told Boggs that Doniphan only had 250 men under his command. Lucas arrived on the 30th with 1,800 men a mile south of Far West. General Lucas to Governor Boggs, November 2, 1838, in *Document Containing the Correspondence, Orders &c.*, 73.
41. Gentry and Compton argue, "The exact number of Saints killed in various skirmishes may never be known." *Fire and Sword*, 358. Apparently somewhere between thirty and forty Saints were killed and possibly one Missourian.

could be entered into they should be safely returned to teir families.[42] They accordingly walked in to the Camp of the enemy not counting their lives more precious than their Brethren & ready to stand betwen them & death if it could be possible to appease the wrath of the enemy or mak a treaty to ameliorate th condition of their Brethren. But scarcely had they reached the Camp when they were met by the officers & in a rough & Savage manner Confined in a Small hollow Square & surrounded by a strong guard of four file[s of] armed men.

They were compelled to lie on the naked ground & covered with the Canopy heaven. As soon as our Brethr were surrounded the enemy my set up a most horrid yell & continued it for hours. The noise was past description & had there been ten thousand wolves yelling for their prey it would not have been equald. T[he] officers & Preists assembled, held a Court martial, & decided that the men they then had under guard should be shot in the presence or their families in the publick Square the next morning at eight oclock. The Prisonors had not the privilege of appeareing at the Court or introduceing witnesses. At [t]his unprecdented transaction Gen Doniphan objected, he being a lawyer, & forth with withdrew his brigade. This checked the horrid design & they Changed the sentence of Death. And conveyed them to Independence Jackson C.O. the Seat of Mobocracy in the former persecution.[43] This gave our beloved Prophet an opportunity of walking upon the land Consecrated & dedicated for the building of the temple, even the Spot of the new Jerusalem which shall be built preparitory to the Comeing of the Son of man & this that his own prophecy might be fulfiled. The design of the enemy no doubt was to destroy these men when they arrived at that place, but the Lord did not suffer it, for their work was not yet finished. ~~After keeping & tantalizeing pretending to some mock trial thy conducted them to~~

---

42. Lucas demanded that the Saints (1) give up their leaders, (2) make appropriation of their property, (3) leave the state, and (4) give up their arms. General Lucas to Governor Boggs, November 2, 1838, in *Document Containing the Correspondence, Orders &c.*, 73.

43. Pratt, *History of the Late Persecution*; and Baugh, "Call to Arms" include sections on the history and legality of state militias.

Our Brethren were thrust in to an old Store house & treated in a rough manner at first & strongly guarded. But after keeping them a few days they Changed their treatment to them & placed them in tavern house & gave them liberty to walk about at their leisure. They rimained here until Nov the 8th when they were ordered to be conveyed to Richmond. They were taken to Richmond & thrust in to Prison & made fast in Chains. General Clark made his appearance & the Prisnors politely enquired the cause of their being thus treated & of the crime allegded against them, for as yet they had not been Indicted & had heard no Charge against themselves. General Clark said he was not able to tell he spent several days in searching over the Statutes & trying to find some thing whereby they might accuse him. But after a fruitless attempt he came to us & informed us that there was no Chance for a Court Martial, & ~~we~~ thy would have to be turned over to the Civil law. Accordingly after a kind of pretended trial which lasted a bout two weeks, [t]here had been a great number of our Brethren taken Prisoners & conducted [to] that place & under went a trial. But at the Close of the trial which was on the 29 of Nov. they were all released or let to bail but 5 persons, viz, Joseph Smith Hyrum Smith. Alexander McRay. Sidney Rigdon. & Caleb Baldwin. These were ordered to be taken to Clay. C.O. liberty jail & to stand trial for treason & Murder. Treason for having stod in our own defence in Daviess C.O. & murder for the man killed in the Bogart battle. Allso P. P. Pratt, Morris Phelps, Luman Gibbs, Darwin Chase, & Norman Shearer who were put into Richmond jail to await trial for the same Crime.[44]

But to return to my self, as soon as I was able I rode to Clay to attend some business & to See how my Father was getting along, w[h]o preivious to any disturbance had moved there for the purpose of tending mill for a time.[45] I found him well & he had not been molested by the enemy. I returned home & soon Started to go to the before mentioned Goverment job. I arrived there safe & found the men at work. But they had labored to great disadvantage for want of a foreman who under-

---

44. Newel quotes here material from "A History, of the Persecution," in *Times and Seasons* 1 (September 1840): 164.
45. Newel now resumes writing what he experienced firsthand.

Clay County (Liberty) jail in Liberty, Missouri, where Joseph Smith, Hyrum Smith, Alexander McRae, Sidney Rigdon, and Caleb Baldwin were held. Courtesy of Church History Library.

stood the buisness. I had to do considerable over, which prolonged the time so that our provisions were so exhausted we had to send to Fort Lvenworth to get a new supply. However, I succeeded in getting the mill done in time to answer the contract & recd the money which I had contracted to build it for. This would have been sufficient to released all my debts & left me a Competence for my family, as I had a house & lot in the City Far West & eighty Acres of land about two miles distant from the City on which I had built & made an improvement.[46]

I returned to Farwest the forepart of Feb [1839]. Found my family well. Yet to my Sorrow ^th^ brethren yet were confined in prison & the enemy were prowling about & doing us all the injury they Could. All-

---

46. It appears Newel felt Joseph's claim was part of what Newel had paid for; hence Newel had 80 acres. Joseph Jr.'s land was the NW 1/4 of the NW 1/4 of section 18 in township 8. Hamer, *Northeast of Eden: Atlas of Mormon Settlement in Caldwell County*, 50, and index of landowners on page 87.

ready our Brethren had Commenced to leave the State & were making everry possible exertion to remove & to devise measures to remove the poor the Widow & Fatherless.[47]

During the summer preivious I had signed a bond with Joseph & others of some hundred dollars, which bond had been taken up & paid. But the dissenters had forged another, & as thy understood the frst & thereby attached my land & property so that I were waiting for me but it so happened they did not find me. I ettled my buisness as soon as possible & went See my Father. I put means in his hands to Convey him & family into th State of Illinois.

returned to my family & made the best shift I could to remove my family. I had no team. I sold my Cook Stove & the only Cow the mob had not killed, for me to hire a team to take my family to Illenois. As I have been absent Considerabl & by the wound on my foot, I have not been an eye witness to many transactions of our enemy & the doings of Officers of the State of M.O. I Shall take the liberty to Copy from the times & Seasons & Such others as from the best of my knowledge have made Correct Statements of facts, as it is what I desig & think essential for the rising generation to understand.[48] At all events I deem it important for my Children to know in future what it has Cost to establish the kingdom of heaven on the earth.

I started from Farwest on the morning of the eighteenth day of Feb. 1839. We journeyed by day & when night Come we spread our beds upon the earth & laid down to repose our weary bodies. Thus we went on, & nothing special occured until we Came within two miles of Huntsville, when the man I had hired to move me Said he could go no farther. His horses breasts were a little sore was his only excuse. He stoped his team & found a family by the name of Pullman who took us in. we I had paid West, for this was the mans name, for moveing me to the Miss River & I was left about half the way there with out means to go further, and in an enemies land from which I had been exiled. I knew not how to extricate my self, but as I had never been forsaken by

---

47. See Hartley, "Missouri's 1838 Extermination Order," and Gentry and Compton, *Fire and Sword*, 447–84.

48. Newel, however, did not insert any of that material.

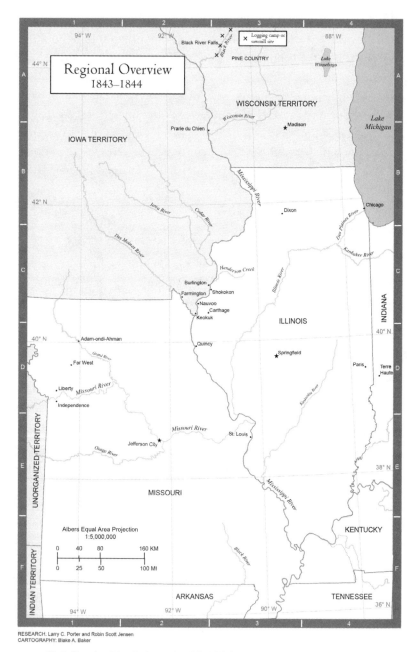

Illinois, Missouri, and Iowa Territory region, 1843–1844. Courtesy of the Joseph Smith Papers Project.

C. C. A. Christensen, *Expulsion of Saints from Far West, 1838* (ca. 1882–84), photograph of panorama. Courtesy of Church History Library.

my heavenly Father I Commited my self & family in to his Care & said in my heart I will trust in him Still.

I Stayed a bout a week at this place when the Lord opened heart of a man in the eighborhood to let his boy go with a team to the river with me. At this time Bro B Youngs family were at the same place & left without sufficient team to carry their goods, & my load was not so much as th team going could carry. Bro Young put on board some of his goods & I again resumed my journey. We had not traveled but a few days when the boys through neglect let their horses get away & could not find them. The oxen thy had left could not bare all the load, so I left by the way part of Brother Youngs good & a part of my own, in the care of a man who appeared freindly, & pursued on.[49]

We arrived safe at the river. Here we met Bro Young on his return to M.O. He had gon on & left his family at Atlass in an all Store house.[50] He invited me to go & stop with them, which I thankfully accepted, &

---

49. Hartley, "Missouri's 1838 Extermination Order," 19.
50. Atlas, Illinois, is roughly thirty miles south of Quincy, close to the Mississippi River. Young participated in a conference in Quincy on April 17 and then

took a team that he had & went back & fetched on the good[s] I had left by the way.[51]

I immediately set to look for a place to locate my family until I should accumulate some thing subsist upon, for I now found my self without money & in a land of strangers. I Concluded to go to Worcester.

---

    left the next day to head back to Far West with five other men. It appears that Newel met up with Young before Young's April trip back to Far West.

51. Brigham Young here offered Newel and his family a place to stay, which they gladly accepted.

PART 4

NAUVOO, 1839–45

INTRODUCTION

Part 4 deals with a lengthy six-year period. It starts when Newel and his family reach the Mississippi River in May 1839, covers their time in Nauvoo, Illinois, and ends with the Church conference in the Nauvoo Temple in October 1845, in which plans for the mass exodus from Nauvoo were announced.

Newel's writing continues to be a mix of his recollections, summaries of what he had read, firsthand experiences, and diary-like entries. He borrows only slightly from published sources. By early 1845 he had brought his autobiography up to date, so the end of part 4 moves to a dated diary format.

Building in Nauvoo, 1907. Anderson Collection, L. Tom Perry Special Collections, Brigham Young University.

Illinois, 27 June 1844. Courtesy of the Joseph Smith Papers Project.

Because of Nauvoo's pivotal position in the course of Church history, records written by its residents while they lived there are of vital interest. Newel's insights into Nauvoo are primarily his own. He provides information about the awful sickness the Saints endured during their first summer at Nauvoo, Lydia's being healed by a handkerchief blessed by Joseph Smith, and Lydia's faith in her patriarchal blessing that kept one of their children from dying.

VERSION 1[1]

[May 1839]. Concluded to go to Worcester [Missouri]. As I was journeying to that place a Stranger rode up to me & Said he had been informed that I was a mill wright [and] if so he would be glad to engage me to make gears for a horse ferry boat for crossing the Miss River. I engaged to go & work for two dollars per day as soon as I could get my family situated so that I could l[e]ave them. I arrived at Worcester that evening. We had a bout a ^peck of^ a little wheat a peck of Corn meal & a little sugar. Of this we made our supper & breakfast. I now began to studey how I should procure some thing for my family to eat while I went to work to earn more. But before I had found any probability of any thing, an old Gentleman by the name of Segget Called in to the Cabin where we had stoped. He after hearing my situation kindly offered to let me have some meal for my family, to provide fire wood for them, &.C. I thanked him for his kind offer & gladly accepted of it. I allso thanked my heavenly Father fo I felt that he was yet mindful of me here in a pennyless situation & among strangers.

I found a more Conv[en]eint house & moved my family the same evening & made preparations to go the next day to do the before mentioned job of work. Sunday morning I arose ate my breakfast & after Committing my family into the hands ^care^ of our maker. I left them & traveled about 30 miles to Clarksville where I was to do the work. The next day, in assisting to move the boat to a Conveinent place to do the work of the gears, there came a squall of wind & the boat got the advantage of us. And in my exertions to save th her I broke one of my ribs so that I could not labor for several days, mor than to draft the work, make preparations &.C.

The next Sabbath I got a horse & went to see how my family were getting a long. I found them well & they ^had^ Corn meal water to eat. Brother Pitkins had moved about 2 miles from where I left my family

---

1. This part is almost entirely version 1, item 5, with several additions copied from the newspaper. Those copied parts are noted in the footnotes. MS 767, folder 1, item 5.

were.[2] I went to see him. Told him my situation. He let me have some money to buy some meat & agreed to buy a Cow for me & wait on me until I should do the work I had engaged to, when I was to pay him. Monday morning I again left my family & rode to place of labor. I now began to work & my side did not hurt me but little. I Stayed two weeks & again went to see my family. They were now in a more comfortabl situation. Bro Pitkins had bought them a Cow & some hens & my wife had formed some acquaintance w[h]o let her have sewing to do, which helped her so that she began to live comfortably. I stayed over night after returning thanks to God fo his mercies & Committing my all to his care & asking a continuation of his mercies to rest upon us. I lef my family & went to finish the work I had on hand, which tok me a bout three weeks longer. On settlement I recd 5.5. dollars which enabled me to pay Bro Pitkins & have some money left.

I soon we[n]t to Quincy where th Father Smith[3] & the most of the twelve & hundreds of the Brethren were stoped I[t] had been contemplated & recommended by Phs Smith while he was in Prison that the Saints make a settlement up the Miss river a bout 60 miles [above] Quincy. The Brethren were makeing preparations to move to that place.

I returned to Worcester & as soon as I coul I hired a ^team &^ moved to Commerce. Bros Joseph & Hiram Smith had now got liberated & were settled here with their families[4]

I shall here take the liber^ty^ to Copy from the Prophets history th account of their sufferings & release from the M.O. Prisons & insert a

---

2. Probably George White Pitkin, whom Newel would have known in Jackson County. Pitkin was the Caldwell County sheriff briefly in 1838. See "Reference" at *The Joseph Smith Papers*. See also Nauvoo Municipal Court Docket Book / Nauvoo, IL, Municipal Court. "Docket of the Municipal Court of the City of Nauvoo," ca. 1843–1845. In Historian's Office, Historical Record Book, 1843–1874, 51–150 and 1–19 (second numbering). Church History Library, Salt Lake City. MS 3434.
3. Joseph Smith Sr., presiding patriarch.
4. Joseph Smith reunited with his family on April 22, 1839. See *JSP*, J1:336.

letter ^or epistle^ which he sent to the church while he was confined in Prison[5]

But to return to my self, I arrived at the new location of the Saints on Sunday a little after noon. My goods were unloaded by the side of the road near the Prophets house [cabin]. As soon as I Could, I went to see him. But I can never describe my felings on meeting with him & Shakeing hands with one w[h]om I had so long & so dearly loved. His worth & his sufferings fill my heart with mingled emotions. While I now beheld him & reflected upon the past & saw the present, I could not but raise my heart in silent but ardent desire that he & his family & his aged Parents might never be torn apart in like manner again, for I knew full well that it had well nigh born them to an untimely grave.

I soon selected a lot & commenced to build or to Cut & hall logs to build a house. I had been here but a few days when Brother Joseph came to my tent & introduced a gentleman by the name of Benjamin Brown, late from Chautauga C.O. N.Y. Brother Joseph soon introduced the propriety & necessity of building mills, as grain was plentyful but, oweing to the scarcity of mills, we had to pay at the rate of eight dols. per bbl for flour & 75 Cts per bushel for Corn meal. I told him I was aware of the propriety of the necessity of mills but had no Capital to buy Irons Stones &.C. But as to the mechanical labor I was ready & could do it. He proposed that Bro Brown furnish Capitol & that we set in operation a mill as soon as possible.

To this he [Brown] agreed & proposed that he furnish money, & that I go directly to Cincinatti & procure a certain Patent for horse power, which he knew was for sale at that place & which he highly recommended. And allso such other materials as should be necessary to put in operation a mill. I agreed to go. The next day we selected a convenient site for the mill & I moved my tent nearer the spot & made preparations to go.

I took passage on board a Steamer & had a quick journey, found the necessary machinery & purchased it & returned to Commerce in less than three weeks. As soon as I returned with th mill aparatus I lost no

---

5. Newel intended to, but never did, insert "Copy of a Letter written by J. Smith Jr. and Others, While in Prison," *Times and Seasons* 1 (May 1840): 99–104.

time in putting it into operation. It was only about eight weeks from th time I first commenced until I had the mill in operation. It performed well. I ground four bush per hour & it was a great help to Brethren.

But Brother Brown's family were taken sick soon after he came to the place & he concluded to buy a farm & said he must sell his share of the mill. As I could not advance the money & would not promise to do it in time for a Certain payment on his farm, he let J. C. Anis[s] have it & took his obligation for the money. Which he afterwords lost, or the said Annis failed to pay. I at the time was verry sorry to have a share of the mill fall into Annis' hands because I knew full well the result that would follow, from former acquaintance with the man. I tried to prevail on Bro. Brown to hold on to the mill a little longer & see if there would not some better way open both for himself & me & allso for the general benefit of the Brethren. But it was all to no purpose.[6]

I had left building my house for the sake of putting the mill in operation & my family were now sick & liveing in a tent. Doct Wilder a man with whom I formed acquaintance on the boat on my return from Cincinatti had boarded with me, allso a young lady my neice [Harriet Stringham] who were both taken sick & allso my youngest child.[7] Sickness prevailed to a great extent so that many suffered for want of proper nurseing many were lying on beds of sickness in tents.[8]

---

6. On December 15, 1839, the high council gave approval for "Brothers Annis, Bozier, and Edmunds" to build "a water mill adjoining the city." Smith, History, 1838–1856, vol. C-1, 1003.

7. Harriet Stringham was the daughter of Newel's sister Esther Knight and William Stringham. Newel and Lydia's youngest child at this point (mid-1839) was James Knight.

8. Because of Missouri troubles and then exposures during the difficult exodus, many Saints faced the summer of 1839 physically run down. Malaria, typhoid, and other river-related diseases caused by unfit drinking water and mosquitoes found easy victims. Many Saints died during July and August 1839. Garrett, "Disease and Sickness in Nauvoo," 171–72. Lydia recalled that "Pestilence and fever were seated at every fireside." Gates, *Lydia Knight's History*, 52. The Smiths took sick people into their home and inside a tent in their yard. Joseph Smith himself fell victim and was sick for two weeks. Hill, *Joseph Smith*, 267–68. When he recovered, he visited houses and tents, blessing the sick. Many experienced remarkable recoveries. He crossed the river, and during a day of blessing on

Some who had lately emigrated from the east & many who had been expeled from M.O. & had suffered the loss of all but their lives now l^a^y on beds of distress. And ma[n]y even died ~~throu~~ being worn out through the persecut, privations, & hardships they had endured. And no doubt their blood will Cry to be avenged of their murderers. Oh M.O. how will thy foul & murderous deed sink the[e] down to perditon & wo, ere thou hast atoned for the blood thou hast shed & the widows & Orph tears thou hast caused to flow & imprisonments & sufferings thou hast caused the Inocent. Thou wouldst gladly become extinct & be no more forever but this cannot be for the blood & sufferings of the Saints wil still cry against you & your sins must come to judgement & your punishment you wilt then a[d]mit is just.

My wife was obliged to attend to the Sick & do all her washing & work. She had done which was quite too much for her delicate constitution,

Doct Wilder was a younger man. He had buried his wife a short time preivious to leaveing Bosston for this place. He came her[e] fo the purpose of sttleing with the Saints & I believe he was a worthy man. He partially recovered of his sickness so that he went to Quincy on buisness, where he took a relapse & died. Harriet, the young la[d]y, began to recover, but our babe continued verry sick. Lydia, my wife, was threatened with a fever a bout this time & there came on a rain which rendered her situation verry inconvenient, as she was obliged to do all her cooking out of the tent. The fever increased, yet necessity compelled her to keep up & to labor much longer than her strength was able to bear. For about two weeks she kept about in this way, when she was obliged to give up & keep her bed.

Harriets health was a little better but she was not able to take care of our sick babe & do what was necearry for the family, so that I could do but little only tend the mill. I knew my family needed a house but

---

July 22 he healed many, even ordering Elijah Fordham back from death's door, who immediately became whole. Joseph Smith blessed a silk handkerchief and sent it to be used to heal victims he could not visit. Smith, *History, 1838–1856*, vol. C-1, 964–65. As shown below, Lydia sought and received such a blessed handkerchief for herself.

at the present I could not build, & sickness made it out of the question to hire. So we were obliged to remain in our tent.

VERSION 3

The sorrows and distress of the saints cannot be discribed at this season. Robbed in Missouri, and now exposed to the deathly "miasma" of the Mississippi, were enough to make the stones shed tears.[9]

VERSION 1

One evening Lydia requested me to go to the Prothet & get a handkercheif from him, or ask him to send her a healing blessing. And, said she, I believe I shall be healed. She would have been glad to have sent for him to come & lay his hands upon her, but did not feel worthy to trouble him, as the multitude of business & Care he had over the Church she knew was more than he was abl to endure wit the sufferings of the Saints he daily. On this account I felt delicate a bout Calling on him. I went out & met met Brother Hollman & talked with him. Returned to my wife & handed her my handkercheif. She tok it but was no better the next day her fever & pain was severe. Doctor Stobey Called on us I requested him to do some thing fo my wife, for her relief he gave her medicine which she took, he alls[o] gave medicine to our babe.

A bout the first of Sept a Small Cabin was vacated & I took my family into it. Lydia was Confined to her bed at the time. She continued to take medicine but got no relief. For near two weeks her Strength failed, & she was rediced [reduced] so low she could not speak aloud. I went to her one evening after She had Sufferd much through the day when she in a whisper [said] Newel I am verry low. If the Lord does not interfere in my behalf, I shall soon be worn out, for medicine does me no good & I am allmost gone. Her strength was now exhausted & she said no more.

I felt that I had not don wright in neglecting to go to the Prophet as she had requested, although I had not told her the handkercheif I gave her was not from him. I left her, went immediately to the Prophet, & requested him to send her his handkercheif with a word of consolation & a healing blessing. Go, said he, tell her the Lord shall bless her & her

---

9. These lines by Newel are not in version 1 or the Allen version; they are only in version 3.

heavenly Father shall heal her. I hastened to my house & went the bed side of my Companion & told all that I had done & the promise that Prophet sent to her. I laid the handkercheif upon her head & prayed th blessing to be sealed upon her. From her Calm appearance it was evident that ther was a Change in her feelings. She soon fell asleep & rested well during the night. in the morning She Said She had felt no pain during the night. At the moment I laid the handkerchief upon her head, the pain ceased & she did not feel as if there was any dissease a bout her at this time. Yet she was weak The next day the Dr. Came to see her he looked at her & examined her pulse & tounge & said he had never seen so great an alteration in a patient in his lif. Said he there is no disease about her let her be a little careful until she recovers her strength & she will get a long. It was but a few days until she was up attending to her sick babe & Cares a bout the house.[10]

[I] must now return to give the mill a passing notice. All my fears were fully realized, for Annis immediately set alltering first this then tht, so that the mill I forsaw would avail neither him self or any one else any thing. I tried to buy his share but to no effect. I then tried to sell mine to him he but with little success. My health began to declin about this time & could take no Care of the mill. After seeing the mangement a few weeks, I came to the Conclusion to give up my Share & have no more to do with it. He gave me a few bushels of Corn meal & I lost my summers labor. He moved the mill up to his place & repaired it until there was nothing left but the Stone & Irons, which he could not use up or alter. It was a great loss to the Brethren who had raised grain & had to go a great distance to get it ground & still kept up the price of meal & fl[o]ur.

My health was poor for about three months so that I could do but little. Some of the time we lived on potatoes & Salt, & some of the time we had bread & water to eat. Our babe still lingered & I have ever believed his mother held him by faith. Fo a long time th neighbors said he could not live & told Lydia She had better give him up fo she would

---

10. Joseph Smith's journal records, "The sick were ministered unto, with great success but many still remain sick & new cases occurring daily." *JSP*, J1:349. See Kenney, *Wilford Woodruff's Journal*, 1:347–48 (July 22, 1839).

wear out her own life & loos her child too. But she could not be prevailed to let him go. Said she, if I k[n]ew the Lord required it I would resign him to His will. But I do not feel that it be at all for his glory or that h require th lif of this Child at this time. But disease has laid heavily upon him & no doubt the destroyer would be glad to take him from the earth for if he can destroy the rising generation he will thereby think to weaken the kingdom of God on the earth.

Oct th 6 [1839] general Conference.[11] Many attended from various parts. My house was to crouded during the Conference that it took all my wifes time to wait upon them, so that she had no opportunity to go to the Conference. And on the last day she cooked the last ~~meal~~ of we had. Just as it was on the table, two more men came in & ate with us, which Cleared the table of the last mouthful. My wife & Harriet with the little Children had not one mouthful to eat. My health had been so poor for some time that I could not procure provisions & it was verry scarce & hard to be got.

She held on to the promises made to her in her ~~hr~~ Patriarchal blessing given by Father Smith[12] & th blessings promised upon the Child in his infant blessing, until I gave up all hopes & thought the child must surely die. It lay verry stupid. One morning when the Prophet was passing, I Called him in to see the Child. he looked at the babe & then to its mother & said there is but one thing more that you can do. Send for Father Harris[13] & undress the Child & have him annointed from the Crown of his head to the Soles of his feet. And if that does not help him you mist give him up for if that will not save him nothing can. Lydia replied, I Cannot give him up! The Prophet said I think it will save him. I went for Brother Harris w[h]o came & administered to the babe as the Prophet directed. Th anointing was effectual, from that time the babe

---

11. At this conference, Newel once again was sustained as a member of the high council. Smith, History, 1838–1856, vol. C-1, 969. Joseph taught that "the righteous will remain with him [Christ] in the cloud whilst all the proud and all that do wickedly will have to return to the earth, and suffer his vengeance which he will take upon them this is the second death." *JSP*, J1:352–53.
12. See our part 2; see also Gates, *Lydia Knight's History*, 34–35.
13. Probably George Washington Harris (1780–1857), a high councilman and city alderman. See "Reference" at *The Joseph Smith Papers*.

amended fast. This was on Monday morning. And on Thursday morning the Prophet called to my house & enquired how the Child was. On hearing, he replied, you know wat has helped him [so] if he should take a relapse, attend to the same ordinance again. Before night the same day, the child was verry ill. it seemed as if the destroyer h^a^d laid hold with a full determination to take th Child. But my wif[e] soon went to the elders. Elders Bennson & Sherwood came & administered to the Child as the Prophet had directed.[14] Whil[e] they were anointing the Child, his countenance Changed & he looked Stead fastly upon them. Had the sun shone in a Cloudy day the Change would not be more visibl[e] than the change was upon the babe. And from that time there seemed to be no more disease upon the Child, but he grew & soon began to walk about. I now came to a full determination that it was best to trust in God a lone for life as well as ^for^ Salvation.

As soon as I had recovered my health so that I could, I [s]ecured some provisions for my family. I commenced to build an another or a saw mill in company with Brother D Hibbard.[15] We commenced to get the timber some time in Jan. As soon as the river opened for stemboat naviation, Bro Hibbard who furnished money & my Self took passage & went to Saint Lewis for Irons. We started the___ of Feb. We had a prosperous journey & by the 6th of April we had our mill in operation & began to make lumber.

At this date ther[e] was a general Conference [1840] by the Saints in this place. We received much good instruction from the Pro[p]het & had a profitabl[e] time. Many of our Brethren Came from different parts to attend the Conference. My house was crowded to overflowing so that my wif did not attend but one half day. The Second day of Conference I took a severe cold so that the next day I was not able to attend. For a house [meeting place] we were obliged to use the grove & the wind was quite cold & boisterous. I cntinued to do buisness in the mill with Bro. Hibbard until the fore part of June when I sold my share to him & built

---

14. Probably Ezra T. Benson (1811–69) and Henry Garlick Sherwood (1785–1867), see "Reference" at *The Joseph Smith Papers*.
15. Possibly Davidson Hibbard (1788–1854). See "Reference" at *The Joseph Smith Papers*.

me a house. I had got a lot & go^o^d picket fence around & garden growing. Yet the Brethren labored und great inconveniance with regard to mills, which induced me to sell my house & lot & try again to build a grist mill, for the Brethren had good crops growing & only thing needful to make bread Cheap & plenty [of] seed, [was], to be a grist mill to manufactor their grain. Bros Rollfe & Jackman Said if I could procure the materials they would assist in doing the labor & we would own the mill in Co [ownership].[16]

House in Nauvoo, 1907. Anderson Collection, L. Tom Perry Special Collections, Brigham Young University.

We had not long settled on this Conclusion when a gentleman from England Came & purchased my house & lot. He paid me money enough to purchase the Stone & Irons for the mill nails &C. I went immediately to St Lewis to procure them while Rollfe & Jackman were prepareing timber fo the mill. I was not gon quite a week. On my return I found all things prosperous.

Home of Wilford and Phoebe Carter Woodruff in Nauvoo, 1907. Anderson Collection, L. Tom Perry Special Collections, Brigham Young University.

There was some sickness, yet it did not prevail to [as] distressing an extent as it did last year. Nor did the sick suffer so great privations, for one years industry of the Saints & reared many comfortable buildings brought withn their command many neceraies & comforts of lif[e], which they were wholly deprived of the preivious year. Prosperity

---

16. Samuel Jones Rolfe (1794–1867) and Levi Jackman (1797–1876). Jackman served with Newel on the high council in Far West.

seemed to attend the labor of the Saints & Crown their industry beyond their expectation.

About the last of Aug or the first of Sept [1840] a Gentleman by the name of J C Bennet came to the place.[17] He was a Dr by practice, had joined the Church a Short time preivious & Came her to reside. He appeared to be a man of Considerable & soon Commenced his professional practice, as it was a time considerable sickness among the Saints. The reason I speak of this gentleman is more particular because of the [n]ecessity I shall hav to make mention of him here after.

We got our mill house up & enclosed the gears mostly ready for operation so that we anticipated soon to be grinding. Bro Jackman & his wif were both verry sick & th man we engaged to build the dam was taken to jail ~~when~~ on an old Kirtland debt, which circumstances had [would have] rendered him free from had justice been administered.[18] This disappointment togather with Brother Jackmans sickness so disappointed us that we failed get the mill in operation ~~at the~~ until the winter set in & froze the river [1840–41], so as to prevent grinding before we Could do the work we had depended on others to do & were disapointed. We had spent our time laboring on the mill so that we had not laid up a winters store of provisions & our means were so exhausted we had not the means to procure it.

We now saw our only allernative was to turn our labor to procure provisions for our families & for the present cease our labors on th mill as there was no prospect its availing us any thing until the opening of Spring or such time as we could build the dam.

About this time Bro Elijah Fordham Came to my house, & seeing the prospect & situation of our affairs, he at first proposed to enter into Co partnership with us assist in finishing the mills.[19] But af[t]er consulting his wif[e] on the subject he declined on the grounds that She was not willing to live near the river. She prefered living on the hill near

---

17. For his arrival in Nauvoo, see Smith, *Saintly Scoundrel*, 50.
18. "A Charter Granted to Newel Knight."
19. Elijah Fordham (1798–1879) was a carpenter. See "Reference" at *The Joseph Smith Papers*; Cook, *Nauvoo Marriages*, 82; Esshom, *Pioneers and Prominent Men of Utah*, 875.

the temple & he concluded to build a horse mill there. He proposed to let us have such things as we wanted to out of his Store & let us do the mechancal labor on on his mil to pay for the goo[d]s he owned.

At the same tim a grist mill across the river in mont rose propeled by horse power which was out of repair. This he want us to put in repair, which we did, & h let us have some provisions. He urged us to trade at his Store as he wished to turn his goods into a mill which he intended to build the next summer. We Concluded to do so, with the agreement to do th gears for his mil to pay for the good[s] purchased of him. Bro Br Rollfe acted as Clerk at the time of our partnership.[20] We gave some orders to those w[h]o had assisted us in the labor of our mill. We got but verry little for our selves, nor if so much as the labor of repairing his mil[l] would amount to.

Soon after we ha[d] made this arrangement with Bro Fordham, we engaged to build a mil for one Allen on the river a bout 7 miles below Nauvoo. We commenced the mill in Dec. [1840?] The inconvenience of being from home & hireing our board induced me to move my family there for the time we should be building the mill. We had good luck & got the m^i^ll in operation. In March Bros Rollfe & Jackman were in Comp [partnership] with me in the job. The same Allen had another mill he wanted repaired & considerable labor done on. The opening of Spring [1841] we saw the situation of our own mill & the river was such that we could not build the dam or do any thing to advantage on it until the latter part of the Season when th water should be low. I concluded to stay & work on Allens mill. Brother allso stayed in company with me. Previous to this Bro Rollfe had sold to us his share in our Nauvoo mill. At the time of our settlement we allowed one hundred dollars Apc at Fordhams.

About middle of March I was taken sick. I was verry low for about one week. My Complant was Severe pain in my breast & sid[e] attended with a severe Cough & fever. After a bout a weeks severe suffering the Lord began to hear our petitions & to rebuke th the disease that was preying upon me. It was some time before I was able to labor much, yet I found my strength gradually increaseing.

---

20. Black, *Who's Who in the Doctrine and Covenants*, 250.

April 6th [1841]. A general Conference at Nauvoo.[21] I attended & we had a profitable meting.[22] At this Conference the revelation from the lord was read showing his people that he required an house to be built unto his name & that it would prove their Salvation, to go too & build it according to the revelation & pattern given through the Prophet.[23] The Brethren generally responded with a hearty Amen & Covenanted to do it according to their abilities or the requirements of the revelation, which is everry tenth according to law anciently given to his Saints & required of them in all ages when he has a people on the earth.

Prosperity prevailed with the Saints in Nauvoo. They had during the last Session of the legislature a liberal Charter granted them which was Calculated to sheild them from many invasions & troubles to which they had ever been exposed by the wicked w[h]o had ever sought to do us an injury & to bring troubl persecution & Death upon the Church.[24] We now had the privilege of making such laws & regulations as was necessary for the good & well being of our City. We alls[o] had a grant for a leigon of our own or for the benefit & Safety of our City & Country. Our Prophet ha confered on him the title & Authority of Lieutenant General which he filled with honor & dignity. The Corner Stones of the temple were laid on [blank].[25]

July 4. Th Nauvoo Leigion made a respectful & noble appearance paraded in Our beautiful City & our Prophet appeared in a most graceful manner at their head. The day passed of well & all seemed delighted

---

21. "Celebration of the Anniversary of the Church," *Times and Seasons* 2 (April 15, 1841): 375.
22. *JSP*, J2:49. "With his family. And several of the Twelve. viz. B[righam] Young H[eber] C. Kimball. W[illard] Richards. & gave instructions how to open organize & adjourn the special conference."
23. This revelation, given January 19, 1841, is now Doctrine and Covenants section 124.
24. Church leaders had lobbied hard with the Illinois legislature and won from it a generous city charter in December 1840. It incorporated the city and granted the Saints broad court, police, and militia powers, making it practically a city-state run by the Church. See Smith, History, 1838–1856, vol. B-1, 1130; Kimball, "Wall to Defend Zion," 491–97.
25. Joseph Smith supervised the cornerstone ceremony.

with the prospect of peace during this season there were no great disturbances with out & in Our City general union prevailed.²⁶

Emigration Continued to flow to our City both from different parts of our union & from the Canadas & from Europ there was considerible sickness prevailing the latter part of summer. Several of our most useful men died & it is a loss to us which cannot be made up to us, they have left a vacancy in our Circl in our Society & City that is felt by all. Among these I would make mention of R B Thompson & D. C. Smith yongest Broter of the Prophet & President of the high Priests Quorum & Editors of our valuable paper the tines & Seasons.²⁷ Their loss will long be felt by & remembered by the readers of that extensively circulated Paper & more especially by their families & intimate freinds.

Cornerstone, Nauvoo Temple, 1907. Anderson Collection, L. Tom Perry Special Collections, Brigham Young University.

D C Smith was young & amiable. He bore a high respectabl office in the Nauvoo Leigion which he nobly filled. I never Saw a man of his age that appeared more noble & inteligent & with whom I bade farewell until the morning of the resurrection with mor reluctance When Oh when will death be shorn of its power & th Destroyer & Spoiler cease to act I would that they might ere long find a day of rest that the mourners might cease to mourn & the tear of the widow the orphan & bereaved might be Stayed.

---

26. "Celebration of the Anniversary of the Church," 375.
27. Robert B. Thompson died on August 27, 1841, and Don Carlos Smith on August 7, 1841.

In Aug [1841] I bought Brother Jackmans Share of our mill & moved back to Nauvoo. The first of Sept I was glad to again get home in the City of the Saints. I was not able to put my mill in operation by water as I had intended as it had taken nearly all my summers work to pay Bro Jackman. But Circumstances occured which induced me so to do, which I do not think expedient name at this time[28] . . . fixed my mill to grind wit[h], August 18. Horse power for the pres[en]t intending as soon as I Could to build a Dam & do [bui]sness by water. During the fall & winter I grou[nd to] some advantage with horses so that my family [live]d Comfortably until ^some^ ~~about the time of high water [an] ox kicked me quit severe on my~~ in Febr [1842] an ox [kic]ked me on my leg so that I was laid up for some [ti]me before I was able to do any thing. High water prevented me from grinding & I was left in rather low [circu]mstances haveing but verry little provisi[on] [on] hand for my family. My health continued [poor] so that I coul not labor to earn but little [?]. I could not d mor than two hours work in a [day] fo a long time. What I could do I keept trying [to pu]t my mill in operation. I had repaird the gears [which was] about all that I could do. The dam was [?]king & I knew not how to build it as I had [no one] to hire & my health was so bad I could [not do] it. In vain I tried to get help. For a while [it see]med as if there was no prosperity for me, no [one] to lend a helping hand in tine of troubl & [ne]cesity.

I tried get some assistance from the Temple Committee ^by loan^. Judge Higbee[29] gave encouragement but Cayhoon utterly refused. He Said he believed it would be an injury to help me for he did not believe the mill could ever accomplish any thing or that there was any privilege or power for mills in the river, & if nobody would help me I would after a while give it up & let it go. But this did not discourage me for I knew the power of water & that it would be the best property in the City if

---

28. The edges of the first few pages are torn, so square brackets will mark where words are missing, and some will contain what seems to be missing. MS 767, folder 1, item 5.
29. Elias Higbee (1795–1843). While in Missouri, he was a Caldwell County judge. He had served on the Missouri high council with Newel. He joined the Nauvoo Temple building committee on October 6, 1840. See "Reference" at *The Joseph Smith Papers*.

it could be put in operation & prove the greatest benefit to the Publick of any thing that Could be done.

A Gentleman by the name of Law[30] Came to the place & had erected a Steam mill & as there was no other mill in the place & people were obliged to have their grain manufactured, he took just such advantage as he pleased. He took about one third for tole. This evil I knew would be at once removed if I could get my mill in operation. Not [that] I wanted to injure Law but I kne[w] justice was du[e] all men & that the laborers rights were due to [?] & that right would wrong no man. With this n[otion? ?] I labored under allmost everry inconvenience & [?] that could be imagined both in body & in mind.

Th[ese] were days of trial to me in regard to my temporal b[usi]ness. For the want of means to hire one months labor [I] was obliged to let my mill lay for months while [my] health was such that I Could not go to do a days [work] to earn any thing from the time I was hurt in [February] until the 18 day of July [1842]. We had not one Dol[lars] worth of provision or Clothing except what my [wife] earned with her hand & needle. We had four Child[ren] at the tine which during the summer all have had the measles & whooping Cough. My wife labor[ed] to take care of the family, yet I never he[ard her] complain or murmur at her situation [?]ny I had no Cow. I owned a blind horse, I had p[ut?] work on my mill in the winter. I had paid twen[ty] dollars for the horse.

The best I could do or the o[nly] way I could procure a cow for my family was my Brother in law Freeborn Demill, [trade] hime the horse for a Cow which would been worth ten dollars in money with an agreement if he could turn the horse to advantage he should let me have five dols worth of provisions. He soon sold the horse for a good price but never found a time give me the provisions.

During this time much of my time was occupied in the buisness of the High Council of which I had been a member ever since its organization. The before mentioned John C Bennet brought great trouble

---

30. Wilson Law (1806–76) was a millwright, merchant, land speculator, and farmer. With his brother William Law, he became a dissenter and opponent of Joseph Smith. He was excommunicated in April 1844. See "Reference" at *The Joseph Smith Papers*.

upon the Church & Sought to lead away & deceive through his Cunning & Deceipt.[31] Many an innocent & virtuous person & an astonishing pass did he deceive before we were enabled to put a stop to his unhallowed career. The Council were in Session a great deal & the iniquity that was proven on Bennet was past description. More especially with the females who were inexperienced & knew not the cunning of the Devil or the deceitfulness of man. Many a female did he bring to irrecoverabl shame Sorrow & the course he took & the measures & devices he practised were such as allmost justify those he deceived & make his crime double.[32]

He allso had a band of associates who were ready at any time testify to the basest intrigues to Carry into effect by Stateing that the Prophet upheld & taught such to be right. When his influence failed he would call on others to prove that thre was no Sin in such a cours as he sought after. And they would testif that Brother Joseph did uphold it & if they would yeild to Bennet it would a great honor & blessing to them. Thus by his cunning & deceit did he deceive & lead astray many & thereby brought great evil upon the Church.[33]

---

31. John Cook Bennett, baptized in Nauvoo in September 1840, rose and fell quickly in leadership roles, including as assistant to the First Presidency and mayor of Nauvoo. He was excommunicated for adultery in May 1842, whereupon he became a bitter opponent of the Church. He published *The History of the Saints; or, an Exposé of Joe Smith and Mormonism*. See Smith, *Saintly Scoundrel*.
32. Several high council meetings were convened to discipline those involved with the "spiritual wifery" doctrine espoused by John C. Bennett. For instance, Knight was appointed as one of the high council representatives to speak either for or against Chaucey Higbee in the trial before the high council for "unchaste and unvirtueous conduct with the widow Miller and others." Higbee had clearly been influenced by Bennett's teachings, and witnesses testified that Higbee had seduced women "and at different times been guilty of unchase and unvirtuous conduct with them and taught the doctrine that it was right to have free intercourse with women if it was kept secret and alos taught that Joseph Smith authorized him to practice these things." Nauvoo High Council Minutes, May 20, 1842, folder 3, 1–2. Higbee was excommunicated.
33. Smith, *Saintly Scoundrel*, 86–90; Dirkmaat, "Search for "Happiness," 94–119; Hales, "John C. Bennett and Joseph Smith's Polygamy," 131–81.

From the time that these evils were proven upon this wicked Clan they began to seek to destroy the Prophet & to over throw the Church. They for a time Sought to secretly decoy or betray the Prophet in to the hands of the blood thirsty, but in ths they were baffled & their designes failed. When they found they Could not succeed in Such a plot, they tried to do it by stirring up Persecution abroad. But show ^to show^ more particular the wickedness of these unhallowed men & the trials Our Prophet & the Church has had to endure I shall Copy from those that have written what I S know to be facts. And my object is that the rising generation & those that are a far off may know in a future day wat it has cost to establish & lay the foundation of this Kingdom upon the Earth in thse the last days, of the power of the Gentile upon the earth. For the Lord will in his own time come out of his hideing place & so great will be the distress of the nations that to those that know not the sufferings that they have caused & wontonly suffered to come upon the innocent, they would allmost be ready to Call upon God to stay the hand of distress & show mercy to the People. Therefore I deem it important that all people have an opportunity understand & know the truth of all that is now passing & of the sufferings of the Saints & the Cost of the establishment of this kingdom.[34]

But to return to my self, it seemed as if after the Lord had suffered me to be brought low & in a State of Privation & trial & saw that I did not Curse God but that I still trusted in hin, he wrought out a way for my deliverance. For in my deepest trials I had not forgotten to Confess the hand of God in all things & still to trust in him & day by day did I go in to my mill & there in Secret ask for the blessings of God to attend me & to bear me off victorious over everry trial that I should be sufferd to come upon me. The only Cow I had, strayed away & I never found her. This left our little Children & selves yet more destitute, for I had not the means to buy another & it deprived us of a great comfort as the milk we got from her was a great help to our liveing.

The reader can better bett judge than any one can describe the the difference betwen liveing on the necessary Comforts of lif[e] & enjoying health & plenty, Seeing prosperity smile on everry hand & all

---

34. Whatever Newel had in mind to include, he does not indicate what it was.

around greet him for his success, & being deprived of health, & misfortune follow after missfortune until all our earthly substance seems to be wasted or to avail us nothing. To see our family in want & not be able to supply the demands of nature & then to see many who in the days of prosperity ^were warm & affectionate become^ cool & indifferent & be treated with neglect because of that which has unavoidably come upon us. I say the Contrast Cannot be described & is only know to those that have passed through ^the^ Same. I have no doubt but Father Job knew something of this situation & allso Th Savior must have known some thing of the Contrast, for we are told that he decended below all things that he might ascend above all things & that in all things he was tempted. Yet he over Came and ~~is set down on high~~ has ascended on high & is amediator & an intercessor & knoweth how to succor t^h^ose that are tempted & afflicted. And if it became necessary for the ancients to suffer & even for the only begotten to experience such like temptations, I am sure I ought not to Complain for ~~if in~~ I am faithful. I doubt not but all will work for my good.

 After I had been contemplateing these things one morning on the 18 of July [1842], while my wif had been prepareing our Scanty meal as we sat at breakfast, I looked out & saw an aged gentleman [John Alley] looking & [ ]ing my mill. After breakfast my little son went out & the old gentleman requested him to ask me to come out. He was a Stranger, a man that I had never before seen. Yet th Spirit seemed whisper me thre was prosperity for me with him. I walked out & after a few words the gentleman proposed to buy a Share of my mill. He asked my price. I told him. He replied that was just what was in his heart to give. I told him my situation & that as I could not set it in operation I would sell one undivided half to him. We at once made a Contract & soon reduced it to writings. He agreed to bear his equal proportion in finishing the mill. Soon returned to Boston, the place of his residence, with the intention of returning again in the fall. He paid me in part so that I was enabled set my mill in operation & supply necessary demands of my family. Thus did relief Come ~~in~~ from an unexpected hand & in an unexpected hour & I did not for get to Confess the hand of God in it & return thanks to him for the same.

On getting my mill in operation, it performed well beyond my expectation. And those that had looked on me with s[c]orn because of Spending my time so long at what they supposed would never avail any thing, now had to confess that it was best to let everry man work at his trade. And that it was for want of a little to do with that I had suffered much & not a miss guided judgement. The Inhabitants also soon found that it proved as I had ever told them great advantage to have the power of water instead of [oxe]n to manufactor their grain for at once the tole was reduced from one third to one eighth. Time passed on & prosperity again began to smile upon us so that our table was covered with plenty & gratitude filled our hearts.

On th 17 of Oct [1842] Lydia gave birth to a little son. He was a fine & promising looking Child. We [nam]ed him Newel after my self. Soon after this [the] Old gentleman, John Aley, returned to this [pl]ace & was truely pleased to see our mill operate. [The] old gentleman s wife & one Daughter had for some time belonged to the Church & for their [ ] he came here with the intention to secure an [ ] with the Church for them, allthough he he did not belong to it him Self. However all things he [saw] in the affairs of the Church did not alltogather please him & concluded to do but little here. He proposed to give up his share of th mill to me on Conditions that I should refund to him what he had paid me for the mill as Soon as Circumstances would make it Consistent fo me to do so. I accordingly gave my obligations to him & again considered my Self benefited, for it was now proven that I had not labored in vain & that I had the best property of it Cost or value in the City. Yet it need much done to have it in a finished Condition.

I had got my winters provisions laid in, bought me a c[ow] & mad[e] necessary provisions for winter before the river froze so as to stop grinding. After winter set in [1842–43] & business in my mill Closed, I began to study how I should occupy my time. I had felt th [s]carcity of lumber & knew the importance of haveing it, as the demands were daily increasing & great quantities of pine was rafted down the river for the building of the Temple & Nauvoo house I came which necessarily must be sawed[.] I determined to try set a Saw mill in operation. I named it

[to] John Scott & he at once joined with my Opinion & he & I went to work to build it in company.³⁵

It was not long before E. Robinson, a man of Capital, proposed to furnish Capital to buy the Irons for the mill & take a share as neither Scott nor myself had Capital & could only do the manu^a^l labor.³⁶ We concluded it would be better to accept of Robinson proposals than to hire money to buy the necessary aparatus to set the mill in to operation. We accordingly [con]tinued our labors & at the opening of Spring [1843] we had the mill nearly ready to put in the Irons & commence Sawing.

A bout this time the before mentioned Robinson went on a mission & mad such arrangements as disappointed us & prevented us from obtaining the necessary apparatus for putting our mill in operation. This was a great disapointment to us & in particular to Scott, who had not as yet been quite so [ ] versed in the School of disapointment as I had. He felt [ ] discouraged that from the time Robinson left [his] labor was of verry little value & I soon saw that all was not moving on the track of prosperity. I proposed to let him take my share of the mill if he would pay me for the time I had labored on it. This he said he Should not do. I then offered to buy his labor on the same terms. He would not Sell on any reasonable terms but, like the dog in the manger, held on while he did nothing & thereby prevented me from doing what I Otherwise Could have done.

On the opening of Spring I again commenced doing buisness in my grist mill & had not the above mentioned disapointments taken place I should have done well. Allso with my Saw mill. The winter has been harder than was ever before known in this place, the rver froze in the month of Nov & ther was Ice Still running on th 6 of Aril at the time of our Conference. I have never before known a Feb. to pass without the boats plying in the river. Under the present circumstances I found

---

35. John Scott (1811–76) was a joiner, farmer, and military officer. In 1842 he lived in the Nauvoo Fourth Ward. See "Reference" at *The Joseph Smith Papers*.
36. Ebenezer Robinson (1816–91) was a publisher and editor for Nauvoo's *Times and Seasons*, 1839–42. He served a mission to New York in 1843. See "Reference" at *The Joseph Smith Papers*.

that nothing could be profitably done with the Saw mill & applyed all my attention to makeing repairs on my ~~Saw mill~~ gristmill.

Considerable of my time was taken up in attending the High Council of which still remained a member, oweing to the dificulty & troubles brought upon us or the Church by those that dissented from us & were ever on the alert to do an injury to the Church.[37]

T Summer passed away & the Sawmil remained as it was. Fall [1843] came on & the want of lumber daily increased. Allso the Temple stood in need of timber being sawed. I proposed to Scott to go & give my share of the mill to the Temple & give some one a chance to put it in operation & no longer let so useful a property ly to waste to gratify the follies of passion. He & I wento the Temple Committee & he & myself both proposed to give the mill in to their hands for the benefit of the temple. This did not alltogather suit the minds of the Committee. Bro Cutler[38] proposed to buy Scotts part of the mill & apply it on his tithing & then put it in to my hands & let me have a chance to put it in to operation. We accordingly entered in to such measures. I gave my obligation to the Committee fo what had been Scotts Share of the mill & soon began [to] put it in ~~operation~~ readiness for operation a the Spring opened & I saw all things around look promiseing with my buisness. Tthe water is unusually high in the river.

There appears to be a scarsity of grain & from appearances there must be some exertion to supply Our City with bread. I went to Burlington & bought flat boat load of grain, but the demands for it wer so great I was induced to make another effort to supply the wants of our Brethren with out their leaveing the Temple & their labors at home to procur bread from the Country. I took passage on board the Maid of Iowa which ascended the Iowa River. I stoped at Wappelo & bought a large quantity of grain. Aas the Steamer returned I put on board as

---

37. "For the Times and Seasons," *Times and Seasons* 1 (February 1840): 56.
38. On October 3, 1840, John Alpheus Cutler was one of three men, along with Reynolds Cahoon and Elias Higbee, on the temple building committee. Cahoon and Cutler supervised construction. Cutler led a group of workmen into the Pineries in Wisconsin, where they cut logs and floated them down the Mississippi River to Nauvoo. See Leonard, *Nauvoo*, 245; Rowley, "The Mormon Experience in the Wisconsin Pineries, 1841–1845," 119–48.

much grain as I could get sacked & in readiness. For the remainder I ~~bought~~ a ~~large flat worn~~d made arrangements to have it conveyed on a flat. The water still continued high so that on my return the steamer found no difficulty in stoping in front of my mill while we took the grain in at the upper door of the mill. Allthough at a usual stage of water, the ground was dry where the boat now floated, yet my mill so constructed that she is safe & doing buisness.

As soon as this grain was secured I again ascended the river & in a few days returned in safety with a large flat loaded with grain. I now concluded I had a bout a suffecient quantity of grain to supply the necessary demands until harvest.

About this time Sister Betsey, my Bro Josephs wife, came to visit us. It may be necessary to here go back & make mention of some particulars respecting my Fathers family.[39] At the time of my greatest poverty & trials about starting my grist mill, both my Father & Bro Joseph lived near by & in vain did I try to get some assistance from them.

During the past winter [1842–43] the order of family organizations was set forth & all people were instructed that it was necessary to set their house or family in order. I had longed felt the necessity of my Fathers house ^or family^ being properly organized. I solicited Fathers Cutler & Cahoon,[40] they being appointed to teach this duty to the

---

39. With new teachings about the eternal nature of families in mind, Church leaders advocated that families should organize themselves in order to help their own members spiritually and temporally. As Newel documents, Reynolds Cahoon and Alpheus Cutler were appointed to teach families how to do that. The organizing meeting for the Young and Richards families on January 8, 1845, indicates what family organizations were for. They gathered in the Seventies Hall and sat according to family groups. The purpose of the groups was to explain how everyone related together through specific common ancestors, to find out how many of particular common ancestors' descendants were in good standing in the faith, and to identify departed relatives for whom proxy ordinances needed to be performed. In the eternities, the group was reminded, all would be governed in family orders, with every man presiding over his own family. See minutes of the organizing meeting of the Richards and Young families, held in Nauvoo on January 8, 1845, in Barlow, *Family Recordings of Nauvoo*, 1–24.
40. Alpheus Cutler (1784–1864) and Reynolds Cahoon (1790–1861). As noted, both were members of the temple building committee.

Church, to appoint a meting at my fathers house, which thy did to the Edification of us all.

However, my Brother Joseph was not present, he haveing moved to Layharp he spring preiveous [1842], a distance of 20 miles. Although I had used everry exertion & made him good & advantagious offers to take hold & assist me in putting my mill in operation so that he might have an interest in the City & be where he Could enjoy the teachings of Our Prophet & be blest with knowledge & inteligence in common with the Saints, I greatly regreted that he could not have been with at Our family interviews.

But to return, his wife Said that he was quite out of health & She feard that he would not long survive. I took some pains to let her understand the principles that had been taught in regard to family order. Told her if Joseph would return to the bosom of the Church it would be better for him & his health would improve. She seemed to beieve what she heard, Said She would use her influence to have him Come back. But to my great sorrow the winter passed [1843–44] & my Fathers family were not organized.

June 2nd [1844] Our enemeis have been determined to do everry thing in their power to destroy us & if possible to flustrate the great work of Jehovah.[41] [June] 20, Our enemies are still on the alert & from appearances the Cheif men in goverment are neither innocent nor ignorant of what is takeing place.[42] O the 27 of June Our beloved Prophet & Patriarch were martyred.[43] I shall Copy from those that have written who were eye witnesses to facts respecting this Awful tragedy as they can do it justice.[44]

---

41. *Nauvoo Expositor*, June 7, 1844; Hedges, "Joseph Smith, Robert Foster, and Chauncey and Francis Higbee," 89–111; Oaks, "Suppression of the *Nauvoo Expositor*," 862–903.
42. *JSP*, J3:295–96; Joseph Smith to Thomas Ford, January 21, 1844.
43. "Awful Assassination of Joseph and Hyrum Smith," *Times and Seasons* 5 (July 1, 1844): 560–61; Brian Q. Cannon, "'Long Shall His Blood . . . Stain Illinois,'" 1–19.
44. Here Newel wanted to rely on what others related about the martyrdom, but he never inserted anything. However, the Allen version of Newel's journal goes into great detail about the martyrdom and then includes the following statement, apparently by Newel.

The Rise of the Latter-day Saints

Memorial of Joseph and Hyrum Smith at Joseph Knight Sr.'s ancestral home in Ninevah (Colesville), New York. Courtesy of Knight family.

The bodies were taken to the mansion and the doors closed, and then the bodies were laid out. I had the privilege of being in the room, and saw the wounds which the /P/rophets received. On the 29th [June 1844] the bodies were put into the coffins, and all who wished, were allowed to see them, when about ten thousand (10,000) passed through the room. /N/ear six in the evening the funeral services were performed, and I accompanied the hearse to the graves. There is a secret connected with this funeral which is not known to all the Saints; although it is generally suspected, and that is, that Joseph and Hyrum were not buried at that time; but the particulars will be made known at the proper time and place.[45]

I have taken up considerable space in telling you the circumstances under which two of the best men that ever lived, lost their lives for the truth's sake. I have known them from boyhood,—have been associated with Joseph from the time before he received the first revelation until the present, and Hyrum has been his constant companion since the Church has been organized.

I have shared in the blessings of the Gospel which they have enjoyed, and been a partaker of the sorrows and troubles, and fierce persecutions which they have endured. I have seen them at home and abroad,—in the discharge of their religious duties; and I have known them as the founders of a great City, and seen their administration of

---

45. See Brown, *In Heaven as It Is on Earth*, 279–304; Bernauer, "Still 'Side by Side,'" 17–33; Johnstun, "To Lie in Yonder Tomb," 163–80.

its government. In every circumstance of life they have ever been true men of God,—humane, upright and just in all their dealings; they loved righteousness and taught it to their followers; their friends loved them for the good they did, and their enemies hated them, because they reproved their sins and wickedness. They died as they had ever lived— faithful and true to that God who has used them as his servants to build up the Church and Kingdom of the Last Days. In the hour of prosperity they taught the people humility and meekness; in the hour of persecution, they practised these virtues and no men have done a greater work on the earth since the days of the Saviour than they have; and their names will ever be held in honorable remembrance by all lovers of truth, virtue, integrity, justice and righteousness; whilst their persecutors will sink in shame, confusion and infamy until they will go down to the place prepared for all doers of wickedness.

O, how I loved those men, and rejoiced under their teachings! It seems as if <u>all</u> is gone, and as if my very heart strings will break; and were it not for my beloved wife and dear children I feel as if I have nothing to live for, and would rejoice to be with them in the Courts of Glory. But I must live, and labor, and try to do good, and help to build up the Kingdom of our God here on the earth. And I pray God my Father that I may be reconciled unto my lot, and live and die a faithful follower of the teachings of our <u>Murdered Prophet and Patriarch</u>.[46]

About the middle of July my Bro. Joseph came to see me. His health was quite poor. He appeared to be declining. I entreated him to return to the City to live. He said if I would give him employment in my gristmill he would Come, for he could not labor or do any other work. I told him if he would ~~be~~ come & do well he should have employment in my mill. He engag^ed^ a house for his family & Soon moved in. As soon as he had Setteled his family & rested a little he Commenced tending my mill, although he was hardly able to set up all day. I had another man employed to assist in the same buisness. He commenced to tend mill on the 26 of August & I paid him 15 dollars a month. Time [went] on & mills performed well.

---

46. For the martyrdom, see Oaks and Hill, *Carthage Conspiracy*; Beam, *American Crucifixion*.

But to the affairs of the Church. The Twelve were mostly gone on a mission at the time of Josephs & Hyrums death. Before they returned Sidney Rigdon came here & claimed to be appointed of God by a special revelation to hin to spercede the Prophet & become the first President of the Church. I shall I shall leave this to be written more pefectly hereafter & for the present confine my pen to myself.[47]

Much of my time was spent in Council so th that the care of my buisness Occupied all my time time when not in Council. In Sept [1844] I went to St Lewis to procure castings & some other necessaries. I had a good passage & soon returned in Safety. All things went on well. For a time my affairs seemed to prosper & I did not forget to return thanks to my heavenly Father for the blessings I enjoyed. On the 26 of Nov [1844] ice commenced to run in the river so that were obliged to stop business.

So that after haveing a little time to rest & settle up my buisness a little, I again began to feel after my Fathers family.[48] I got my Father to Call his Children to gather & with all the energy of my Soul did I exhort them to be engaged in those things which are most necessary for our salvation. And I greatly desired to see my aged Father arise & honorably Stand at the head of his family, set his house in order that he might be first in his own kingdom & make it honorable in the sight heaven. Yet

---

47. Newel's son Samuel, almost twelve, witnessed the transformation, as did Newel's nephew Oliver DeMille. Hafen, "Samuel Knight"; and the Oliver DeMille sketch in "One Man's Family: Oscar DeMille."
48. In October 1844, Nauvoo tradesmen organized to promote manufacturing. One committee looked into erecting a dam across the Mississippi River, and on January 7, 1845, the committee added Newel Knight to its membership. The temple committee and surveyors became involved. A plan for the dam was drawn up consisting of fifty-three piers, each forty feet long, ten feet wide, and fifteen feet apart. Averaging twelve feet in depth, the planks were to be put down between the piers, and the spaces were to be covered with planks also, "the whole forming a permanent dam, and a bridge forty feet wide and eighty rods long." On February 11, a committee proposed that citizens be invited to subscribe twelve thousand days work for constructing the dam. Shareholders in the dam met on February 20, and on February 27 "some of the principal men" met at the site of the dam. Jessee, *John Taylor Nauvoo Journal*, 16, 36, 39, 44, 45, 46. For years Newel had wanted the dam built, but construction never started.

all my endeavors seemed to be in vain. The winter [1844—45] passed & the family remained as they were. This has been mor greif to me than all the poverty I have ever experienced for when I look upon my aged Father & see his head already white with hardships & Cares of upwards of 70 years I wanto see him begin to put on the armor of righteousness & magnify the preisthood & Stand with his family in their proper lot.

O[n] th 12 of Feb [1845] the ice was broken in the river so that my mills again commenced operation. I again gave Joseph employment in my grist mill. His health had gradually improved from the time he commenced work for me. Time passed on, yet complaint daily increased from the customers of my mill. It became evident that Joseph did not give satisfaction as a miller. I therefore Came to the conclusion, as his health was so improved he could at various business, to discharge him from the mill. As soon as this came to my Fathers [attention] he Called his family to gather & first Called on me to Covenant to ~~hear~~ Obey his Council & let him stand at the head of my buisness & dictate the affairs of my mill. I told him that nothing could delight me more than to see our family properly organized & to see hin at the head. That I was ready to hearken & obey everry thing that was in accordance withe the laws of the kingdom & to hold hin at the head of his kingdom & to honor him as such.

But, before I could Covenant to give my temporal business over to him, it would be necessary for him to become responsible to my Creditors as ther were Considerable debts standing against me which I should not be able to meet only from the resourses of my mills, which if properly managed with the same prosperity I had hithertoo had, I should no doubt be able to meet. Tthat as these debtes had been contracted by me for the express purpose of ~~getting~~ ^benefitting^ the mills, it would be doing them injustice to let my property go out of my Controll until they were made secure or satisfied. Neither could I do my self & family justice to enter in to such measures until I should be honorably discharged from debt & have to my family some provisions for a subsistance, as we had struggled hard ^to^ get our property. I should be glad to enjoy it in peace & in righteousness. However I did not conceive that any of these things ought to or need hinder us from all that could be required in regard to a proper organiz^ation^ of family. After I had finished my remarks, little ~~until~~ more was said & we again dispersed.

On the 01 of April [1845] one of the gudgeons of my sawmill broke.⁴⁹ I was obliged to go to St Lewis to procure another. I took passage on board a Steamer which soon Conveyed me there in safety. I procured such articles as I chose & again embarked for home.⁵⁰

I now found a little at rest from a multiplicity of Cares & buisness which daily occupied my attention. When at home I gave my self to reflecting upon the situation of my Fathers family. Aall the day long did I ponder & at night Sleep departed from me. I Called upon God & desired that he would guide me & direct me by his holy Spirit so that I might not er[r]. It was foreign from my desire to treat lightly the Council of my Father or to greive him. I had therefore still employed Joseph although it had been to my disadvantage but to do according to his request in all my affairs and not appear expedient to me. I therefore sought earnestly to know what the Lord would that I should do. The situation of the family bore me down with greif & pained my inmost soul.

I saw that my Father was old & according to the common lot of man he could not long survive. I saw & knew also that Joseph did encourage him to or use stratagem to cause hin to make such requirements of me as before mentioned & that he did seek advantage of me in other respects & to turn the influence of the Brethren against me. I felt bad. I was alone as it were in my Faters family. I searched my self to see if I had given occasion for this. I could not feel tat I had. I knew my intentions were & ever had been good. I could do no more than to commit all in to the hand of God & trust the event with him, praying that the understanding of my ^father^ be enlightened & that he may yet

---

49. A gudgeon is a metal journal (the part of a machine shaft or axle supported by a bearing) mounted in the end of the main shaft, so the wheel (usually a waterwheel) may turn on bearings.
50. On April 19, 1845, Lydia sent Newel's apology to the high council "in behalf of my husband . . . whom I love and reverence" for his absence at that meeting. "He is sick," she said, "quite confined to his bed with a severe cough and fever." Newel requested they consecrate a bottle of oil for him. Two weeks later he felt well enough to attend the council's meeting. Nauvoo High Council Minutes.

honor the Preisthood & Stand honorably at the head of his family or kingdom. And that Joseph may allso come up honorably in his proper lot. And that I may be kept in all my aged Father, whom I love & delight to honor, know that it is & ever has been my theme to do right & deal justly. And may the Lord preserve him & let his old age be crowned with with everry good thing & his life be prolonged as long as life shall be desired by him. And I would that Joseph may yet see the truth as it is & that all things that have been wrong ^be right & be^ may be forgotten & that union & love & Confidence may exist betwen us which becometh not only Saints but which is doubly binding upon Brothers.

Oh Lord wilt thou give me patience & Wisdom & let thy holy Spirit direct me in all things for these things do weigh heavily & peirce like a pointed dagger to my heart. All the privations losses & Persecutions which I ^have^ passed through from our Eenemies abroad cannot Compare with the Sorrow & bitterness of soul that the situation of my Fathers family gives me. I can only Commit all in to the hands of our great Creator who guideth the destinies of the Children of men on the Earth.

Saturday, May 24, 1845.[51] The Capstone of the Temple was laid this morning at a little past Six O Clock in the morning, after a little more than four years hard labor of the Sants, during which time we have passed through scenes of persecution too great to be panted by man, & the blood of our best ~~friends~~ men have Stained the floor at Carthage Jail & he earth has drunk their blood. While our enemies have been thus cruelly satiateing themselves, The brethren have been laboring by day & watching by night to accomplish the house which the Lord hath Commanded them to build unto his most holy mane. The mornig was cool, Clear & beautiful: the Saints rejoiced while the band echoed forth their sweetest strains of music upon the top of the walls. When the Stone was placed there was a united Hosana to God & the Lamb Amen

---

51. Here, inserted into the journal, is a half sheet or scrap of paper. It contains Newel's comments based on his reading and borrowing from an article in "The Capstone of the Temple," *Times and Seasons* 5 (June 1, 1845): 926.

^&^ Amen shouted three times which not only gave joy to the Saints but filled heavens with gladness.⁵²

The Twelve & other authorities of the Church were present to witness & direct the scene. President Young made some appropriate remarks & as it was the Seventh day, the same that God finished his work & rested, so the Saints might do the same. A new hymn was sung & all hearts rejoiced in the hope that the wrath of our enemies might be stayed intil the building shall be completed & the faithful receive their endowments therein.⁵³

This day Mrs Caroline, Wif of William Smith, was buried⁵⁴

An address delivered by Elder Orson Pratt one of the Quorum of the Twelve. I shall if

Bro Heige is willing her[e] insert the speech delivered by him on the 15 of June 1845 as reported by G L Watt.⁵⁵

June 14ᵗʰ, [1845].⁵⁶ My health is considerably improved & my buisness seems to prosper. A general time of peace & prosperity seems to smile upon the Saints. Crops lok well. An abundant harvest promises to reward the faithful laborer for all his toil. The Temple is progressing finely. good inteligence from Europe & the Iselands of the Sea & various parts of the world. I think a more general time of prosperity never daund upon this kingdom

July 1st All is well with the Saints as a People. Properity attends them & health is tolerable good in the City.

[July] 13. As to my business I am prospered & fell to give thanks to my heavenly Father for all blessings I enjoy.

July 27, 1845. Just one year one month & one day have elapsed since our beloved Prophet & Patriarch fell martyrs to the cause truth. I have

---

52. See William Clayton, journals, May 24, 1845; Anderson and Bergera, *Joseph Smith's Quorum of the Anointed.*
53. Anderson and Bergera, *Nauvoo Endowment Companies,* xi–xlii and table 1.
54. Newel took this information from a very long article in the same issue of the *Times and Seasons.*
55. Newel never added this speech to his manuscript, leaving the remainder of the page blank.
56. Here the narration resumes on the next regular page. Because Newel had brought his record up to date, he now writes dated, diary-like entries.

this day visited the Jail & viewed the place where they were so bound & Cruelly murdered. My Wif & my self went into the room where the out rag[e] was commited. The Scared walls & blood still crimson on the floor (in spite of all the efforts that have ben made to erase the & cleanse the blood from the floor) stand as a bold testimony against the Nation that suffers all to pass unnoticed. Me heart was filled with emmotions that I cannot find language to express. Pen cannot paint the scene.[57]

July 31. Blessings are bestowed upon us as a People. Less sickness hav has prevailed [than] any previous season since the Saints began to settle here & infact ther is less than at any place from which we have inteligence in all the Country a round. In this the words of our martyred Prophet are verrily fullfiled, for at a time when sickness prevailed to so great an extent that there not well ones enough to take Care of the Sick, Our Prophet Joseph exhorted the Brethren & Sisters to be faithful & put their trust in God & all their afflictions should work for them an exceeding & eternal weight of Glory, & time would come that it should be said & the report should go forth that Nauvoo is a healthy place. Thousands can now bear testimony of the fulfillment of this prophecy & many of the Brethren who at that time lay sick in tents, haveing the year befor been deprived of all their rights as Citizens in the State of M.O. & had barely escaped with their lives, are now in good Circumstances, Surrounded with the blessings life health & plenty.

As to my Self I have labored hard & th^r^ough the blessing of my heavenly Father I hope soon to see my family situated comfortably. My mill is now in a properous condition so that we are comfortable for food & raiment, so that if Brother Clap[58] performs the job of building a house for me acording to Contract by the first of Sept I shall have the satisfaction seeing my family comfortably situated.

Aug 1ˢᵗ, We had an excellent discourse delivered by Elder H C Kimball ^and^ well calculated in its nature to instruct encourage & s[t]

---

57. See Jessee, "Return to Carthage," 3–19; "Martyrdom of Joseph and Hyrum Smith," 301–2; Laub, "George Laub's Nauvoo Journal," 151–78; Taylor, *Witness to the Martyrdom*.
58. Possibly Benjamin L. Clapp.

imulate the Saints to atten to such duties as will prepare them for usefulness in life & prepare them for an exaltation in the Celestial world.

[August] 8 I am truely glad to see the peace & union that exists among the Brethren. The High Council Continue to meet as usual, but I am happy to say that [f]requently of late have little to more than to lift our united petitions to the most high for peac & prosperity to attend their people & for the spread of truth, & the establishment of righteousness upon the earth.

[August] 18 There was never a more eventful day than the one in which we live. The past Spring & Summer has such a Catalogue of events by water & calamities by land the report thereof is a vexation.[59] Freedom & the rights of man are trampled upon with impunity & it seems that mercy find no admittance & justce no place among the nations of the earth. Truely the Sants have great reason to rejoice for the peace & good order that prevails in our City & according to the words of the Prophet the time will come when he that will not take up his sword against his Neighbor will have to flee to Zion for Safety.

I have got my Celler dug & all of my part ready for Brother Clap to perform his part but to my great disapointment he is not on hand acording to Contract. My Father's health is good & I still feel a pleasure in administering to his wants. May he be blest & live long upon the Earth & yet to see many good days is the desire of my heart, Amen.

[August] 25th I have been makeing every preperation ~~on my part~~ to secure to my family a comfortable house, for the sickness & privations that we have endured in consequence of the persecutions of our enemies haveing been from tine to time obliged to leave all & barely escape with our lives in Common with the Saint ^has rendered us in circumstances that a comfortable house to us would be to us of great worth^. I have bought pine lumber for Sash, window, door Caseings, doors &C. And hired Brother Foster to make it ready for the house so that if Bro Clap had not disappointed me I should soon have had the pleasure of Seeing my family Comfortabl. But he has not commenced to lay up the walls which is a great disapointment to me.

---

59. See *Times and Seasons* 6 (August 15, 1845): 999.

Sept lst. The time has arrived that Bro Clap should according to agreement ~~should~~ have done the job of puttind up & encloseing my house ready for the inside finish. But he has not commenced the walls & but verry little preperations on his part appear to be makeing. Our children are Sick, our family large & in circumstances that we greatly need a better place to live ^in than^ that we now have.

[Sept.] 7, Sabbath. We had an excellent discourse delivered & instructions well Calculated to enliven & unite & Stimulate the ~~bethr~~ Brethren to tose thing which are necessary to their best intrest here & secure to them an exaltation in that plac where the wicked Shall not have dominion.[60] My Children are Still sick with the whooping Cough & the Chills & fever. My wife is allso confined. She has a fine Son [Jesse] born last night. Both are doing well.

[Sept.] 12 My business is prosperous & the health of the Brethren I think is generally better than it has ever been any Season Since we have lived here. Yet there is Some Sickness in our City, but I think far less according to the no of inbitants than in any Town or City About. Our Children are sick. Newel[61] had a fit to day, he has partially recovered from it. My wife is getting a long as well could be expected.

We suffer great inconvenience for house room, & from the littl preparation Bro Clap is makeing I think there little propect of haveing a better one. Had he fullfiled the Contract made

Jesse Knight, Newel's son, became one of Utah's earliest wealthy businessmen. Courtesy of Knight family.

---

60. On September 9, 1845, the Council of Fifty voted to organize companies to leave for Utah. *JSP*, A1:465–69.
61. Newel and Lydia's son, born 1842, here is almost three years old.

betwen him & my Self I Should now have had the pleasure of Seeing my family Comfortably situated, which after the many toils & privations we have Suffered would be a precious boon to us. The patience with which Lydia has ever borne all the Scenes of Sufferings & privations we have passed through Seems to lay a double obligation upon me to make her Comfortable now. And after advanceing pay to Bro Clap & makeing Such Calculations as I have, it is not possible fore build a Comfortabl dwelling if he fails to fulfill his Contract.

[Sept.] 15th [1845]. Our enemies begin to fear lest in the midst of the blessings which our persevereance & industry is Crowning us we shall be Surrounded with the blessings of plenty Peace & quietness, & that if they do not do as wicked men have allways have done, too many of the Candid & Honorable men of the Earth will lay Shoulder to the wheel & that Mormonism will be more than a match for them. The Temple is in a great State of forwardness & a more general appearance of prosperity never dawned upon a People. A Golden havest rich & abundant is on hand & the Brethren are united in accomplishing those things which the Lord hath Commanded us to do.

As I before Said the wicked begin to think their Craft in danger & lust after fruits of the industrious labors of the Saints & to try the old method of obtaining it.[62] They have Commenced mobbing & burning houses on the out parts of our Settlements. thinking no doubt it will all be winked at or Sanctioned by the administrators of the law, as have been all roberies, murders & every kind of wickedness which have been from time to time practiced upon the Church of Jesus Christ of latter day Saints.

Oct 1. Our enemies, or rather the enemies of the kingdom which God hath set up on the earth, are rageing & doing all that is in their power to destroy the Saints from off the Earth. So violent have been their measures & seemingly aided or abet[t]ed by those who hold the

---

62. In September 1845, arsonists, proudly labeling themselves "anti-Mormons," torched more than a hundred buildings and burned out the Saints living at Morley's Settlement, two dozen miles south of Nauvoo. See Hartley, *1845 Burning of Morley's Settlement*. Inspired by their success, they vowed to burn other Latter-day Saint settlements, including Nauvoo.

reins of goverment that all our brethren whose lives have been Spared have been compelld to flee from every part of the C.O. [county] into the City for Safety while their houses & Chattels have been given to the flames, their horses Cattle Sheep hog &C have become an easy prey to their enemes togather with their numerous feilds of grain.

While I write my hand & heart trembling at the picture or reality of the acts of men who are made in the likeness of God & ought to be noble & like him ^in^ their motives allmost forbids, & quite makes me blush to record their acts. So violent have been the works & so little heed has goverment paid to our Cries & petitons for redress of ou[r] wrongs, that the only way possible for us to check the flame & Stay the hand of persecution & thereby save the lives of the innocen babe, the sprightly youth, to gather with the middle-aged & the Silver headed veteran who once fought with a Washington to plant the Standard of freedom & Spread the banner of liberty in this glorious land, I Say the only possible means Checkng the fury of this nation has been to Sign a decree that the People Called latter day Saints in mass leave this boasted land of liberty that they neither sow nor reap again upon their possessions.

O Columbia! Oh boasted land of America! how hath thy glory faded, thy honor fled. How will the Nations a far off reproach thee when thy foul deeds ~~play in~~ in gore written in letters of blood go forth for they cannot be concealed. The Widows Cry & Orphans greif will burst everry land & u^n^cover everry act, that thy works may appear naked in the eyes of all Nations. But those whom thou now persecutest & drivest out from thee & alltogather despisest & hath refused them an Asylum or one cheering hope of justice, shall yet rise in magesty & Glory & Shine forth glorious & powerful as the Sun when thy glory hath departed.

First meting in the Temple.[63] On Sunday the 5 day of Oct, through the indefatigable exertions, unceasing industry, & heaven blest labors in

---

63. Feeling the pulse of antagonistic sentiment in the region, the Twelve decided that the Saints must pull out of Nauvoo and relocate somewhere in the West. On October 5–8, 1845, in the almost-finished Nauvoo Temple, they presided at the Church's first general conference held in three years. About five thousand

the midst of trials tribulations, poverty & worldly obstacles, solemnized in some instances by death, about five thousand Saints had the inexpressible joy & gratification to meet for the first time in the house of the Lord in the City of Josph. From mites & tithing millions, had risen up to the glory of God, as a Temple where the Children of the last kingdom Could Come together & praise the Lord.

It certainly afforded a holy Satisfaction to think that since the 5 of April 1841, when the first Stone was laid amidst the most straitened Circumstances, the Church of Jesus Christ of latter day Saints had witnessed their bread Cast upon the waters or more properly their obeidience to the Commandments of the Lord, appear in the tangible form of a temple entirely enclosed, windows in, with a tenpory floors pulpits & Seats to acommodate so many persons preparatory to a General Conference. No General Conference haveing been held for three years past according to the declaration of of our martyred Prophet:

"There shall be no more baptisms for the dead until the ordinance can be attended to in the font of the Lords house & the Church shall not hold another general Conference untill thy can met in Said house. For thus Saith the Lord."

President Young opened the Services of the day in a dedication prayer presenting the temple thus far Completed as a monument of the Saints liberality fidelity & faith

Lord we dedicate this house & Our Selves unto thee. The day was occupied most agreeably in hearing instructions & teachings & offering up the gratitude of honest for so great a privelige as worshiping God with in instead of with out an edifice whose whose beauty & workmanship will Compare with any house of worship in America &

Saints attended. As President of the Twelve, Brigham Young opened the services by offering a dedicatory prayer for the temple thus far finished. On the second day, members sustained general and local officers of the Church, including Newel to continue as a high councilor. That day and during the next two, speakers explained why and how the Saints must vacate Nauvoo by the next spring. "Conference Minutes," *Times and Seasons* 6 (November 1, 1845): 1008–16. Newel here quotes from "First Meeting in the Temple," *Times and Seasons* 6 (November 1, 1845): 1017–18; the quotation ends with "whose motto is Holiness to the Lord."

whose motto is Holiness to the Lord. On the 6 [Oct. 1845] was held the a general Conference in the house of the Lord the minutes which I extract as reported[64]

---

64. Newel here intended to copy from "Conference Minutes," *Times and Seasons* 6 (November 1, 1845): 1008–16, though he never did. This ends MS 767, folder 1, item 5. We conclude our part 4 here so that part 5 can deal with the Nauvoo exodus story, which this conference announced and launched the preparations for.

PART 5

THE NAUVOO EXODUS AND THE "MOUNTAIN EXPEDITION," 1845–46

INTRODUCTION

Newel's material thus far primarily has been his autobiography based on his recollections, some published sources, and several diary-like entries. But, from here on, the last two parts of version 1 (items 5 and 6) are in diary format. His entries are dated, regular, and usually detailed, providing insights into important episodes not well covered in Church history. For the 1846–47 period of Church history, at least a dozen diaries have become important sources of information, such as those penned by Hosea Stout, William Clayton, John D. Lee, Patty Sessions, and Louisa Barnes Pratt.

From the Church's October 1845 conference until early January 1846, Newel's diary makes contributions in five arenas. First, it documents how hard it was for the common people to become properly outfitted and supplied for vacating Nauvoo and nearby areas. Second, his diary is the best insider's account of the massive spring exodus from Nauvoo, the main phase of the exodus, which historians overlook. Third, he writes heartfelt tributes, eulogies, and prayers about the course of the

Restoration, the persecutions, the forsaking of Nauvoo and the temple, and the Saints' situation as a modern version of the children of Israel in the wilderness. His powerful literary expressions, reflections, and meditations regarding the Saints' forced exodus are unequaled. Fourth, Newel provides rare documentation about the "mountain expedition," which the Twelve sent ahead from the Missouri River in July 1846. And, fifth, Newel's diary is the best record we have of the Ponca encampment; his record shows that the nearly five hundred souls were not, as is often implied, a disobedient, misled group.

Our featured text, Newel's version 1 (MS 767, folder 1), has a gap for almost four months between October 6, 1845, and February 1, 1846. However, the Allen version contains narration, evidently written by Newel, which covers the gap period. It fits like a missing puzzle piece into Newel's version 1 account. Both pieces interlock where each is telling about Newel's business dispute with Elijah Fordham, which contributed to preventing Newel's family from leaving Nauvoo with Brigham Young's advance company in February. Therefore, the missing Newel statements as found only in the Allen version begin the diary entries here in part 5.

The Nauvoo Exodus and the "Mountain Expedition," 1845-46

ALLEN VERSION

1846. January 31. For the last two week my time has been altogether taken up in laboring in the Temple. It is expected that the time will be short in which the Saints can have the privilege of receiving their endowments, as our enemies are prowling about on every side, like ravening wolves, and in fact they have only been held at bay during the whole winter, by the prayers of the Saints; and as the brethren generally have been faithful in laboring to build the Temple, that the Lord might have a place prepared in which to give blessings, and endow the Saints with power from on high. President Young says no time shall be lost, for as they have been faithful in building, so the servant of the Lord shall be faithful in waiting upon them.

We attend in the Temple both day and night, and I can truly say it is better to be a waiter in the House of the Lord, than to enjoy all the glittering wealth this world can afford. My soul has been filled with the love of God. I feel his spirit burning within me day by day. The blessings I have received during this winter, have doubly repaid me for all I have done towards building this house. I think the brethren generally feel in their hearts to say, the Lord has not been slack concerning his promises for the power of God is manifested in withholding our enemies from us.[1]

In the meantime, I found it necessary to be settling my temporal affairs . . . [Elijah] Fordham insisted that he should have his pay so that he could be prepared for the move in the Spring, although it should bring me to beggary. I told him I did not believe in that principle,—I did not think it my duty to take the last bit of bread from my children, under the peculiar circumstances we were placed in, although I acknowledged that he should have his due. But he had assisted us /from/ his abundance, and ought not to demand it of me in my poverty. If the Lord would prosper me in disposing of my property I should be able to satisfy not only him but all my creditors, who should be amply rewarded for waiting on me, as I did not want any man to lose on my account. He still insisted that I should pay his full demand, and I proposed to leave the matter in the hands of some judicious brethren, and would abide by their decision. I told him I was not satisfied with the demand he made

---

1. Leonard, *Nauvoo*, 261.

upon me, but as he had lost his accounts I did not wish to injure him and would rather pay him more than less than what I owed him, so long as it did not bring my family to suffering to do so.

Bro Fordham chose Edward Hunter, Isaac Higbee and Bishop Hale as referees,[2] and I had intended choosing some of the members of the High Council who were laboring in the Temple the same as myself, attending to the ordinances of the Lord's House. I was engaged there at the time bro Fordham called and told me he was ready for a settlement, and the brethren at the place designated. It was inconvenient for any of us to leave, so I chose to go alone rather than hinder any of them in their duties.

VERSION 1

[109] I entered the room where they were waiting for me. Told them it had so happened the men I had selected were at the time engaged so that it would not be expedient for them to be present. And as I did not wish to hinder time either of my self or Brethren and had ever looked upon Brother Fordham to be an honorable man, I arose and made a statement of facts as above written. Told them I would abide the decision of the Brethren who were present, thinking to cut short the affair and supposed it would be done in righteous[ness]. In fact I had so much confidence in Bro Fordham I cold not believe he intended any wrong torards me, but to my surprize he arose and deemanded as his account at least three hundred dollars. He said he had talked with his wife on the subject and they had concluded it was at least three hundred dollars and thought likely it might be three hundred and fifty.

Brother Rollf[3] was present, said h[e] acted as clerk at the time this debt was contracted and knew or was confident the true account, if it could be found, would not exceed one hundred dollars, for he could [not?] be much deceived as to the orders he gave or the debts that were cancelled with Brother Fordham. He allso stated it was not our

---

2. Isaac Higbee was a bishop and a justice of the peace in Nauvoo, and Johnathan Harriman Hale was a Nauvoo bishop, city assessor, and tax collector. See "Reference" at *The Joseph Smith Papers*.
3. Samuel Jones Rolfe, who at some point was president of the Nauvoo priests quorum.

fault he did not receive his pay for all we traded with him according to agreement. Brother Fordham insisted that the referees he had on hand should give a decision not only whether I should py him immediately but how much his acount should stand. They acordingly decided that I should pay the above mentioned Elijah Fordham one hundred and fifty dollars immediately and one hundred more as soon as I could or some time here after.

Feb 1rst [1846].[4] This day a number of persons met at my Fathers for the purpose of a family interview and to understand each others feelings. As Father had been Called upon to go the following day to the temple to receive his Sealing and anointing, my Step Mother refused to be Seald to my Father. I took some pains to get the family to gather that we might all know each others feelings and understand the cause of my Fathers and Mothers separation. I arose and made a statement of my feelings and intentions, also showed the necesity of such a separation being fully understood by all parties. I first called upon Father to [express] his feelings. He said he loved and respected Phebe but she was not satisfied to abide with him and he had agreed [110] to let her go. I asked her the Cause of her dissatisfaction. She said She respected the old gentleman, believed he was a good man, he had ever been kind to her and as a good man she ~~honored~~ ^respected^ him. But did not love and honor him as her head and bosom Companion and for this reason alone she was not Satisfied to a bide wit[h] my Father.

I [t]hen told them all I wanted them to express their feelings to wards me. I did not know at the time why my feelings were thus inpressed that I should be thus particular, but the sequel will show. Mother [Phoebe] said She had no feelings against me. She believed my mo^t^ives and intentions had ever been good towards her self and family. Said She Could find no fault with me and that the above reason alone was all she had

---

4. After Newel's mother, Polly Peck Knight, died, Father Knight married Phoebe Crosby Peck Knight, the widow and first wife of Polly's brother Benjamin Peck. Hence, Father Knight's second wife was his sister-in-law. In a few days, the administering of temple ordinances would cease, so, as Newel explains here, Phoebe's reluctance to be sealed to Father Knight caused some family concerns that involved Newel and his other Peck relatives related to Polly Peck Knight, Father Knight's first wife.

for not abideing wit my Father. I told her that reason ought to make her free, yet if she was satisfied to abide with my Father I should have no objections. As such I should honor and respect her. But as her feelings were to leave I should say amen and still respect her and wishe her well.

[T]he Children Henrietta ^Rich^, Hezekiah ^~~Rich~~^ and Sarah Peck were present. They said they [had] not ought against me. We agreed to close our interview by prayer, asking the blessings of God upon eache other in the presence of Ezekiel and Electa Peck,[5] Thomas Rich and wife, and Fathers family. My Wife went home with in company with uncle and Aunt Peck. I took my horse and buggy and went 9 miles out on the prairie to get my ^oldest^ Sister Anna [DeMille] to go to the temple with my Father and act as proxy for my Mother, whose remains were the first of the Saints the earth opened [t]he bosom to receive in Jackson CO., M.O.

Feb 2nd. Monday morning took my Sister Anna to the temple to meet my Father according to previous agreement. When Father came, Phebe was with him. [She] said she wanted to talk with some of the Twelve.

I went to attend to usual labor in the temple until we were called in to Council by our President [Brigham Young], who stated us that the Spirit [111] dictated that it was time to Commence our intended move into the wilderness and soon bring our labors to a close in the Temple, to which the Council all agreed.[6]

About the time this Council Closed, one of the Twelve Came to me and said that Phebe had ~~agreed~~ concluded to be Sealed to Father, provided my oppression to her could cease! She told them ^the Twelve^ she was willing to be sealed by the Old gentleman but not by his Children. I replied I had never oppressed her, neither did I wish to rule or oppress her, but if they were agreed I should not hinder their union. But

---

5. Ezekiel Peck was a brother of the deceased first wife, Polly Peck.
6. According to Brigham Young's Manuscript History, on February 2 the Twelve, the Nauvoo Trustees, and a few others (including Newel) met in council and "agreed that it was imperatively necessary to start as soon as possible. I counseled the brethren to procure boats and hold them in readiness to convey our wagons and teams over the river, . . . for if we are here for many days, our way will be hedged up. Our enemies have resolved to intercept us whenever we start."

the reader can better judge than I discribe my feelings on hearing the above statement, after what transpired yesterday. Suffice to say they were Sealed and received their annointing.

At this time I owened a grist and and saw mill worth 25 hundred dollars. A few days previous to this I had been offered a trade for my m^ills^. I laid this before the Brethren. They counciled me to take it, allthough it was not more than on fourth the real value of my property, this being the only source I had to fit for the journey.[7] It was agreed that I leave my labors in the temple and attend to the above business.

Brother Nobls[8] and my self started the next morning to go and see the man [Joseph Andrus] who had made the offer for my mills, distance about 20 miles. I accomplished a trade and started for home. A man by the name of Mathews who had formerly belonged to the Church but had turned away was at that place (Laharp).[9] He got up a false account and f[o]llowed with a Constable who was a friend to the enemies of this Church, who attached a good horse I had taken from the man who bought my mills. I arrived home late in the night. I found the Brethren busily engaged prepareing for the journey.

Feb 6. Got the deed of my mills, house, barn, and so fort[h] made over to Joseph An^d^rus.

[Feb] 9. I started with Ira Willis[10] to go and get the oxen, Cows, waggons and such property as I had taken for [112] my mills. We returned. I paid the before mentioned Elijah Fordham two hundred and thirty dollars, which was all but twenty dollars of the demand he claimed against me. This 20 dollars he and his Wife acknoweledged to be an order they had taken from one Nickerson, which I had never given.

In the mean time my Wife was busily engaged prepareing for the journey. She had got our tent, waggon cloths, s[t]ock &C all in readiness, provisions and goods packed, and all things about ready for the journey.

---

7. Flanders, *Nauvoo*, 338. See also Leonard, *Nauvoo*, 561.
8. Possibly Joseph Bates Noble, who had been the Nauvoo Fifth Ward's bishop.
9. La Harpe was twenty-three miles east of Nauvoo.
10. Ira J. Willis was part of the original Colesville Branch, was with it in Jackson County, and was related to the Knight family network.

When one Hiram Kimball[11] who at the time held a note against me for some [iron] castings which on useing fell to peices in our hands. I had given the note before I had proved the Castings or found them to be bad. I tried to settle with him. I offered him good property to the amount of the note [but] he would take nothing but the money. This I had not, neither Could I get it. As law and justice were out of the power of a Mormon at this time, there was no alternative for me. Although, had justice taken place I should have recovered damages of him.

^Feb 13th^. He attached my teams and waggons which hindered me for the present from the journey. I used my best of my endeavors to make sale of my property to obtain money to satisy his demand which togather with st Cost was about 65 dollars. It was on the 13th day of Feb [t]his Kimball attached my property. The best I could do. I had to sacrifice property I had allowed two hundred dollars in the trade of my mills to satisfy his demand. It may not be improper to here state that the above mentioned Kimball was living at Nauvoo at the time the Church settled there. He was a poor man or a bankrupt. He took every possible advantage of the poor brethren and had mad himself rich from their necesities. In the mean time he had joined the Church but could now strike hand with our oppressers. The Lord reward him according as his works have been. This togather some little affairs I had to settle, left me rather destitute of the necary comfort ^requisite^ such a journey required yet my yet I was encouraged to persevereance by the glorious hope of geting beyond the reach of our oppressors.[12]

[113] I made every possible exertion to make sale of property to get the money for Kimball before the Constables sale arrived. The Constable knowing the injustice of the affair gave me all the lenity the case would admit, but the best I could do I was obliged to sacrifice property. I had allowed two hundred dollars for in the trade of my mills to settle

---

11. Hiram S. Kimball, a resident in the area long before the Latter-day Saints created Nauvoo, was baptized in 1843. His wife Sarah Granger Kimball was one of the originators of what became the Relief Society. By 1846, Kimball operated a Nauvoo iron foundry.
12. Instead of entries between February 13 and April 6, Newel provided the following brief summary of his efforts to get into a position to remove from Nauvoo in the spring.

the above affair, which detained me until April. I now saw my Creditors satisfied and again began to Calculate and arrange the little I had left to the best advantage I could for the journey. I could only fit my self with two waggons, 3 yoke of oxen, & 3 Cows. My family consisted of 9 Persons, viz my Self & Wife, 5 sons & 2 Daughters, besides widow Edwards, an aged Sister that had lived with my family for some time.[13]

April 6. To day was appointed fo general Conference but it rained so steady there was but little business done. A few Persons met, Chose a President [and] Secty &c for the meting & adjourned.

[April] 7 the rain continued allmost unceaseingly Conferrence again adjourned.

[April] 8th. The day was quite pleasing. Conferrence met, acknowledged the Authorities of the Church as usual, & general anxiety was manifested by the Saints to fulfill all that the Lord had Commanded to be done, both in this place & in going out from this Nation. Nothing unusual took [place] until just as the Congregation was dismissed, when Bro O Hide Called the attention of the People, said he had just received a letter containing a rifle ball. The letter did not disclose its Author but left all to conjecture for themselves both its Author & intent.

My teams waggons & all things were now about ready to start the journey. But it seems that I cannot go & leve all my kindred. Some of my Cousins Called on me this evening, Said they knew no way that they move. They could not bear the Idea of my going & leaveing them as they were my Children as it were in the gospel. They were among the first or nearly so who had embraced the gospel in this kingdom in these last days on the earth. Were led by me with the first branch of the Saints that emigrated to Jackson CO. MO in 1831 My heart yearned over them. I asked God to give me wisdom that whereby a scheme might be [114] devised for their good. I at length told them if they would all be agreed and hearken to Council, they Could all go & get to a location or resting place of the Saints in time to raise sufficient to sustain their their families the esueing year. We accordingly agreed to meet the following day to enter in to arrangements to this effect.

---

13. Newel was 46; Lydia, 24; Samuel, 14; Sally, 10; James, 8; Joseph, 6; Newel, 4; Lydia, 2; and Jessie, about 1. The widow Edwards is unidentified.

[April] 9th. I went to Benjamin Slades, my Cousins, & from there about one mile to Freeborn Demills, my Bro. in law. Found them all anxious to go west, but they had but little to prepare for such a journey as they were among the first of the Saints that embraced the gospe in this dispensation and the first who emigrated to Jackson C.O. MO. & had been robed & driven from time to time by our enemies. The Competance they once had was gone y[e]t they felt no less anxious to be gathered with the People of God and be numbered with those that have made a covenant with him by sacrifice. They with he rest of the Saints were obliged to flee from Jackson CO in the Cold & inclement season of the year 1833. ~~they~~ ^we^ were obliged to leave many of ~~their~~ ^our^ effects & necessaries of life, which we by our industry had accumulated for the Comfort & Conveinience of our families, which to gather with the hardships & privations we have suffered from time to time ^from the hand of our enemies, Leaveing the State of MO. in the Cold dreary winter of 1838 in common with the Saints, had greatly impaird our Constitutions so that we had not that strength to labor & accumulate the the things of this life as we once had.

Yet the pleaseing prospect of getting beyond the tyranny and oppression of our enemies & from the banner so deeply staind with the blood of innoce, from the soil thad was allready crimsoned with the blood of martyered Prophets, & from the air that had so oft been rent with the Cries & mournings of the bereaved Widow & Orphan of the aged Father & heartbroken Mother for the loss of her beloved Child, with the virgins sighs & with grief of thousand of the fair Sons & Daughters of this People, yea, I say the hopes of finding an assylum for the Oppressed although it should be in the wilderness or among the red men of the forest or in the lone vally of the Mountains bouy[e]d our Spirits up & seemed to nerve us with [115] youth ful vigor.

Brother Demill [said] he was ready to enter to enter in to any measures that should be advisable. After some Conversation I told them the best & only measures I Could devise was the following: as but few had teams & the necessary means for the journey, it would be imposible for all to go at once. But if they would be agreed & all lay too wit[h] united energy, the summer should not pass away until they with families should be located at a resting place for the Saints & with all have sufficient raised by their industry with the blessings of heaven to attend their labors to sustain their families the ensuing year.

I shall first propose that all our most able men & teams take their farming tools, seeds of all kinds, & grain &c. ^as many families as shall be expedient at the time^ & go as soon as possible to a resting place which probably will not ex[c]eed 2 hundred mile & put in Crops at the earliest moment. While some few of our Older men Stay to take Charge of the families & leave with the[m] team sufficient so that, as soon as they have settled & their affairs & made wath [what] necessary preparations they can, they may all be moved across the Mississippi or the great Father of waters that gives such a Commanding aspect to our beloved City that we are about to bid farewell for a season. And there be in readiness for ebarking on board, not our splendid ships that float loftily upon the ocean nor upon the elegant steamers that ply so fearlessly upon the majestic waters that bound our devoted City that we are forced to abandon because of our faith in Christ & the virtue & integrity that lives in the bosoms of the Saints, but as soon as we get the soil broke, our grain & seeds in so that we can, we will leave some to tend the crop while the remainder take the teams & return for the families that are wating to embark on board our plain yet safe & & commodious common waggons drawn by oxen, save now & then a few horses & mles, the only way of Conveyance into the wilderness where we expect to be hid up for a little season while the indignation of the Lord passes over.

If you all agree to thes proposals I will abandon the idea of Crossing the mountains this [116] y[e]ar although I have made everry arrangement to this effect, & [will] use all my means & efforts to assist in moving you to a place of safety. For it would afford me the greatest pleasure of any object to see those that have long suffered to gather, removed to a place of safety that they may of that number that shall sanctify themselves through obedience to the law, even that of a Celestial, & be prepared to receive an inheritance on that Consecrated land when that blessing is given to the Saints, which is promised after much tribulation. My friends appeard Satisfied, said they believed the above measures the best that could be devised & the only way that some of them could be comfortably removed & sustaind.

I left them to determine the matter & returned home. As the day was pretty far spent I told my wife the arrangements we had made notwithstanding it was a disappointment to her & would probably involve us in many inconveiniences which we should a void by makeing our journey to the mountains this year. She Cheerfully consented. I now f[e]lt a pleaseing prospect of seeing my connexions all Comfortably situated beyond the reach of their oppressors, which afforded me a pleaseing sensation.

[April] 12th. Twelvth I went to meting my Brother in law Freeborn Demill. He informed me that the Slades & Cleaveland ^my cousins^ had concluded they could on [during] the Course of the Season get away them selves.[14] And [they] thought perhaps they could accumulate a little more to their personal advantage by doing so & did not Conclude to join the Com. as above proposed. Some of my uncles did not incline to join us. Bro Demill said he Could not bear the idea of haveing me leave him. My Father allso was not in a situation to move ^until he could sell^. I did not want to leave him. I told Demill allthough they should all leave but him, If he would stick to his integrity he should not be left, for I would even for his sake & the sake welfare of his family underg[o] or [not] abandon the Idea of Crossing the mountains this year. I would leave considerabl flour & provisions I had prepared for that expedition, & Carry what I [117] could for him.

He had one yoke of oxen & a verry light waggon which, with what I could take for him, would Carry [the rest] so that our families could live until we could raise mor. And after we had ploughed & put in our seeds & grain I would leave him with the our boys to tend the crop & I would take team & return & fetch up my Father & his family. Demill joyfully agreed to the above, for, said he, it is impossibly for me to go with out assistance & I cannot bear the thought of staying. We parted. I went home with a sorrowful heart reflecting upon the situation of my friends, for I knew if everry one went his way they would bring suffering upon themselves & it might be a long time before they would all

---

14. Father Knight's sister, Mary Knight, had married Aaron Slade Jr. Their children were Newel Knight's first cousins. Of them, Benjamin, Anna, Clark, and George Washington Slade joined the Church. Anna Slade married Henry A. Cleveland.

find a resting place with the Saints. But I had done all I could ad I could do nothing mor but commit them into the hands of our great Creator who holds the destines of all men.[15]

[April] 13th. I went to the temple with my Wife & Children to take our last view & farewell of that noble & magnificent building, which will Stand as a monument of everlasting honor to the Saints who have labored with all diligence to build it, that the Lord might have an house to his name in this place & endow his Saints with power from on high, which he has done in his holy temple, which the righteous ^temple & City^ are obliged to leave for the present, which will stand as a testimony against this nation.

[April] 14th. I covered my waggons & got all ready to lod them for the journey. Bro Demill came to see me. He had need of lumber to make a box ^to his waggon^ [and] Iron to repair it, which I gave him. I alls gave him money to b^u^y nails. I told him go to with his might & get ready as soon as possibl, for I should be waiting on expense for him. So he went his way rejoicing with the fond hope of soon being out from under yoke of tyrrany & oppression of this Nation. Sister Edwards who was at this time liveing wit us & expected to go with us, concluded to go to Bro Lewises[16] so that I could carry mor fo Demill. [118]

[April] 15. I went to the Ferry to see when I could Cross. Agreed with the Ferryman take my effects the next day. I returned, loaded my waggons & got all ready for a ^to^ start.

[April] 16th. The wind blew. I took my oxen, got a waggon, & went to Demill. Helped him about packing & getting ready some of his go[o]ds, provisions, & so forth & put in to my waggon to carry for him. To day the governors troops were in our City prowling about like demons in humane form with pretended claims, Claims on Bro

---

15. In the Allen version, its addendum contains the following: "This may certify that Newel Knight is entitled to the privilege of the Baptismal Font having paid his tithing in full to April 12th, A. D. 1846. (Signed) Wm. Clayton Recorder, by J. Whitehead Clerk. City of Joseph, March 13th 1846."
16. Three months later, the Lewises would be in the wagon train Newel captained for President Brigham Young.

Binghams property. They took his Cattle & waggons & drove them out to Carthage.

Friday the 17th The morning was Clear the wind Calm. I arose befor day, fed my Cattle, yoked them, & Started just as daylight began to dawn. I with my family Commited ourselves & our all in to the hands of our make[r] for protection & bade farewell to our Comfortable home & all our earthly possessions, save the little we took with us. When I arrived at the ferry the boat had just left the shore. The wind rose & blew so hard all day we were obliged [to] lay by all day in our waggons To day the troops were in & took 4 of the Brethren out to Carthage & thrust them in the jail where our b[e]loved Prophet & Patriarch fell victims to the Cursed Crew of demons in human form. I went to see my Father and bid him farewell. I left with sufficient APCS [?] to Collect to support him comfortably until I should have time to return for him.

[April] 18th. Just as the Sun began to dawn upon us we found our selves safely on board the Ferry with our effects, & bade farewell to the shores of our beloved City. We crossed safe. I drove on a little from the landing & stoped to wait for Brother Demill. [I] intended to go & help him but the wind rose & blew so hard the boat Could not Cross. I remaind all day with my family. I pitched my tent & felt to offer thanks that all was as well is it was & that we were thus far preserved on our journey.

19th. Sunday. The day is fair the wind favorable fo Crossing the River. I went over on the boat & once more had the satisfac[t]ion of walking [119] through the Streets of the City of Joseph & bholding great works he had so nobly reard & laid the foundation of before his Martrydom. I went to Bro Demills to see how he was getting along for the journey. Stayed all night & assisted him until it was time to return to my family, who I had left in a tent with the Care of my Cattle & waggons.

[April 20]. I returned at evening to my family on the 20 & found them all well & all things Safe.

21est. I stayed all day with my family, watching fo & expecting Bro Demill.

[April] 22. Crossed the river again. Went to see what detaind Demill. I assisted him in getting his effects loaded & down to the river.

He Crossed safe. The same evening, drove up to my tent & stoped for the night.

[April] 23rd. One of my oxen was gone, so we were obliged to tarry all day in search of him. I found I had to take so much for Demill, my team could not hall it. I tried to get another yoke of Cattle But Could not. I found an opportunity to b^u^y a horse & pay such property as I Could command by sacrificeing about one 3rd. I did it.

24th. We left Mississippi a bout noon. We ascended the bluff. Here we all halted & took a farewell view of our delightful City that we had seen & helped to rear even from its infancy. We also beheld the magnificent Temple rearing its lofty tower towards the heavens, which speaks volums in honor of the wisdom & greatness of our Martyred Prophet who was the founder of this magnifficient temple, as well as the persevereance, econe^m^y, & industry of the Saints who have had to labor with the sword in one hand & their tolls [tools] in the other ever since the Commencement of this noble house. We allso took a farewell look of our Comfortable homes we had labored so hard to rear for the Comfort of our families.

While beholding & pondering upon all this, [I] felt to [express] the gratitude of my heart to our heavenly Father that we had got thus far on our journey. I felt my dependeance upon God & asked his protecting Care to be over us on our Journey. Yea, my heart did swell with in me [120] because of the things which I beheld. For I beheld, with one glance of the eye from the eminance where I stood, the noble works of Joseph the Prophet & Seer & Hiram the Patriarch with whom I had been acquainted even from their boyhood. I knew their worth & mourned their loss. I had allso seen their Martyred, mangled bodies, & knew that they now laid in yonder silent resting place mouldering back to dust. And the hands yet wreaking with their blood wer now arrayed against the Saints.

And while I returned thanks fo our preservation, I did not forget the Brethren that were left & mor especially the poor who had not the means to leave & to go out from under the yoke of tyrranny of this Nation. And while I Pondered in my heart I felt to offer up the following Prayer:

O God the eternal Father I ask thee in the name of Jesus thy Son to let thy blessing rest upon us who are now here standing upon thy footstool & Covered with the heavens. For by this our presen situation & Sacrifice we do witness unto the[e] that we ar determined to be faithful unto thee all the remainder of our days upon the earth & to be gathered with thy People, even those that have made a covenant with thee by sacrifice. Therfore, we ask thee to forgive all of our Sins our frailties & unworthiness to which the we have become subjects through ^the^ weakness of our natures[,] for we confess our weakness & depravity before thee. Wilt thou give unto us thy holy Spirit to enlighten our understanding & let thine Angels guard us on our journey & thy presence go before us.

Preserve us from the Power of the destroy[er,] from Sickness & from accidents & from evils of everry kind. And incline he hearts of the People favorably towards us & to all thy Saints as we are journeying through to the wilderness. Wilt thou soften the hearts of our enemies even as thou didst Phario towards the Children of Israel.

And wilt thou O God, the Eternal Father, bless the the poor among the Saints the Widow & the Fatherless. Send men from the North & from the South, from the east & from the West, to b^u^y their houses & their lands, their furniture & all that is left in the hands of [121] of the Committee[17] for the benefit of thy needy Saints, That thy People may be provided with Teams & waggons, with Provisions, with Clotheing & with every needful thing fo their journey.

Wilt Thou remember in mich [much] mercy my aged Father. Give thine Angels concerning him & provide all needful blessings for him untill I shall see him gathered with thy Saints in a land Peace wher the wicked do not rule. And even then Let thy gentle Spirit guide & thine holy Angels guard him even down to the vally

---

17. In January 1846, the Twelve assigned Almon W. Babbitt, Joseph L. Heywood, and John S. Fullmer to be trustees in Nauvoo to find buyers for unsold Church and private property.

of death, & in the morning of the first resurrection let him Come forth & be Crowned & receive an inheritance with the Sancified.

Grant to bless thy Saints in so much that they may all soon be gathered from among their oppressors, that they be not partakers of the sins of this wicked Nation & receive not of her plagues. And do thou unto our enemies according to thine own pleasure & thy decree which is unalterable. The Cup they have filled to thy People, fill to them doubled & let the Blood of our Martyred Prophet & Patriarch & of all of our Martyred Brethren be avenged. O Lord, thou seest that in Consequence of our enemies thy People at this time are an afflicted & a poor People. Therefore let thy Special blessings rest upon them. Have mercy upon them & deliver them from their enemies. And deliver our Brethren from prison, for at this time the Scared walls & blood stained flor of Carthage Prison holds the bodies of thy Saints, even that Prison wher our bloved Prophet & Patriarch fel[l], a Sacrifice to the wicked & which blo[o]d & Scars stand as a testimony against the Nation that passes by unnoticed such unheard of Cowardice treachery & Bloodshed. Therefor wilt thou O Lord deliver our Brethren out of that Prison that they may again be restored to the bosom of their families & Brethren, for through the malice of the Wicked & not for Crime wer they thrust in to Prison.

As thy People have labored faithfully to build an house to thy name & are driven from it by Our enemies, let that house [122] let that house stand betwen thee & thy People & Our enemies, that whatsoever thy enemies do to that house do thou even so to them. Who so shall bless that house do thou bless them & who so shall Curse that house let them be Cursed.

O Lor[d] God of Israel, wilt thou remember thy ancient Covenant People & as our journeyings have to be among the remnants of that Scattered & long dispersed People, even among the Lamanites who at this time ar a wild uncivelized race having no knowledge of a redeemer or of the resuretion, I ask [t]hee in the name of thy only begotten that thou wilt move upon their hearts & let the prayers of their righteous Fathers begin to be answered upon their heads that th^e^y may be favorably inclind to wards thy Saints. And may they in due time Come to a knowledge of their Redeemer & of the incorrect traditions of their forefathers. And Wilt thou give thy Servants wisdom that they may act in all prudence toward thy Chosen Seed, & ^may^ thine Anointed ones honor thee & be preserved as the apple of thine eye.

Bless thy Saints who are in far Countries & upon the Island of the Sea, & prepare the way that thy Sons & thy daughters may come from far Countries & bring their rich treasures with them to beautify an house & City which thy Saints will yet build unto thy name, notwithstanding at this time they are scatered & sorely oppressed by their enemies. Therefore wilt [thou] bless thine afflicted People at this time, & in all their journeying let thine Angels guard & thy presence go before thy Saints. And may thy Saints be faithful to remember their Covenants with the[e] & to do them & to Sanctyfy themselves through obediance to thy law. So that when thou Shalt see fit to Call them forth out of their hideing place, or the Secret Chamber thou hast prepared for them, they may be prepared to Come forth with Songs of everlasting joy to Share on that blessing which thou hast promised should follow after much tribulation, even the redemption of Zion.

And as this thy Servant, with all of his immediate connexions who have empraced the gospel in these [123] last days, have been driven by our enemies from that land ~~by our one~~ togather with hundreds of thy Saints, I ask a special blessing upon us & greatly desire that some of us may yet live to return & receive an inheritance on that consecrated land which shall be an everlasting inheritance for us & our Seed after us.

Again, I commit my Self & Family in to thy Care, O God our heavenly Father, with all our Cattle & effects, which [we] acknowledge [are] a gift and blessing from thee. And I ask thee to take us & our all in to thy Care from this time & preserve us from the power of the destroyer & from all harm. Let no evil befall us & give me thy servant wisdom that I may do thy will & honor thee in all that I do.

And wilt thou preserve my wife & little ones through all our journeyings. Let them live to be gathered upon an everlasting inheritance from whence I have been driven. Let us help to build that holy City unto thy name & prepare us with all thy Saints for a place in thy Celestial kingdom & to thy great name shall be all the honor & glory ascribed through the merrits & in the name of thine only begotten, both now & forever. Even so Amen & Amen.

[April 24, 1846].[18] We again resumed our journey until nearly night when we stoped & camped by the wayside.

[April] 25, We arose in go[o]d Spirits & after our breakfast was over our Cattle well fed & all thing in readiness, we started on traveled about 5 miles from Farmington & camped for night.

[April] 26. Traveled through Farmington. This is considerable of a Town about 20 miles from the Mississippi river. The roads are extremely bad. I broke one of my wagon wheels ^about two miles west of this place,^ fixed in som^e^ false spokes & drove on to a conveinient place for Camping [and] Stoped for the night.

[April] 27. Drove on to a little town Called Boneparte 5 miles west of Farmington where I stoped to get my waggon repaired. Pitched my

---

18. Because their livestock could feed on the prairie grass and plants, the exiles from Nauvoo took better routes across Iowa than the one used by Brigham Young's Camp of Israel. They started across Iowa on April 24. In terms of today's maps of Iowa, Newel drove through Farmington and at Bonaparte did not cross the Des Moines as Brigham Young's company did but instead followed the river's northern shore to Bentonsport and then Keosauqua. On May 6 they camped close to Pearson's Western Hotel, probably in Keosauqua.

After waiting out high waters, they crossed the Des Moines, then traveled the Camp of Israel's route on county roads around Richardson's Point and along the Fox River. Where Drakesville is today, they left the Camp of Israel's route that bent southward and went west instead, on what was becoming the main alternate route heading to Mount Pisgah. They drove west along a high-ridge road between the Fox River and Soap Creek, passing near present-day Unionville and Moravia. On May 10 they crossed Soap Creek. The next day they rolled up onto a broad and extensive prairie and an amazing panorama suddenly burst into view: wagons, people, and livestock spread out all across the prairie. After traveling along the high ground between the Chariton River and White Breast Creek, about six miles south of present-day Osceola, they intercepted the Camp of Israel's newly imprinted trail to Mount Pisgah. They arrived at the Mount Pisgah encampment on May 25.

tent on the bank of the Desmoine & stayed over night. The rain poured dwn like torrents during the night.

[April] 28. It rained al day so that we could not travel. [124]

[April] 29 & 30th. The river was so high we could not cross.

May 1 & 2ond [1846]. The river continued up so that the Ferry did not think Safe Crossing.

[May] 3rd. Sunday, we Crossed the Desmoine river. Drove about 12 miles & Camped for night, the knight was quite rainy.

[May] 4. We traveled a few miles over the worst road I ever saw. Met Bro Gleeson on his way from the Camp to Nauvoo.[19]

[May] 5. We Continued our journey met Brother Taylor returning from the Camp. It truely rejoiced my heart to see him & hear go^o^d news from the Camp of Israel. The road is allmost impassable on account of frequent rains.

[May] 6. We Camped Close by Pearsons Western Hotell. Here it rained nearly all night. In the morning my Wife Sold some Crockerry, towels &C to recruit ours & Bro Demils Provisions.

[May] 7, 8, & 9th. The traveling was so bad & my loads so heavy we traveled but little. Our load had got damp. We dried them & fited up again for Travelling on the 9th.

[May] 10. We Crossed Soap Creek in Appenooce C.O. passed Sister Allen who lay verry sick in a tent supposed to be dying.

[May] 11th. Monday morning, after travelling a short distance we found our selves on the broad & extensive Priarie. Here we could look forward for miles & behold the Prairie spoted with wag gons, Cattle, horses & Sheep, Men, Women & Children, who all seemed to be in good Spirits as if nerved for the journey by his omnipotent arm. And had it not been for the reflection of the poor who are yet behind & have not the means to get away, I should have rejoiced with all my heart. Thus was joy on one hand & Sorrow on the other mingled in my bosom while I Pondered upon the things around me. Joy because of the thousands who have been enabled thus far to take their journey from their oppressors where the wicked shall not rule nor oppress the Saints

---

19. Probably John S. Gleason.

& again. I lifted m[y] heart in fervent prayer to bless the Camp of Israel in all their journeyings:

> Give the Saints patience o Lord God of Irael. Be thou their front & rear wall, a lamp to their feet, & a guide to their path, until they shall all find a resting [125] place where the oppresser shall cease & they that have wasted thy people with out mercy shall have no more dominion. Send men to buy the property thy Saints have to sell that thy people may be provided with means to leave their oppressore & the Nation allredy Crimsoned with the blood of righteous men. May the weather be favorable & let the elements Conspire to favor thy people in their journeyings. The pit that our enemies have dug for us, let them fall there in. Let them be snared & taken in the net they have spread for thy Saints. And now our Father, I dedicate my self & family & all that we have into thy Care & ask the[e] to give wisdom & understanding unto this thy [s]ervant, that all he does may be don in the name of the Lord & acceptably before thee. Give health to my family, strength & patience, as their journeyings may demand. Give us with all thy Saints everry needful blessing even so, Amen.

The rich & variegated Prairie looks as if nature had done her best to Cheer the weary & attract the admiration of the raveler, while our Children amuse themselves with the sweet & beautiful flowers which grow spontaneous. It gives a refreshing fragrance to all & serves to Cheer us on our way.

[May] 12, We stoped to wash & bake &C.

[May] 13. Pursued our journey passed the last house wher white man lives. Pitched our tent & Stayed until the 15 on account of rain[,] when we again resumed our journey Slowly.

[May 16]. Nothing special occuring untill on the 16 we Crossed a trace we did not understand, but as we saw teams before us we followed the largest road.

[May] 17. We found we were too far north & had traveled nearly two days out of course. We forded a Creek which we supposed to be white breast & went on bending our Course towards the Courses we designed to go or supposed the Camp [Mount Pisgah] to be.

[May] 18. Traveled all day.

[May] 19. Traveled a few miles & stoped our teams. I took my horse & went to find the road that led to the Camp. Found it & returned to my waggons and family a little before night.

[May] 20 Wednesday. The rain fell s[o] fast we did not attempt to travel until nearly non [noon] on the 21.

[May 21]. We resumed our journey until the evening of the 23rd.

Sunday the 24. The rain prevented traveling the fore part of the day. In the afternoon we went a few miles. Brothers G A Smith & A Lyman rode out & met us about 2 miles from the Camp.[20] The first salutation from them was "there Comes [126] the oldest mormon now liveing" (haveing refference to my age in Church & Preisthood), accompanied with "how do you do Bro Newel" &c &c. Truely did the Prophet say the Countenance of a friend rejoiced the heart of man & truely the salutation of a friend is like o^i^1 or the balm of gil[e]ad to a friend, was theirs to me After talking a while they invited me to drive on & they would accompany us to the Camp. I thanked them but told them as the day been some rainy we had not washed & Changed our clothes & I thought we had better Stopt, Stay over night & make ourselves Clean & prepare to go in to the great Camp of Irael on the following morning. They consented bade us good evening & re[t]urned.

[May] 25th.[21] We arose & after a verry heavey shower milked our Cows, eat our breakfast, & started in good Spirits for the Camp. Just

---

20. Apostles George A. Smith and Amasa Lyman.
21. The Camp of Israel had reached this location on May 18, so they had been there only six days by the time Newel arrived. Here they were setting up a farming settlement, as they had done at Garden Grove, for those not properly equipped to go farther west. Leaders tried but failed to borrow wagons and teams from the Pisgah campers to enable the Twelve and a selected company to push ahead for the Rockies that season. Located on the Middle Fork (Thompson River) of the Grand River, Mount Pisgah was named by Elder Parley P. Pratt after the biblical elevation called Pisgah (Deuteronomy 3:27), from whose summit at Mount Nebo Moses viewed the promised land. The site is located 5.5 miles northeast of today's town of Afton, Iowa. Mount Pisgah saw a continual turnover of residents. At its largest, it contained two thousand Saints and had several thousand acres of prairie land fenced for cultivation. Saints vacated the settlement by 1852.

before we arrived Bros G A Smith & A Lyman two of the Twelve again Came out & met us. And after a cordial salutation with them we passed on to the Camp. We came first to Father [William] Huntingtons, which about half reared. Here we beheld a sample of economy & industry unequaled by any other People on earth. And saw the smileing countenance of many a friend & heard their kind salutations that truely made the wilderness seem like the garden of Eden, & the busy hum of the ploughman, the sound of the axe, the industry of the Brethren, all seemed to say the wilderness will soon blossom like the rose & become a fruitful field.

We drove on a short distance & pitched our tents & considered ourselves at home.

As I had bee[n] obliged th [to] Sacrifice so much, not only in Selling my mills but allso again I was obliged to make great Sacrifice to Satisfy the demands of the before mentioned Kimball & Fordham & pay some other demands, besides waiting for & assisting Bro Demill to come to place, I did not expect to be able to Cross the mountains this year. But intended to stop at this pl Stake or resting place for the present & do all I could to gather up my Fathers family to this place, that they may be out of the reach of the gentiles & be prepared to go up to the standard of liberty to the ensign of the nations, wher it shall be reard, & allso to share in that blessing which is promised after much tribulation. For in poverty I have labored [127] & sought to keep the commandments of God. And notwithstanding the slowness of many of my kindred to keep the Commandments & arise & Shake of the yoke of oppression & bondage that they may continue to be of that number ^who^ are gathered to gather, haveing made a Covenant by Sacrifice, My bowels of Compassion still yearn over them.

And as I said I had labored in poverty, I had allso labored in Spirit by night & by day that they may be saved in the kingdom of God, for I could not bear the Idea that one soul of them should be lost or that they should loose the Crown that is laid up for these righteous who have been the first laborers & ^have^ been faithful in this kingdom from the beginning, through all the scenes of trial & persecution we have had to pass, if they continue faithful unto the end The Crown is yet befoe but blessings will soon be ours if we continue faithful. I now felt to offer up the thanks & gratitude of my heart to our heavenly Father for the preservation of our lives & health & for the privilige of meeting with the Church in this resting place.

After dinne[r] [I went] over to see President Young, Elder Kimball & others. The first salutation I had from Phs[22] Young was "how do you d Bro Knight have you fetched your mill with you?" "No sir," Said I, "I lacked team so I left[it]." "Well," said he, "are you going over the mountains with us to build another?" I replied, "if you say so." "Well," Said he, "I say so." I Afterwards had a talk with Elder Kimball. He Said I had better prepare to go on the best that I could. I told him my situation & why I was thus unprepared for such a journey. "Yet," said I, "at what is required of me I never look back but will make everry exertion & do all I can."

After enjoying a short interview with the Brethren I returned to my family. Told my wife we had got [128] to prepare to Cross the mountains. This was quite unexpected to her, yet with her usual Calmness & fortitude She replied, "I am ready to do or to go where ^or what^ ever you are conciled [to] do for, notwithstanding our means are small, the Lord is able to preserve us insomuch that we Shall not perish. I had rather trust in the Lord in keeping Council, allthough we have but little, than to depart from it for the prospect of mor ease & plenty. If Brother Young says go I should not expect a^n^y prosperity in Staying." We accordingly began to make Calculations for a further journey.

This Place the Brethren Called M.t. Pisga.[23] It is Situated a little east of the middle fork of grand river or on its bluff. It is about [ ] miles from the City of Joseph. The land is owned by the indians who freely have given the Brethren liberty to Settle here. There William Huntington Sen. is appointed to Preside here, C C Rich & E T Benson for his Council. From the present appearance & industry manifested by the Brethren, they will be Crowned with an abundant harvest in the fall for their families to subsist upon during the winter & to recruit & load up many for a mountain voyage next Spring.

---

22. Phineas Young.
23. Mount Pisgah, Iowa.

There is allso a resting place situated on the East fork of grand river about thirty miles from this place Called Garden Grove, wher a goodly number of the Brethren have stoped to raise a Crop this year. Bro Samuel Bent is appointed to Preside, Aaron Johnson & David Fulmer are his council.[24] It will be their object the[r]e same as at Mt. Pisga to raise provisions & do all in their power to aid & assist in establishing the Church in a safe resting place some where in the region of the moun^tains^. [129]

I told Brother Demill I could not assist him to go any further, for my team was not sufficient to carry provisions sufficient ^to^ sustain our families through, nor was it suitable ^to^ go even with my own family. I told him if he would assist me a bout going on ^I thought^ it would prove a blessing to him and ^be^ an advantage to me, for I would go and prepare a place for him to come and should be under obligation to use all my endeavors to hereafter assits him in getting up to the standard of liberty.

In the commencement of our journey I found I had taken so much load for Brother Demill my team could not draw it. I was obliged to mak the best shift I could. Oxen I could not get with out going some distance in to the Country and paying cash for them. This [I] could not do, for I had not money enough to half buy one yoke of oxen. I found an opportunity to buy a horse and turn out a new Saddle. I had some bedding, a rifle, pair of ^otihn^ [?] and so forth to gather with ten dollars cash. to ^twice^ the amount Not withstanding I had to pay a bout twice what the horse was worth, I thought it better to do it than leave Demill. My wife left some things and we by this means and by occasionally doubleing teams we got through, so that Brothr Demill will have provisions enough to last his family till harvest.

The assistance I asked bro Demill was to take the above mentioned horse, a stone [stove], some Chairs, and some other articles I could not carry ovr the mountains and let me have one yoke of oxen. I told him I thought he could take the horse and harness, and such property as [I] could let him ^have^, in to the country and trade them for young cattle which he could break in the course of the winter and have a better team

---

24. Bennett, *Mormons at the Missouri*, 39.

to go in the Spring tha[n] he could have by keeping his oxen. So that it would be a present advantage to me ^and^ result in the same to him in the end. But all this was to no effect. I could get no assistance from him atall, but on the contrary he rather censured me for now leaveing him and not doing still more for him. But this I was obliged to do for I had allready done all that my circumstances would admit of. For I had left of my own goods and provisions to fetch his, so that I shall be obliged to sell off our Clothing and all that we can live ^dispense^ with out to recruit provisions for the journey.

I now commenced fitting up and prepareing my loads and waggons for a further campaign, intending, as I could trade nothing here, to go on to the settlements[25] and there trade my horse for oxen ^and^ get provisions fo^r^ the journey.

[May 31]. Sunday the 31 the People assembled for meting. After a short adress by G A Smith, President Young arose proposed that this meting be a general Conference for the purpose of attending to the general Church buisness. It rejoiced my heart to see the wisdom & prudence with which he had managed & was still managing for the benefit of of this People. May the Lord ever give unto him a double portion of that Spirit that supported Joseph through his life for the burden is great he has to bear. [130]

June 1st [1846] Monday morning. I had intended to cross the river to day but rain prevented.

[June] 2. One of my oxen was gone. I spent nearly all day in search of him.

[June] 3. I got my Cattle togather, my oxen yoked and all things about ready for a start, when Brother [Thomas?] Grover came up and said he wished I would wait till the following morning so that he could go in company with me. I waited for him.

[June] 4. Thursday morning, all things being now ready, I with my family bid farewell to mount pisga and again commited my all ^my self^ in to the hands of my creator and asked his blessings to rest upon my

---

25. The settlements Newel mentions were those south of Mount Pisgah in northern Missouri, those located by the Missouri River (where they were headed), or those down the Missouri River in the state of Missouri.

family, ^my self^ my Cattle, and all that I possessed. And to give unto me wisdom, knowledge and understanding that I may do all that I do in the name of the Lord. I drove on about three miles and stoped to bait my cattle. I waited some time for Brother Grover. He did not come I left my family to take ^Care^ of my teams and went back to mount Pisga to learn what detained him. When I got there I learnt that he had sent back to the farmer [former] first resting place of the Saints [Garden Grove], a distance of about thirty miles for a chest of tools. He was daily expecting it.

I went back to my family and waited untill sunday the 7.

[June 7]. Brother Grover did not come. I went back again to Mount Pisga. The day was pleasant. I attended meting. Elder O Hide arrived to day from Nauvoo. He addressed the congregation. Went ^to^ Brother Grovers. The Chest of tools had not arrived. I told him I could not wait for him much longer [and] as I should be obliged to go out in to the Country to trade, it would be expedient for me to be on the journey soon. He was not willing for me to go and leave him. Said he would go on the next morning ^day^.

[June] 8. Towards evening Brother Gover came on [and went with the Knights].

[June] 9. Tuesday morning, Brother we started on our journey. The road was tolerable good and the weather favorable for traveling. We passed by Bro O[rson] Prats Co.

[June] 10. Crossed the west fork of Grand river.

[June] 11. Crossed Platt.

[June] 12 passed Father John Smiths Co. They had stoped on the acount of sickness. Tthe same day we passed through an Indian town of the Potowatome nation situated on the Otowa ^Nodaway^ river.[26] They come out in great numbers to see us pass and expressed every mark of friendship towards us. They generally looked well and healthy and

---

26. John D. Lee said that the village had fifty wigwams and that "some few lots of grounds were enclosed by Pole fenses & tilled by the squaws." Lee, diary, June 8, 1846. The Pottawattamie Indian village site is two miles west of today's Lewis, Iowa, on a ridge overlooking the spot where Indian Creek flows into the East Nishnabotna River.

allthough they could speak but little English I could read much from their appearance. Their countenance bespoke inteligence all though it was shrowded in native simplicity. The appearance of these red men of the west brought many ^re^flections and caused my heart to flow with gratitud to God that he has given me an existence upon the earth in this momentous ^age^ for it truely is a day of great events, a time that the ancient Prophets looked down upon with deep intrest and wrote their most enlivening strains, and offered up the inmost desire of their souls for the accomplishment of the work that is required of this generation. For in this generation shall Israel be restored and the kingdom of [131] God set up on the earth and shall prevail. The Red men of the forest will ere long come to a knowledge of a redeemer and the Gentile yoke shall be broken from off their necks. For according to the knowledge that we have gained from the book of mormon, they are of the blood of Israel and for them is reserved great blessings which are soon to be poured out upon their heads.

[June] 13. We passed Elder Taylors company. They had encamped to stay over the sabbath.

[June] 14. Passed Elder [William] Claytons Co. The same day we Crossed Isthtabotany river.

[June] 15. We traveled all day.

[June] 16. Tuesday. We came up to the Camp. They had stopped nea[r] the Missouri River at Council bluffs. The Brethren had commenced a boat to ferry over the River. I went to see some of the Twelve and found it would be nessary to go in to the Country to trade as soon as we could.

[June] 17 Brother ^Grover^ and myself arose in the morning and after asking Our heavenly Father to protect us and to turn the gentiles favorably towards us that we might obtain grain and Cattle and all such things as was needful for our journey in exchange for such property as we had to carry with us, we committed Our selves, Our families, our Cattle, and all that we posse,^sse^d in to the Care of our Creator and started on.

[June] 18. We came to a settlement where we purchased Cows and grain &c for our journey.

[June] 20. We spent the days in shelling and put up our grain.

[June] 21. Sunday morning started to go to the Camp of the Saints where we had left our families. We travelled about forty miles,

[June 22]. Arrived safe, and found our families all well on Monday P M about four oclock.

[June] 23 & 24. The wind blew high with some rain. The air was quite cold for the season so that it rendered the situation of our women and Children quite inconveneient, y^e^t they manifested patience and resignation in the midst of privations, sufferings, and hardships which they unavoidably had to endure. The thoughts ^of^ being freed from the iron yoke of tyrrany and oppression of those that had so often rendered us houseless and homeless and left us destitute upon a merciless world, and had added to this the most barbarous and cruel murders ^that has ever been recorded on the page of history,^ and that to of our best and most worthy men, buoyed their spirits up and gave them fortitude to brave the most appalling storms and dangers of the western wiles.

How sweet is liberty to the oppressed and how joyful shall this People be when when they can build houses and inhabit them and plant vineyards and eat the fruit there of, when they can worship God and none shall dare to rend their rights asunder, when the blood of martyrs shall cease, and the tear of the widow and Orphan be stayed. We are true Americans. Our fore fathers have fought and bled for liberty and [132] their children are rightfull heirs to that freedom they so nobly won. God, liberty, and patriotism is our motto. For it we intend to live and for it are ready to die.

[June] 27. Two years to day have passed in to eternity since our honorable Prophet and patriarch fell martyrs by the most cowardly cruel and yet unheard of barbarity that ever put forth the the puny arm to accomplish the work of death upon the noblest men that ever had an existance upon the earth. Sad indeed is ^the^ remembrance of that cruel deed to this People. Our present situation, scattered as we are near the wide wilderness priarie, shrinks into Oblivion, or seems but a light momentary thing in comparison to that dreadful scene. When O Lord shall thy people be wholly ^be^ dilivered from blood thirsty men? Me thinks I hear the spirit whisper, hold on to thy integrity a little longer the and the victory will be yours, for in the last days shall my kingdom be established and prevail.

[June] 28 Sunday. I atended meeting. Pesident Young and Elder Kimball addressed the Brethren in verry appropriate manner. Their discourse was well calculated to encourage the honest to persevere in well doing. The Brethren met in the afternoon to attend to arrangements for the journey.

[June] 29. Moved up to president Youngs Co.

[June] 30.[27] The United States officers came here.

July 1[1846]. I intended to go to the S̶a̶w̶ mill and prepare to go down to the river to assist in ferrying, but a meting was called to give to officers an opportunity of laying their business before the people. They had come to enlist soldiers for the California frontiers country. President Young told the brethren the hand of God was in this move and it would prove a great blessing to them if they would enlist and make the number of soldiers called for. President Young said he would return to mount pisgah and lay the affair before the brethren there and have them come on and join with the Soldiers here.

July 2. I moved down to the river. Here I pitched my tent and assisted in making a road to ascend the bluff, working on the boat, swiming cattle across the river, and so forth, untill wednesday the eighth when I crossed my waggons, family, and cattle over the river.

[July 8]. Drove on about four miles to the general encampment of the saints.[28] Stayed over night with my family.

[July] 9th. I went to the river again to assist the brethren in crossing. Assisted until saturday night when returned to my family. Spent the sabbath with them. Toward night the brethren were called to gather.

---

27. After meeting with Jesse Little, a Latter-day Saint representative in the East, President James K. Polk authorized the formation of a Mormon battalion to fight in the Mexican-American War. During the first two weeks in July, US Army recruiters from Fort Leavenworth visited the Saints' encampments and invited the Church to enlist a battalion of five hundred men. Captain James Allen and three dragoons (cavalry men) rode to Council Bluffs and on July 1 gave Brigham Young the enlistment offer.

28. The Cold Springs Camp. This was located four miles from the west bank landing in present Omaha, Nebraska. It provided a camp headquarters for most of July. See Bennett, *Mormons at the Missouri*, 68, 363n1.

Inteligence was [told] that president Young had arrived from mount Pisgah at the general encampment on the other side of the river. [133]

[July 10].[29] A general attendance of the brethren ~~of the~~ was requested at that place the following day [meaning July 10] for the purpose of makeing up the companies of volunteers for the California expedition.

[July] 13. Monday morning I went to the place of appointment where president Young, Elder Kimball, and others made a statement of the affair showing the advantage it would give us to go and defend that country. The day passed off well. Volunteers ~~seemed~~ were on hand which loudly spoke the patriotism that lived in the bosoms of our people and their willingness to defend their Countries rights, not withstanding we have been cast out as exiles.

At this time when war seems to threaten the nation, on every hand the great men of the earth begin to feel after the Mormons, notwithstanding their eyes have been blind and their ears deaf to all the petitions and entreaties of the Saints for these many years. They have suffered the innocent to be hounded, in Chains and groan in prisons, virgins to be rob[b]ed, female innocence and virtue to be insulted, the blood of Martyrs to stain the earth from which they receive their daily bread which has caused the innocent the widow and the orphans cries to ascend into the ears of the Lord of Sabaoth, and all so placed him who holds the destinies of the nations of the earth at this time on high to gather with many witnesses whose souls are with t[h]ose that John saw under the altar of God crying day and night to be avenged of their enemies who dwell on the earth.

Yea, I say at this time when the Lord seems to be about to come out of his hideing place to vex the nation. They begin to awake to a sense of what they have suffered upon ^the^ innocent, so much so as to send men after us into the wilderness to intreat of us to go and defend the nations rights, that has thus wantonly expeled us from our rights and and comfortable homes. It truely affords the saints satisfaction that they have the privilege of showing by their works that honor and patriotism that has ever lived in their bosoms and burns in their veins

[July] 14 ^and^ 15. Stayed with my family.

---

29. MS 767, folder 1, item 7.

[July] 16.³⁰ President Young called the brethren to gather to lay before them further arrangements for the general good of this People. He proposed that those that were fitted for crossing the mountains should organize and be on the march as soon as they could [and] that another company go to grand Island³¹ and there make a settlement and put in crops so that there may be sufficient resting places for the Saints in their journings through the wilderness. And all such as are not prepared for a further journey at this time stop near this place, and [134] do all they can to bring on the remainder of the Church and prepare to sustain them selves and Cattle through the winter as well as possible. After this meting was closed I went work on the road as it was necessary that considerable labor should be done before the road was finished.

[July] 17. I crossed the river in hopes to trade for a yoke of cattle but did not accomplish it.

[July] 18. Fixed my yokes to yoke my cows and make necessary preparations for crossing the mountains. For president Young's request is that I shall go on for the purpose of erecting mills, preparing for a

---

30. As noted above in our introduction, on July 9 Brigham Young sent Bishop George Miller up the Platte River, heading a "mountain expedition" to advance as close to the Rocky Mountains region as possible. Then, a week later, both Brigham Young and Heber C. Kimball organized two more wagon trains to push west to reinforce Miller's party. Neither Young nor Kimball themselves went with those companies. Young enlisted Newel to go in his company, his "fifty" as it was called, and to captain it. The captains of the seven "tens" in Newel's "fifty" were Anson Call, Jerome B. Kempton, David Lewis, Solomon Hancock, Louvrin H. Dame, Erastus Bingham, and William Mathews. According to Newel's roster (below) of his fifty, it included 217 people, sixty-one wagons, 244 oxen, twenty-two horses, 127 cows, and nearly a hundred sheep. Wagons averaged 3.5 people each and 4 oxen. The Knights traveled in Captain Kempton's ten. It was small, having only four families, twenty-three people, and seven wagons. The Knights had two wagons, six oxen, four cows, and the only horse in that ten. Being captain of a train of five dozen wagons and so much livestock meant he had to be on horseback a lot.
31. Grand Island, in the Platte River, was nearly two hundred miles upstream. The forty-mile-long island could graze cattle, was well timbered, and had buffalo. Young wanted Bishop Miller to explore that site. But by the end of July, various discouraging reports made Young abandon the Grand Island idea. Bennett, *Mormons at the Missouri*, 63–64, 66, 67.

carding machine, and so forth. And as I could not get oxen sufficient to draw my loads, I resolved to yoke my cows and never cease my exertions until I had accomplished all that was required at my hand.

[July] 19. This morning president Young, Elders Kimball and [Willard] Richards returned to our Camp, called the Brethren togather in the after noon to attend to arrangements for organizeing a company to cross the mountains, and to impress upon Brethren the necessity of being faithful and diligent in all things that are entrusted to their care. And in particular to have the herdsmen be diligent in attending to their duties. As the Indians corn is infenced it required great attention to keep our Cattle from destroying it.

Monda 20. I worked on the road.

[July] 21. Started on for the mountains.

[July] 22. Stoped at Elkhorn river. This is considerable of a stream about a hundred yards wide and so deep that we could not ford it. It is a bout 22 miles from the Missouri River. As there was no ferry boat we got a raft of dry logs and floated our wagons across on it. This evening president Young, Elders Kimball and Ricchards arrived here to organize or give us the nessesary instructions for organizeing and Crossing the mountains.

[July 23] Early in the morning the brethren assembled on the Bluff a little east of the river to attend to the above named buisness. ^President Young called for a nomination for some who should be duly appointed to lead a company over the mountains or to some good valley or good and safe location in the region of the mountains. The following persons were nominated and unanimously appointed Captains to lead the first Compa[n]y duly organized by the regular authorities of the Church of latter day saints: Joseph Holbrook John A Miksel [Mikesell] and myself Newel Knight.^

After the Council was over, Brothers Young, Richards, Kimball, and Hollman came to my tent where Brother [Jerome Boneparte] Kempton had "dressed the fatted calf" and Sister [Maria] Kempton and my wife had made it ready for our breakfast. And I felt thankful for the privilege of entertaining the best most honorable men of the earth, for I look upon their honor to far out shine any monarch that sits upon any earthly throne.

But to return to the subject or the business of the day, after breakfast was over we resumed the business of Crossing the river. And after Our President & ^his^ Council had given us such instructions as thy deemed proper for us, they they bade us farewell & returned. As soon as we had all safely crossed the river we proceeded to arrange the Company in tens so that all things might be in order for travellin in the morning. The following is a correct Copy of each ten. [135]

A schedule of the first fifty first ten on their way over the mountains, July 23 1846, Elkhorn Creek:

	Family	Wagons	Oxen	Pigs	Horses	Calves	Cows	Sheep
Joseph Holbrook Hanna Holbrook Judson Tolman Sarah Tolman Charolotte Holbrook Joseph L. Holbrook Catharine Barton	7	2	12	1	0	0	7	
Anson Call Marry A. Call Bosco Call Vasti M. Call Chester Call Abigail Wiley	6	2	6	2			7	
Harvey Call Mary Ann Call Francis Call	3	1	4				1	
Josiah Call Henrietta Call	2	1	2				1	
Ransom Shepherd Adaline Shepherd Jacob Shepherd Mary Shepherd Samuel Shepherd	5	2	7			1	3	
Fornatus Dustin Rosaline Dustin	2	1	2			1	1	

The Nauvoo Exodus and the "Mountain Expedition," 1845–46

Chandler Holbrook Eunice " " Diania " " Maria " " Eunice " " Orson " " Joseph " "	7	2	10		1	2	6
Cyris Call Sally Call Sarah Machem Homer Call Omer Call	5	1	4				1
Dwight Hardin Phebe " " George " " Charles " " Alma " " Elizabeth " " Phebe E " "	7	1	2				2
Hiram Mace Elizabeth " " Larenerd " "	3	1	2				1
Anson Call Capt of the first ten. R Shepard Clerk							

2nd Ten

	Family	Wagons	Oxen	Cows	Horses	Sheep	Colys
Newel Knight Co Lydia " " Samuel " " Sally " " James F " " Joseph " " Newel " " Lydia " " Jesse " "	9	2	6	4	1		2
Groam ^Jerome^ Kempton Maria " "	2	1	2	1			

James Porter Betsey " " Lydia Ann Elizabeth " " George " " James " " Martha " "	7	2		2			
Jacob Houtz Lydia " " Mary " " Lucinda " " Asa Rice " "	5	2		3			
Geroam B. Kemmpton, Capt							

3rd Ten

	Family	Wagon	Oxen	Horses	Cow	Calves	Sheep	Mule
David Lewis No Doritha " " Araminta " " Preston " " David L. sister Mary Arkins Neviah " "	6	3	8		1	4	4	2
Beson Lewis Elizabeth " " John " " Wm Lewis Martha " " Elizabeth " " Frederick Bainbridge	7	3	10	3	14	9	21	2
Neriah Lewis Rebecca " " Wm " " Marion " " Robert " " Sarah Hendricks Tabitha " " Wm Bryant	8	3	12	2	5	4	8	
Anthony Blackburn Betsey " " Thomas " " Matilda Patterson	4	1	6		2	3		

Isaac Hill Clara " " Nancy " " Elizabeth " " Lucinda " " Mary " " Wm " "	7	1	2		3	2	
David Lewis, Capt. and Clerk							

4th Ten

	Family	Wagons	Oxen	Horses	Cows	Calves	Sheep
John A Miksel Catherine Miksel George Miksel	3	1	4		3		
I H Miksel Margaret " " Joseph " " John A " "	4	1	2				
Asa Barton Mary " " Martin Dewitt Sarah " "	4	3	10	2	3		
John G Wilkins Nancy " " Alexander " " Jane " " Ausker " "	5	1	4		3		
George Sweet Mary Ann Sweet Henry " " Keziah " " Robert " " Phebe " "	6	1	4		2		
Solomon Hancock Phebe " " Alta " " Solomon Jr " " Elijah " " Jacob " " Isaac " "	7	2	6		2		
Solomon Hancock, Capt. Asa Barton, Clerk							

5th Ten

	Family	Wagon	Oxen	Horses	Cows	Calves	Sheep
Louvrin H Dame Sophia " " Phidelia G " " Laura A " " Wesley W " " Tamson P " " Simon B " " Sally M Wade Minerva Wade	9	4	17	2	6	5	11 1
Wm. H Dame Lovina " "	2	1	4		1		
Daniel Drake Patience " " Orison " " Horace " " Sarah I Wilson	5	2	10		6	1	6
W G Paine Sarah " " Eunice " " Sarah I P " "	4	1	4		1	1	7
Daniel N. Drake Cyntha P " " Lucy " " Sylvia Johnson	4	1	4		1	1	7
Dames Teamsters Martin Crandell John O Augers Wm. B. Maddock							
Louvrin H Dame, Catain, Elkhorn, July 1846							

6th Ten

	Family	Wagon	Oxen	Horses	Cows	Calves	Sheep
Erastus Bingham Lucinda " " Sanford " " Meria L " " Willard " " Edwin " " Brigham " "							
Thomas Gates Sen	8	3	12	2	4	10	18

Jacob Gates Mary Gates Elizabeth C Gates	3	1	4	2			
Mary Freeman Ed " " Roxana " " Oscar " "	4	1	6	2			
Olive B. Bingham Olive L " " Erastus P " "	3						
Rodney Badger Nancy " " Nancy M " " Lydia " "	4	1	4	1	1		
Maria Bleliss Louisa " "	2	1	4		1	1	
Fielding Garr John T " " Wm H " " Abel W. " " Caroline M " " Sarah Aaura " " Mary V " " Benjamin T " "	8	3	12	2	5	5	40
Erastus Bingham Capt 6th Ten, Elkhorn July 23 1846							

7th Ten

	Family	Wagon	Oxen	Horses	Cows	Cattle	Sheep
Wm Mathews Elizabeth " " Thomas " " Elizabeth " " John " " E C " " M C " " N C L " " E L " "	9	4	12	3	6	3	

Pyton Nowlin Merrert " " B W " " I P " " Aanda " " Wm. C. " " V. C " " N P " " IV Now, black Samuel Now[lin], black Lovina Now[lin], black	11	4	16	Mules 8 Horses 1		8	
David Calvert Wm " " Wm " " Ann " " Ellen " " Samuel " " Nancy " " Farah " " M T " " Julia " "	10	1	6		2	2	
Elkhorn July 23, 1846. Wm Mathews Cap., P W Nowlin Clerk								

[140] [July] 24.[32] The remainder of our company get over the [Elkhorn] river a little before noon.[33] After calling our company to gather to give the necessary instructions for travling and camping at night, ^on

---

32. The Platte River flows easterly nearly the length of Nebraska and empties into the Missouri River thirty miles south of where Winter Quarters was later located. Soon after leaving their assembly location by the Elkhorn, Newel's company reached the Platte. From then on, their route ran near and parallel to the Platte's north side to where the Loup Fork River flows into it. For more than a week, the wagons followed the poorly defined road until they met up with the Miller and Emmett companies on August 2 at the Loup Fork River. Regarding the sites where Newel's company watered, traveled, and camped, we have been unable to match them to sites identified by William Clayton in his trail guide written the next year. At the Loup Fork River, finding a fording place proved difficult.
33. Solomon Hancock estimated the Elkhorn River was 150 feet wide. Journal History, July 23, 1846.

~~the bank of plat river~~ ^we started on [and] traveled a bout eight miles and encamped for the night ^on the bank of ~~a stre~~ of the Plat river^.

[July] 25. We traveleld untill about noon when we stoped to bate our teams. Here we called the Brethren to gather to learn whether our guns ammunition and all necessary preparations for our safety were were in readiness. After which we traveled until it was time to camp for night.

[July] 26. Sunday we traveled about half the day when we found a suitable place to stop. Encamped by a slue. The water was not quite as good as the river yet it was passable. We stayed until the following morning ^by the river side^;

[July] 27. Again resumed our journey. The day was verry warm. Just after we stoped at evening, an ox kicked Brother Call and injured his leg considerable. He is Capt of the first ten in our camp. Brother Shepherd called on me to baptize him for the recovery of his health, this evening.[34] He has been ill for some time. This is quite a commodious place for camping. The ^west^ bank of a strem called [ ] forms a wall on one side, situated so that our long circle of waggons ^oposite^ forms a safe and bautiful pasture for our ^cattle^ to graze upon. With in this circle is a cool clear spring of water which cannot fail to invite the weary traveller to stop and refresh him self. Fire wood is allso on hand. In fact it seems as if nature has done her best to provide a comfortable hotel for emigrants here on this lone long wilderness priarie.

Our course has been west or ^n^early so from Elk horn. We crossed the bottom a distance of a bout 8 miles where ~~where~~ we struck the Platt. The soil is generally sandy an fertile. The grass in many places two feet higher than the cattles backs. Up to this time the bottom has been quite level. We have not ascended or decended at any one place four feet. There is but little timber and that is altogather willow and Cottonwood or principally so. The Platt is considerable of a river. Its bottom is sandy. The water is clear and good. The bank generally commodious fo watering cattle.

---

34. Baptism for health was a healing ritual common among Latter-day Saints from 1841 to 1922; see Stapley and Wright, "'They Shall Be Made Whole,'" 69–112.

[July] 28. We traveled a bout 14 or 15 miles. The road lays so far from the river we were obliged to drive the whole distance without water. Here we again struck the river and found good place for camping. We passed some verry singular looking sand banks, which verry much resembled an Oregon Company at the distance. The sand is from them. The traveller could hardly be convinced to the contrary. We had a refreshing shower last night which coled the air so that it has been comfortable traveling to day.

[July] 29. Traveled about 10 miles. Found a place to water Cattle a bout 6 miles from where we stayed last night. Our encampment to night is on the rivr just ~~were~~ at the entrance of a little branch which heads between the road and river.

[July] 30. We got our teams in readiness in good season and started on. ^The soil has been sandy and rather barron. ~~tody untill towards~~ [Toward] evening it appeared mor^. Traveled untill about noon. We found water for our Cattle just at the entrance of a creek which we soon forded.

While here resting and bateing our Cattle some of the brethren requested that a meting should be called, which was done. Meting was opened by brother Solomon Hancock [141] singing one of his California songs. It appeared that the organization of our Company had not been fully understood by some, which togather with the misunderstanding of some things or jeaousies that some thing wrong would exist, had rather disturbed the feelings of some few of our company. We gave all an opportunity to exppress their feelings. The Captains ^proposed^ ordrs and regulations for the Camp, but there seemed to be rather a division of feelings among the brethren and our meting broke up rather in confusion. ^~~a young man who was with us but had never~~

Just after this meting closed, John T Garr, a young man who was with us but had never been baptixed, came to me and requested me to administer the ordinance to him which I did. We got our teames in readiness and again pursued our journey. It so happened that we did not find water at a suitable hour for camping, which greatly disturbed the uneasy spirit that had showed its self at the above mentioned meting. Some wanted to stop without water, while others insisted it would not injure our teams so much to drive an hour after dark as it would to stop with out ~~wood~~ water.

In the midst of this, Solomon Hancocks boy fell from his waggon and broke his arm. The forward teamsters were not apprized of tis accident until they had come near to Beaver Creek where they designed to stop.[35] It was thought expedient to go on there as there ~~had~~ ^were^ some sick in the forward ~~teams~~ ^waggons^ who verry much needed water. This gave great dissatis with some. Suffice to say some went on and others stoped with out wood or water while their Children were crying with thirst. We arrived a[t] the Creek bout ten in the evening where we found a good place to water our Cattle and ^a^ convenient place for camping, making a distance of travel for the day about 18 miles.

[July] 31. The remainder of our company came up. After breakfast we called the brethren to gather with a determination to have an understanding of all matters pertaining to our journey, and if there ~~there~~ was any root of bitterness in our camp to root it out and plant a root of peace and union instead thereof. Capt Miksel spoke first of the necessity of there being a union of feelings ~~and~~ among us. After which I arose and after setting forth in ^short^ the organization of the Church and showing the strength and power of union and the necesity of this Camp ^~~and alls the present organization of this Company~~^ being agreed and acting for one general good, not only for the preservation of our horses and cattle but allso that we ourselves ^may^ enjoy the Spirit of God ^and^ continually have his presence with us and his angels to go before us. That we may be kept from the power of the destroyer and not fall a prey ^to any enemy^ or be overcome with any evil. I endeavored to give the brethren a correct understanding of the organization of this Company and the great benefit it would be to all that were faithful in performing the ^journey^, it being recorded on the Church record [of] president Youngs first company regularly organized to cross the mountains.

---

35. This likely is what William Clayton's guide calls Beaver River, which he says is 103 miles from Winter Quarters and about ten miles from the old Pawnee village, where Bishop Miller was at work. See Kimball's edition of Clayton, *Emigrants' Guide*, 44–45.

I wanted them to act like men and be valient in all that is [142] entrusted to us, for if we do not prove ourselves faithful in this expedition we cannot expect to be entrusted with more ~~of~~ ^or^ be counted faithful stewards over what he hath ^~~been~~^ commited to us. Not ^only^ so but it would greatly facilitate the emigration here after if we accomplished the journey this season so that we can put in and raise good crops the coming year, as it would supercede the necesity[of] carrying a years provision over the mountains as we have to at the present time.

After I had finished my remarks, Capt Holbrook arose and said he fully coincided with with what had ^been^ said and exhorted the Brethren to be careful to give heed to Council and to be faithful and diligent in what was commited to them. After which we called a vote to ascertain whether they would all agree to lay aside all jealousies and hardness, and after haveing a full understanding of the design of this Company and our feelings and designs towards each other, ~~we cal~~ we wanted to know whether the officers and organitation should stand as they now are or as president ^Young^ has organized us. To which they voted unanimously. ~~I now felt return thanks to my heavenly Father for the union that has been effected among us. we now commenced to r~~ [Then] when the following resolutions unanimously adopted: Resolved that we unanimously uphold ~~the~~ our officers & that we are Satisfied with our present organization & also that we go on in union & ley all feelings that have existed in consequence of missunderstanding ^some two or three week previous^.

Soon after our meting closed, George Miller, who had gone a head and had stoped about 6 miles beyond, had heard we were at this place and came to see us. He said ^Charles Crissman [Crismon], Capt of his 50 who had returned from the Springs [Cold Springs] with us, fetched directions to him from ~~President Young to~~^ President Young [who] had sent instructions to him to Preside over us and that we should wait until his Com were ready to go on, which would detain us a number of days. And this being ^contrary^ to any directions President Young gave us, it was agreed by our Co unanimously that I should go back and see President Young. Miller said he would go with me.

The next day, [probably August 1], soon after we stoped, Miller sent a messenger to our Camp requesting all the Capts of our Co to come to his Camp to council with him, which we did. He agreed to be at our Camp the next day at ten oclock to go with me to see President Young. Next day [August 2] he arrived about noon, said he had concluded to send Mr. [John] Kay and not go himself.

Kay and myelf started on our mission and arrived at the springs [Cold Springs] about noon on Tuesday [August 4]. The Camp there were just starting to find a location up the Missourie river where they can winter their their Cattle. He [Brigham Young] and his council attended to our business so that we started the next day about non for our Camp. Arrived there in safety about 5 in the evening on Friday [August 7]. Crisman had given Miller wrong information with respect to our Com[pany]. But, it was so late in the season it was deemed [143] wisdom for us to stop and winter in the vicinity of the Pawnee village, by the Council there.[36]

August 1[1846] our ^Camp^ drove up to the loup fork of Platt distance about 5 miles here we stoped until Tuesday the 4 [of August] to set our waggon tire and do such blacksmithing as was needful for our journey, when the Camp drove up the river about 4 miles, where they forded the river it with safety.[37]

About two miles distant from where they forded the river was an old missionary station. The Indians there were of the Pawnee nation who were mostly out on a buffalo hunt. A little before we came to this place the Sue Indians with whom the Pawnees had for some time been at variance had burnt the Pawnees Village and drove the Missionaries away.[38] Bishop Miller was stoped with his Company at the old Missionary Station. He said he had contracted with the Missionaries for grain, Iron, and so forth, which they had left, and [he] advised that our Co should take as much of the same in to their waggons as they passed as they could hall. Accordingly they did so and all things seemed to move well. We all safely forded the river and camped for the night.

---

36. These next comments Newel should have prefaced with "meanwhile, while I was gone, my company." He refers to his company as "they" and tells what his company did on dates when he was not there: August 4 to 7.
37. On August 4, Newel left to consult with President Young.
38. Bennett, *Mormons at the Missouri*, 85.

This evening [August 4] Brother Kimball's Co arived to the river where they camped, intending soon to cross the river.

[August] 5 this morning Bishop Miller sent an express to our camp requesting an interview with us before we proceeded on our journey. Caps Holbrook and Micksel, with such of our Co as were not for to guard our Cattle and waggons, went to his Camp. They agreed to wait untill his [Miller's] Company got over the river and allso Brother Kimballs.

It was thought advisable that the Camp move about 2 miles up the river to find ^a^ more convenient place for camping, in which move a spirit of division showed its deformed head. Capt Lewis who had been appointed Seargeant of the guard gave orders for the move, when Capt Micksel, he being the only one of the three first Capts [of Newel's seven tens] present, ~~present~~ gave contrary Orders to what Capt Lewis had done, saying Miller had given him orders to arrange the Company as he was doing. All and started on with his team, ordering the Capts. of tens to follow with their respective Cos. Micksel drove on to the designed ground for camping and commenced forming a circle. Capt Lewis saw the move and rode up, requested Capt Micksel to stop, ^turn back^ and form according to his directions. But Micksel utterly refused and Commanded the whole Co. to come to him. Capt Kempton ^and Co^ of the second ten, and who had charge of my teams in my absence, followed Miksel. Some others fell in the rear. Lewis refused to join the circle formed by Micksel and formed another a few yards distant, where the remainder of the Co stoped ^with him^. Capt Holbrook did not arrive with ^his^ waggons untill after dark.

This evening both Kimballs and Millers Company drove up to our camp, after which the respective Capts of each Co [144] met and attended to placing sufficient guard around our encampment and see that all necessary preparations were made for our safety, as the Pawnees had just returned from their hunt. It was thought nessesary to be well prepared lest they might attack us. The night was clear and beautiful.

[August] 6. Capt Miller gave orders to have all the Iron returned, which our Co. had taken. The request was promptly attended to. This evening the Indians robed two of our boys, who were out on guard for the safety of our Cattle, of their arms and guns and mules. A posse of men went in pursuit of them but to no purpose.

[August] 7.³⁹ There was nothing special occured, all hand were waiting for the ^return^ of their messengers who had been sent to president Young. They [we] returned in the evening and brought the following information ^and letter^ from him. The following is a Copy of the letter:

Omaha Nation—7 miles west of the Missouri River, Aug 4ᵗʰ 1846.

> To Bishop George Miller & the Capts of fifties at Pawnee Village and west. Brethren. We have received Bro Miller's letter of the first inst and shall endeavor to comply with his request concerning the Ordinance. We are satisfied that it will be impratical for any ~~of you~~ Company to attempt to cross the mountains this fall. S[o] you will have to be diligent to prepare for winter. so as to secure feed for your Cattle before the Idians fire the priaries to gather the buffalo which they will do as soon as the grass is dry enough. it will be wisdom for you to settle as near to gather as circumstances will permit to be able to resist any encroachment from the Indians. When the weather is cold enough you may do well to send back some of your teams to winter in this vicinity and load up with grain ^again^ in the spring. We shall be able to come up with you before you will ^want to^ leave Pawnee in the spring. If there is a good chance for hey [hay] at Pawnee perhaps ~~you~~ you can not do better than to stop in that neighborhood.
>
> You are on fishing ground & have the best ^of^ nets & hooks, spread your nets cast your hooks & live by fishing & leave not one ~~foot~~ ^inch^ of ground unoccupied. You have long wanted a chance to fish & now you can spend the winter at it and no telling how many you may salt before spring. You will do well organize a council of twelve men to superintend the affairs of the Church with you temporally and spiritually and see that offenders

---

39. Newel and John Kay returned on August 7, meaning their round-trip to Brigham Young's camp and back took them three days. They, the "messengers," brought with them a letter from Young and the council, which is a revision of the August 1 letter noted above that apparently was not sent.

of the law ~~are brought~~ do not go unpunished. We would suggest ~~that~~ for your consideration that Geo Miller Preside assisted by Newel Kight. Joseph Holbrook Titus Billings Hiram Clark [145] Bartholomew, Anson Call ^David Lewis, John A Miksel, Solomon Hancock^ Erastus Bingham, Thomas Gates, Charles Chrisman, A^s^el Lathrop. or sufficient of them to constitute the Quorum of twelve.[40]

According to the best knowledge we have, we are now disposed to recall our recommendation of making to Larime or the [Grand] island. This for there is danger of the fires cutting off supplies for your stock and we would like to you as near as that we may visit ~~you~~ each other occasionally this winter. We speak some things in parables.[41] Brothers Knight and Kay will explain. In behalf of the council. we remain your brethren in the Gospel. Signed Brigham Young President, Willard Richards Clerk

P.S. Bro Miller you will ~~do well~~ secure the kegs in your possession keep them safe let them not be opned til further instructions.[42]

[146] August Saturday the 8th. A Conference was called to give all an opportunity of hearing the above named letter, allso to give them ~~an oppo~~ ^the necessary^ instructions for organizing and establishing our selves in a proper manner for our safety and best intrest. Alls[o] to give all an opportunity to act for them selves in regard to accepting those men suggested by Brother Young to act as a council for this People. They were all unanimously voted for by the congregation and a general union seemed to prevail, not withstanding their disappointment in regard to crossing the mountains this year.

[August] 9. The Brethren assembled under a commodious arbor which they ^had^ erected to sheild them from the schorching sun to worship God and attend to such instructions as would be for our good and advantage both spiritually and temporally. Meting was opened by singing, prayer by Brother Anson Call, after which Brother Hiram Clark

---

40. Bennett, *Mormons at the Missouri*, 86–87.
41. This reference to speaking in parables might refer to the fishing instructions, which might refer to Indians, not fish, who could be taught that winter.
42. *Kegs* probably refers to gunpowder.

gave a short address, followed by Brother Gates and President Miller, who gave us particular instructions in regard to giveing heed to Council and the necessary course we would have to pursue in order to gain the friendship of the Indians and sustain ourselves and cattle through the winter. After which several of the Brethren expressed their satisfaction with the council and advice which had been given. Meting closed by singing and prayer by Brother Solomon Hancock.

BIBLIOGRAPHY

Almond, Philip C. *Heaven and Hell in Enlightenment England*. Cambridge: Cambridge University Press, 1994.

Anderson, Devery S., and Gary James Bergera, eds. *Joseph Smith's Quorum of the Anointed, 1842–1845: A Documentary History*. Salt Lake City: Signature Books, 2005.

———, eds. *The Nauvoo Endowment Companies, 1845–1846: A Documentary History*. Salt Lake City: Signature Books, 2005.

Ashurst-McGee, Mark. "Moroni: Angel or Treasure Guardian?" *Mormon Historical Studies* 2, no. 2 (Fall 2001): 39–75.

Ashurst-McGee, Mark, David W. Grua, Elizabeth Kuehn, Alexander L. Baugh, and Brenden W. Rensink, eds. *Documents, Volume 6: February 1838–August 1839*. Vol. 6 of the Documents series of *The Joseph Smith Papers*, edited by Ronald K. Esplin, Matthew J. Grow, and Matthew C. Godfrey. Salt Lake City: Church Historian's Press, 2017.

"Awful Assassination of Joseph and Hyrum Smith." *Times and Seasons* 5 (July 1, 1844): 560–61.

Bibliography

Backman, Milton V., Jr. *The Heavens Resound: A History of the Latter-day Saints in Ohio, 1830–1838.* Salt Lake City: Deseret Book, 1983.

Barlow, Ora Haven, comp. *Family Recordings of Nauvoo, 1845 and Before, Including Minutes of the First LDS Family Gathering.* Salt Lake City: O. H. Barlow, 1965.

Baugh, Alexander L. "A Rare Account of the Haun's Mill Massacre: The Reminiscence of Willard Gilbert Smith." *Mormon Historical Studies* 8, no. 1 (2007): 165–71.

Baugh, Alexander L., and Michael S. Riggs. "'That They Might Rest Where the Ashes of the Latter-day Saints Reposed': The Far West Missouri Burial Ground." *Mormon Historical Studies* 9, no. 1 (2008): 135–42.

Beam, Alex. *American Crucifixion: The Murder of Joseph Smith and the Fate of the Mormon Church.* New York City: Public Affairs, 2014.

Bennett, John C. *The History of the Saints: Or, An Exposé of Joe Smith and Mormonism.* Urbana and Chicago: University of Illinois Press, 2000.

Bennett, Richard E. *Mormons at the Missouri: Winter Quarters, 1846–1852.* Norman, OK: University of Oklahoma Press, 1987.

Bernauer, Barbara Hands. "Still 'Side by Side': The Final Burial of Joseph and Hyrum Smith." *John Whitmer Historical Association Journal* 11 (1991): 17–33.

Black, Susan Easton. *Who's Who in the Doctrine and Covenants.* Salt Lake City: Bookcraft, 1997.

Bradshaw, M. Scott. "Joseph Smith's Performance of Marriages in Ohio." *BYU Studies Quarterly* 39, no. 4 (October 2000): 7–22.

Brown, Samuel. *In Heaven as It Is on Earth: Joseph Smith and the Early Mormon Conquest of Death.* New York: Oxford University Press, 2014.

Buerger, David John. "The Development of the Mormon Temple Endowment Ceremony." *Dialogue: A Journal of Mormon Thought* 20 (1987): 33–76.

Burgess, Harrison. *Labors in the Vineyard.* Salt Lake City: Juvenile Instructor, 1884.

Bushman, Richard. *Joseph Smith: Rough Stone Rolling.* New York: Alfred A. Knopf, 2006.

Cannon, Brian Q. "'Long Shall His Blood . . . Stain Illinois.'" *Mormon Historical Studies* 10, no. 1 (2009): 1–19.

Cannon, Donald Q., and Lyndon W. Cook. *Far West Record: Minutes of the Church of Jesus Christ of Latter-day Saints, 1830–1844.* Salt Lake City: Deseret Book, 1983.

"The Capstone of the Temple." *Times and Seasons* 6 (June 1, 1845): 926.

Bibliography

"Celebration of the Anniversary of the Church." *Times and Seasons* 2 (April 15, 1841): 375–77.

"A Charter Granted to Newel Knight to Erect a Wind Dam in the Mississippi, April 9, 1842." In *Records of the City Council of the City of Nauvoo, Illinois, Commencing A. D. 1841*. Church History Library, Salt Lake City.

Christensen, Clare B. "Before and After Mt. Pisgah." Salt Lake City: privately published, 1979.

Clayton, William. Journals. Church History Library, Salt Lake City.

———. *The Latter-Day Saints' Emigrants' Guide*. St. Louis: Mo. Republican Steam Power Press–Chambers & Knapp, 1818.

"Conference Minutes." *Times and Seasons* 6 (November 1, 1845): 1008–16.

Cook, Lyndon W. *Nauvoo Marriages: Proxy Sealings, 1843–1846*. Provo, UT: Grandin Book, 2004.

"Copy of a Letter written by J. Smith Jr. and Others, While in Prison." *Times and Seasons* 1 (May 1840): 99–104.

Corrill, John. *A Brief History of the Church of Christ of Latter Day Saints, (Commonly Called Mormons;) Including an Account of Their Doctrine and Discipline; with the Reasons of the Author for Leaving the Church*. St. Louis, MO: "Printed for the Author," 1839.

Davidson, Karen Lynn, David J. Whittaker, Mark Ashurst-McGee, and Richard L. Jensen, eds. *Histories, Volume 1: Joseph Smith Histories, 1832–1844*. Vol. 1 of the Histories series of *The Joseph Smith Papers*, edited by Dean C. Jessee, Ronald K. Esplin, and Richard Lyman Bushman. Salt Lake City: Church Historian's Press, 2012.

Davidson, Karen Lynn, Richard L. Jensen, and David J. Whittaker, eds. *Histories, Volume 2: Assigned Historical Writings, 1831–1847*. Vol. 2 of the Histories series of *The Joseph Smith Papers*, edited by Dean C. Jessee, Ronald K. Esplin, and Richard Lyman Bushman. Salt Lake City: Church Historian's Press, 2012.

"Death of Newel Knight," *Deseret Evening News*, May 25, 1907, 6.

Dirkmaat, Gerrit J. "Searching for 'Happiness': Joseph Smith's Alleged Authorship of the 1842 Letter to Nancy Rigdon." *Journal of Mormon History* 42, no. 3 (July 2016): 94–119.

Dirkmaat, Gerrit J., Brent M. Rogers, Grant Underwood, Robert J. Woodford, and William G. Hartley, eds. *Documents, Volume 3: February 1833–March 1834*. Vol. 3 of the Documents series of *The Joseph Smith Papers*, edited by Ronald K. Esplin and Matthew J. Grow. Salt Lake City: Church Historian's Press, 2014.

Bibliography

Document Containing the Correspondence, Orders &C, in Relation to the Disturbances with the Mormons; and the Evidence. . . . Fayette, MO: n.p., 1841.

Esshom, Frank. *Pioneers and Prominent Men of Utah: Comprising Photographs, Genealogies, Biographies.* Salt Lake City: Utah Pioneer Books, 1913.

"Extracts from H. C. Kimball's Journal." *Times and Seasons,* published in installments.

"First Meeting in the Temple." *Times and Seasons* 6 (November 1, 1845): 1017–18.

Flake, Kathleen. "The Development of Early Latter-day Saint Marriage Rites, 1831–1853." *Journal of Mormon History* 41, no. 1 (January 2015): 77–105.

Flanders, Robert B. *Nauvoo: Kingdom on the Mississippi.* Urbana: University of Illinois Press, 1975.

"For the Times and Seasons." *Times and Seasons* 1 (February 1840): 56–57.

Gates, Susa Young. *Lydia Knight's History: The First Book of the Noble Women's Lives Series.* Salt Lake City: Juvenile Instructor Office, 1883.

Garrett, H. Dean. "Disease and Sickness in Nauvoo." In *Regional Studies in Latter-day Saint Church History: Illinois,* edited by H. Dean Garrett, 171–72. Provo, UT: Department of Church History and Doctrine, Brigham Young University, 1995.

Gentry, Leland, and Todd M. Compton. *Fire and Sword: A History of the Latter-day Saints in Northern Missouri, 1836–39.* Salt Lake City: Greg Kofford Books, 2010.

Givens, Terryl L., and Matthew J. Grow. *Parley P. Pratt: The Apostle Paul of Mormonism.* New York: Oxford University Press, 2011.

Godfrey, Matthew C., Brenden W. Rensink, Alex D. Smith, Max H Parkin, and Alexander L. Baugh, eds. *Documents, Volume 4: April 1834–September 1835.* Vol. 4 of the Documents series of *The Joseph Smith Papers,* edited by Ronald K. Esplin and Matthew J. Grow. Salt Lake City: Church Historian's Press, 2016.

Godfrey, Matthew C., Mark Ashurst-McGee, Grant Underwood, Robert J. Woodford, and William G. Hartley, eds. *Documents, Volume 2: July 1831–January 1833.* Vol. 2 of the Documents series of *The Joseph Smith Papers,* edited by Dean C. Jessee, Ronald K. Esplin, Richard Lyman Bushman, and Matthew J. Grow. Salt Lake City: Church Historian's Press, 2013.

Greene, John P. *Facts Relative to the Expulsion of the Mormons or Latter Day Saints, from the State of Missouri, under the "Exterminating Order."* Cincinnati: R. P. Brooks, 1839.

Hafen, A. K. "Samuel Knight: Oct. 14, 1832–Feb. 11, 1910." Washington County Historical Society, March 1960. wchsutah.org/people/samuel-knight1.pdf.

Bibliography

Hales, Brian C. "John C. Bennett and Joseph Smith's Polygamy: Addressing the Question of Reliability." *Journal of Mormon History* 41, no. 2 (April 2015): 131–81.

Hamer, John C. *Northeast of Eden: Atlas of Mormon Settlement in Caldwell County, Missouri, 1834–39*. Independence, MO: John Whitmer Books, 2011.

Harper, Steven C. "'A Pentecost and Endowment Indeed': Six Eyewitness Accounts of the Kirtland Temple Experience." In *Opening the Heavens: Accounts of Divine Manifestations, 1820–1844*, edited by John W. Welch, 327–71. Provo, UT: Brigham Young University Press; Salt Lake City: Deseret Book, 2005.

Hartley, William G. *The 1845 Burning of Morley's Settlement and Murder of Edmund Durfee*. Salt Lake City: Primer Publications, 1997.

———. "1839: The Saints Forced Exodus from Missouri." In *Joseph Smith: The Prophet and Seer*, edited by Richard Holzapfel and Kent Jackson, 347–90. Provo, UT: Religious Studies Center, Brigham Young University; Salt Lake City: Deseret Book, 2010.

———. "Missouri's 1838 Extermination Order and the Mormons' Forced Removal to Illinois." *Mormon Historical Studies* 2, no. 1 (Spring 2001): 6–27.

———. "Mobbed from Jackson County, Missouri, in 1833." In *History of the Saints: The Mormon Wars*, edited by Glenn Rawson and Dennis Lyman, 21–47. American Fork, UT: Covenant Communications, 2014.

———. *Stand by My Servant Joseph: The Story of the Joseph Knight Family and the Restoration*. Salt Lake City: Deseret Book, 2003.

Hedges, Andrew H. "'All My Endeavors to Preserve Them': Protecting the Plates in Palmyra, 22 September–December 1827." *Journal of Book of Mormon Studies* 8, no. 2 (1999): 14–23.

———. "Joseph Smith, Robert Foster, and Chauncey and Francis Higbee." *Religious Educator* 18, no. 1 (2017): 89–111.

Hill, Donna. *Joseph Smith: The First Mormon*. New York: Doubleday, 1977.

History of Carroll County, Missouri. St. Louis: Missouri Historical Company, 1881.

"History of Joseph Smith." *Times and Seasons*, published in installments.

Jennings, Warren Abner. "Zion Is Fled: The Expulsion of the Mormons from Jackson County, Missouri." PhD diss., University of Florida, 1961.

Jenson, Andrew. "Dewitt." *Historical Record* 7 (1888): 603–8.

———. *Latter-day Saint Biographical Encyclopedia: A Compilation of Biographical Sketches of Prominent Men and Women in the Church of Jesus Christ of Latter-day Saints*. 4 vols. Salt Lake City: Andrew Jenson History Company, 1901–36.

Bibliography

Jessee, Dean C., ed. *The John Taylor Nauvoo Journal*. Provo, UT: Grandin Book, 1996.

Jessee. Dean C. "Return to Carthage: Writing the History of Joseph Smith's Martyrdom." *Journal of Mormon History* 8 (1981): 3–19.

Johnson, Clark V., ed. *Mormon Redress Petitions: Documents of the 1833–1838 Missouri Conflict*. Provo, UT: Religious Studies Center, Brigham Young University; Salt Lake City: Deseret Book, 1992.

Johnstun, Joseph D. "'To Lie in Yonder Tomb': The Tomb and Burial of Joseph Smith." *Mormon Historical Studies* 6, no. 2 (2005): 163–80.

Journal History of the Church of Jesus Christ of Latter-day Saints, Church History Library, Salt Lake City.

Juvenile Instructor Office. "Newel Knight's Journal." In *Scraps of Biography*. Vol. 10 of the Faith-Promoting Series. Salt Lake City: Eborn Pocket Books, 2010.

Kenney, Scott G., ed. *Wilford Woodruff's Journals, 1833–1898*. Midvale, UT: Signature Books, 1983–85.

Kimball, James L., Jr. "A Wall to Defend Zion: The Nauvoo Charter." *BYU Studies* 15 (Summer 1975): 491–97.

Kirtland High Council Minute Book. MS 3432. Church History Library, Salt Lake City.

Kirtland Camp. Journal. Church History Library, Salt Lake City.

Laub, George. "George Laub's Nauvoo Journal." *BYU Studies* 18 (Winter 1978): 151–78.

Lee, John D. Diary. Robert Glass Cleland, and Juanita Brooks, eds. *A Mormon Chronicle: The Diaries of John D. Lee, 1848–1876*. 2 vols. San Marino, CA: Huntington Library, 1955.

Leonard, Glen M. *Nauvoo: A Place of Peace, a People of Promise*. Salt Lake City: Deseret Book, 2002.

Lum, Kathryn Gin. *Damned Nation: Hell in America from the Revolution to Reconstruction*. New York: Oxford University Press, 2014.

MacKay, Michael Hubbard. *Sacred Space: Exploring the Birthplace of Mormonism*. Provo, UT: Religious Studies Center, Brigham Young University; Salt Lake City: Deseret Book, 2016.

MacKay, Michael Hubbard, and Gerrit J. Dirkmaat. *From Darkness unto Light: Joseph Smith's Translation and Publication of the Book of Mormon*. Provo, UT: Religious Studies Center, Brigham Young University; Salt Lake City: Deseret Book, 2015.

BIBLIOGRAPHY

MacKay, Michael Hubbard, Gerrit J. Dirkmaat, Grant Underwood, Robert J. Woodford, and William G. Hartley, eds. *Documents, Volume 1: July 1828–June 1831.* Vol. 1 of the Documents series of *The Joseph Smith Papers*, edited by Dean C. Jessee, Ronald K. Esplin, Richard Lyman Bushman, and Matthew J. Grow. Salt Lake City: Church Historian's Press, 2013.

MacKay, Michael Hubbard, and Nicholas Frederick. *Joseph Smith's Seer Stones.* Provo, UT: Religious Studies Center, Brigham Young University; Salt Lake City: Deseret Book, 2017.

"Martyrdom of Joseph and Hyrum Smith." *Millennial Star* 46 (May 12, 1884): 301–2.

Moore, Beth Shumway. *Bones in the Well: The Haun's Mill Massacre, 1838, a Documentary History.* Norman, OK: Arthur H. Clark, 2006.

Nauvoo High Council Minutes, LR 3102 22, Church History Library, Salt Lake City.

Oaks, Dallin H. "The Suppression of the *Nauvoo Expositor.*" *Utah Law Review* 9 (Winter 1965): 862–903.

Oaks, Dallin H., and Marvin S. Hill. *Carthage Conspiracy: The Trial of the Accused Assassins of Joseph Smith.* Chicago: University of Illinois Press, 1975.

Parkin, Max H. "A History of Latter-day Saints in Clay County, Missouri, from 1833 to 1837." PhD diss., Brigham Young University, 1976.

Petersen, Lauritz G. "The Kirtland Temple." *BYU Studies* 12, no. 4 (1972): 400–409.

Porter, Larry C. "The Colesville Branch and the Coming Forth of the Book of Mormon." *BYU Studies* 10 (Spring 1970): 365–85.

———. "The Colesville Branch in Kaw Township, Jackson County, Missouri, 1831 to 1833." In *Regional Studies in Latter-day Saint Church History: Missouri*, edited by Arnold K. Garr and Clark V. Johnson, 281–311. Provo, UT: Department of Church History and Doctrine, Brigham Young University, 1994.

———. "Organizational Origins of the Church of Jesus Christ, 6 April 1830." In *Regional Studies in Latter-day Saint Church History: New York*, edited by Larry C. Porter, Milton V. Backman, and Susan Easton Black, 149–64. Provo, UT: Brigham Young University Press, 1992.

———. "Reverend George Lane—Good Gifts, Much Grace, and Marked Usefulness." *BYU Studies* 9 (Spring 1969): 321–40.

———. "A Study of the Origins of the Church of Jesus Christ of Latter-day Saints in the States of New York and Pennsylvania, 1816–1831." PhD diss., Brigham Young University, 1971. Also available as Larry C. Porter, *A Study of the Origins of the Church of Jesus Christ of Latter-day Saints in the States of New York and Pennsylvania, 1816–1831.* Dissertations in Latter-day Saint History. Provo, UT: Joseph Fielding Smith Institute for Latter-day Saint History; Provo, UT: BYU Studies, 2000.

Pratt, Parley P. *History of the Late Persecution Inflicted by the State of Missouri upon the Mormons.* Detroit: Dawson and Bates, 1839.

Pratt, Parley Parker, Jr. *Autobiography of Parley Parker Pratt.* Salt Lake City: Deseret Book, 1938.

Pratt, Parley P., Newel Knight, and John Corrill. "'The Mormons' So Called." *The Evening and the Morning Star, Extra*, February 1834, 1–3.

Riggs, Michael S. "The Economic Impact of Fort Leavenworth on Northwestern Missouri, 1827–1838." *Restoration Studies* 4 (1988): 124–33.

Robinson, Ebenezer, and Don Carlos Smith. "A History, of the Persecution, of the Church of Jesus Christ, of Latter Day Saints in Missiouri." *Times and Seasons*, published in installments.

Rogers, Brent M. "To the 'Honest and Patriotic Sons of Liberty': Mormon Appeals for Redress and Social Justice, 1843–44." *Journal of Mormon History* 39, no. 1 (2013): 36–67.

Rogers, Brent M., Elizabeth A. Kuehn, Christian K. Heimburger, Max H Parkin, Alexander L. Baugh, and Steven C. Harper, eds. *Documents, Volume 5: October 1835–January 1838.* Vol. 5 of the Documents series of *The Joseph Smith Papers,* edited by Ronald K. Esplin, Matthew J. Grow, and Matthew C. Godfrey. Salt Lake City: Church Historian's Press, 2017.

Romig, Ronald E. *Early Jackson County, Missouri: The "Mormon Settlement" on the Big Blue River.* Independence, MO: Missouri Mormon Trails Foundation, 1996.

Rowley, Dennis. "The Mormon Experience in the Wisconsin Pineries, 1841–1845." *BYU Studies* 32, nos. 1–2 (1992): 119–48.

Smith, Andrew F. *The Saintly Scoundrel: The Life and Times of Dr. John Cook Bennett.* Urbana: University of Illinois Press, 1997.

Smith, Hyrum. "To the Saints Scattered Abroad." *Times and Seasons* 1 (December 1839): 20–24.

Smith, Joseph. History, 1838–1856, Volume A-1. Church History Library, Salt Lake City.

———. History, 1838–1856, Volume B-1. Church History Library, Salt Lake City.

———. History 1838–1856, Volume C-1. Church History Library, Salt Lake City.

———. Journals. Church History Library, Salt Lake City.

Bibliography

Smith, Joseph, to Thomas Ford, January 21, 1844. Joseph Smith Collection. MS 155. Church History Library, Salt Lake City.

Shipps, Jan, and John W. Welch, eds. *The Journals of William E. McLellin, 1831–1836*. Urbana and Chicago: University of Illinois Press; Provo, UT: BYU Studies, 1994.

Stapley, Jonathan A., and Kristine Wright. "'They Shall Be Made Whole': A History of Baptism for Health." *Journal of Mormon History* 34, no. 4 (Fall 2008): 69–112.

Taylor, Mark H. *Witness to the Martyrdom: John Taylor's Personal Account of the Last Days of the Prophet Joseph Smith*. Salt Lake City: Deseret Book, 2017.

Walker, D. P. *The Decline of Hell: Seventeenth-Century Discussions of Eternal Torment*. Chicago: University of Chicago Press, 1964.

Wayment, Thomas A., ed. *The Complete Joseph Smith Translation of the New Testament: A Side-by-Side Comparison with the King James Version*. Salt Lake City: Deseret Book, 2005.

INDEX

A

Abbot, Lewis, 65
adultery, 138
Allen (client), 133
Allen, Inez Knight, xxii
Allen, James, 190n27
Allen, Lucette, xxii
Allen, Robert, xxi–xxii
Allen, Robert E., xxii
Alley, John, 140
Andrus, Joseph, 167
Aniss, J. C., 125, 128
apostasy, 105, 137–39
Atchison, Capt., 60, 62, 70

B

Bailey, Calvin, 81–84
Baldwin, Caleb, 111–13
baptism for the dead, 158
Beaver River, 203
Bennett, D., 54
Bennett, John Cook, 132, 137–38
Benson, Ezra T., 130, 184
Bent, Samuel, 185
Bible, lost books of, 30
black man, burned alive, 93–94
Boggs, Lilburn, 59–60
Book of Mormon, 10, 20
Brown, Benjamin, 124–25
Brunson, S., 79–81

C

Cahoon, Reynolds, 144–45
Caldwell County, Missouri. *See also* Far West, Missouri
Newel leaves, 115–18

Index

Caldwell County, Missouri (*continued*)
    Newel's life in, 95
    persecution in, 106–13
    Saints begin to leave, 114–15
    Saints move to, 97–98
Call, Anson, 201, 208
Camp of Israel, 179n18, 181, 182n21
Chase, Darwin, 113
cholera, 69, 70–71
church, to be built in Independence, 51
Church of Jesus Christ of Latter-day Saints, The. *See also* persecution
    growth of, 20
    organization of, 10–11
    reorganization of, 71
    understanding foundational years of, xii–xiii
Clapp, Benjamin L., 153, 154–56
Clark, General, 113
Clark, Hiram, 208–9
Clay County, Missouri
    Newel returns to, 90, 91–94, 96
    Newel's debts in, 99, 100–101
    Newel's employment in, 101, 104, 105–6, 113–14
    Newel's life in, 95, 97
    Newel's property in, 66, 99
    persecution in, 62, 97
    Saint-owned property in, 66n150
    Saints flee to, 60–61
    Saints leave, 97–98
    Saints settle in, 61–71, 75
Cleveland, Alanson, 56
Cleveland, Anna Slade, 172
Cleveland, Henry A., 172
Coe, Joseph, 37
Colburn, Emily, 45–46n107

Cold Springs Camp, 190n28, 204, 205
Colesville Branch
    driven from Independence, 63, 65
    establishment of, xiv
    Joseph Smith visits, 42
    leaves for Kirkland, 32–33
    letter from Joseph Smith and John Whitmer to, 17–19, 26–28
    relocates to Independence, 35–37
Commerce, Illinois, 123
Conference(s)
    in Fayette, 21–23, 31
    in Independence, 41
    in Kirtland, 33–35
    in Mount Pisgah, 186
    in Nauvoo, 157–58, 169
    at Pawnee village, 208–9
Copley, Leman, 33
Corrill, John, 57
Council Bluffs, Iowa, 189–93
Cowdery, Oliver, 50
Crismon, Charles, 204
Culver, Aaron, 24, 39n91
Culver, Esther Peck, 39n91, 75, 76, 97, 98, 99
Cutler, John Alpheus, 143, 144–45

D

dam, 148n48
DeMille, Anna Knight, 4, 7, 166
DeMille, Freeborn, 7, 104, 137, 170, 172, 173, 174–75, 185–86
DeMille, Oliver, 28
De Witt, Missouri, 108–9
Dibble, Philo, 56–57
Doniphan, Alexander, 112
Dunklin, Daniel, 50, 53, 60, 63–64

Index

E

Elkhorn River, 193–200
endowment, 70, 71
Enoch, prophecy of, 30
Evening and the Morning Star, The, 43, 46, 49
evil spirit(s)
    cast from Martha Long Peck, 24–25
    cast from Newel Knight, xiv, 14
exodus. *See* Mormon exodus

F

family order, 144–45, 148–51
Far West, Missouri
    Hyrum Smith speaks in, 101
    Newel leaves, 115–18
    Newel moves to, 102–3
    Newel visits, 101–2
    persecution in, 106–13
    Saints begin to leave, 114–15
    settlement of, 105
Fishing River revelation, 69
Fordham, Elijah, 132–33, 163–65, 167
Freemasons, 28
Fulmer, David, 185

G

Garr, John T., 202
Gates, Susa Young, xxiii
Gibbs, Luman, 113
Gilbert, Algernon Sidney, 37, 53, 57, 58, 70
Gilbert, Elizabeth, 45–46n107
Gilliam, 69
Gould, John, 50

Grand Island, 192, 208
Greene, John P., 106
Grover, Thomas, 186, 187–88

H

hail, stops oncoming mob, 67–68
Hale, Isaac, 17
Hale, Johnathan Harriman, 164
Hancock, Solomon, 202, 203, 209
handkerchiefs, healing through, 126n8, 127–28
Harris, Emer, 23
Harris, George Washington, 129
Harris, Martin, 37
Harvey, Don, xxii
healing(s)
    of Electa Peck, 33
    of James Knight, 129–30
    of Lydia Knight, 106, 127–28
    of Martha Long Peck, 24–25
    of Newel Knight, xiv, 14
    of Oliver DeMille, 28
    performed by Joseph Smith, 125–26n8, 127–28
    of Philo Dibble, 56–57
    through handkerchiefs, 126n8, 127–28
Hebrew school, 86–87
Hibbard, D., 130
Higbee, Chauncey, 138n32
Higbee, Elias, 136
Higbee, Isaac, 164
high council, xv, 71, 76–77, 102, 137–38, 143, 150n50, 154, 164
"History of the Church," 1–2
Holbrook, Joseph, 193, 204, 206
Hunter, Edward, 164

Index

Huntington, William, 183, 184
Hyde, Orson, 50, 169, 187

I

Independence, Missouri. *See also* Jackson County, Missouri
    church to be built in, 51
    commerce in, 42
    construction begins in, 38
    first winter in, 39–41
    mill in, 50
    persecution in, 47, 48–50, 52–62
    Saints flee, 58–60
    Saints relocate to, 35–37
    settlement in, 42
Indians, 187–88, 205, 206–7

J

Jackman, Levi, 131, 132, 136
Jackson County, Missouri. *See also* Independence, Missouri
    expulsion from, 2
    persecution in, 64–66
Jesus Christ, visits Kirtland Temple, 89
Johnson, Aaron, 185

K

Kay, John, 205
Kempton, Jerome Boneparte, 193
Kempton, Maria, 193
Kimball, Heber C.
    called to high council, 71
    in Council Bluffs, 190
    and Mormon Battalion, 191
    and mountain expedition, 192n30, 193

Kimball, Heber C. (*continued*)
    in Mount Pisgah, 184
    Newel Knight borrows from diary of, 2, 67n151
    speaks in Nauvoo, 153–54
Kimball, Hiram S., 168
Kirtland, Elisha, 76
Kirtland, Ohio
    courtship of Newel and Lydia Knight in, 77–79
    gathering in, 32–33
    Hebrew school in, 86–87
    Lydia Knight goes to, 85–89
    marriage of Newel and Lydia Knight in, 79–81
    Newel arrives in, 76
    Newel's activities in, 86–87
    Newel's time in, 73–74
    Newel travels to, 76
Kirtland Temple, 76, 86, 87, 89–90
Knight, Betsey, 144, 145
Knight, Eli, 75
Knight, Elizabeth, 4
Knight, James Philander, 103, 125, 126, 128–30
Knight, Jesse, xv–xvi, 155
Knight, Joseph, Jr., 4, 66, 104, 144–45, 147, 149
Knight, Joseph, Sr.
    background of, xiii–xiv, 4–5
    and family order in Nauvoo, 144–45, 148–51
    fares well in Clay County, 113
    following death of wife, 39n91
    health of, 154
    remarriage of, 65
    sealed to Phoebe, 165–67

Index

Knight, Lydia Goldthwaite Bailey
    biography of, 74, 81–86
    as caretaker of Newel's papers, xix, xx
    courtship with Newel, 77–79
    employment of, 123
    gives birth to children, 99, 103, 141, 155
    healing of, 127–28
    history of, xxiii
    illness of, 97, 98, 99–100, 106, 126–28
    and illness of James Knight, 128–29
    marriage to Newel, xv, 79–81, 86
    and Mormon exodus, 167, 172, 184
    nurses sick, 126
    patriarchal blessing of, 90–91
    and revision of Newel's journals, xxii–xxiii
Knight, Nahum, 4, 7
Knight, Newel
    chastised by church officers, 45–46n107
    as Church elder, 74, 88
    courtship with Lydia, 77–79
    death of, xv
    debts of, 99, 100–101, 104, 132–33, 163–65, 167, 168–69
    early years and family of, 4–5
    evil spirit cast from, xiv, 14
    financial challenges of, 137, 139–40
    happiness and familial harmony enjoyed by, 8–9
    healings performed by, 24–25, 28, 33, 56–57
    illness of, 75, 76, 97, 133, 136, 137
    injury of, 105–6
    journals and autobiography of, xi–xiii, xvii–xxiii, 1–3

Knight, Newel (*continued*)
    life of, xiii–xvi
    marriage to Lydia, xv, 79–81, 86
    marriage to Sally, 5–6
    revelation for, 35, 47n111
    as witness of Restoration, xii–xiii
Knight, Newel, Jr., 141, 155
Knight, Phoebe Crosby Peck, 65
Knight, Polly (Newel's sister), 4, 20–21
Knight, Polly Peck (Newel's mother), xiii–xiv, 4, 36, 39
Knight, Sally Colburn
    confirmation of, 16
    death of, xv, 75–76
    gives birth to Samuel, 43–44
    loses infant, 10
    marriage of, xiii, 5–6
Knight, Sally (Lydia's daughter), 99
Knight, Samuel, 43–44, 76, 96

L

Lake Erie, 33
Law, Wilson, 137
Leonid Meteor shower, 60n132, 61
Lewis, David, 206
Louisville, Kentucky, 93–94
Lyman, Amasa, 182, 183

M

McCarty, Richard, 53, 57
McLellin, William E., 40n94, 57, 58
McRay, Alexander, 111–13
Mexican-American War, 190n27. *See also* Mormon Battalion
Mikesell, John A., 193, 203, 206

225

Index

Miller, George, 192n30, 204–5, 206, 207, 209
mill(s)
   to be built in Salt Lake Valley, 184
   in Caldwell County, 99–101, 103, 114
   in Clay County, 97, 104, 105–6
   in Independence, 50
   in Jackson County, 66
   in Kirtland, 96
   in Nauvoo, 124–25, 128–29, 130–33, 136–37, 140–43, 147, 149, 167
   Newel advised to leave work in, 6
Mississippi River, 122, 127, 143n38, 148n48, 171, 175
Missouri River camp, 57–71, 75
Missouri War, 106–13
Morley, Isaac, 57, 103
Mormon Battalion, 190–91
Mormon exodus
   Knight family leaves Nauvoo, 174–79
   Knight family's route, 179–82
   mountain expedition, 192–209
   plan for, 171
   on prairie, 180–81
   preparations for, 166–74, 188
   stop in Council Bluffs, 187–93
   stop in Mount Pisgah, 182–87
mountain expedition, 192–209
Mount Pisgah, 182–87

N

Nauvoo, Illinois. *See also* Mormon exodus
   apostasy in, 137–39

Nauvoo, Illinois (*continued*)
   business dispute with Elijah Fordham in, 163–65
   general conference in, 157–58, 169
   illness and healings in, 125–28, 129–30, 133
   Joseph Knight Jr. returns to, 147
   Knight family disagreements in, 165–67
   Knight family leaves, 174–79
   mills in, 124–25, 128–29, 130–33, 136–37, 140–43, 147, 149, 167
   Newel arrives in, 124
   Newel builds house in, 154–56
   Newel's hardships in, 137, 139–40
   Newel's occupation in, 124–25, 128–29, 130–33, 136–37
   notable deaths in, 135
   persecution in, 156–57, 170
   prosperity in, 131–32, 134–35, 152, 153–54, 155, 156
   teachings on family order in, 144–45, 148–51
Nauvoo Temple, 134, 143, 151–52, 157–59, 163, 173, 175
Noble, Joseph Bates, 167

P

Page, Hyrum, 21–22
Partridge, Edward, 30, 37
Pawnee village, 205–9
Peck, Electa, 25, 32–33
Peck, Ezekiel, 25
Peck, Hezekiah, 24–25, 44, 166
Peck, Martha (Polly) Long, 24–25, 44–45
Peck, Phoebe Crosby, 165–67

INDEX

Peck, Sarah, 166
persecution
   in Caldwell County, 106–13
   in Clay County, 62, 97
   faith in face of, 63
   in Harmony, 16–17, 20–21, 23–24
   in Jackson County, 47, 48–50, 52–62, 64–66
   in Nauvoo, 156–57, 170
   rain and hail stops oncoming mob, 67–68
   redress for, 60–62, 63–64, 68–69
Peterson, Ziba, 28–29
Phelps, Morris, 113
Phelps, W. W., 37, 50, 58
Pitkins, Brother, 122–23
Pixley, 48
Platte River, 200n32, 201–2, 205–6
Polk, James K., 190n27
Pottawattamie Indian village, 187–88
Pratt, Orson, 26
Pratt, Parley P., 28–29, 41n95, 54, 63, 113
Prindle, James, 99
printing press, 103

Q

Quincy, Illinois, 123

R

revelation(s)
   Fishing River revelation, 69
   given to Joseph Smith and Sidney Rigdon, 29–30
   given to Parley Pratt and Ziba Peterson, 28–29

   Martha Long Peck speaks against, 44–45
   for Newel Knight, 35, 47n111
Rich, Charles C., 184
Rich, Henrietta, 166
Richmond, Missouri, 66–67
Rigdon, Sidney, 29–30, 37, 38, 111–13, 148
Robinson, Ebenezer, 142
Robison's mill, 105–6
Rolfe, Samuel Jones, 131, 133, 164–65

S

sawmill, 130, 141–43, 167
Scott, John, 141–42, 143
Searcy, Colonel, 68–69
seer stone, 22
Segget, 122
Shearer, Norman, 113
Shepherd, Ransom, 201
Sherwood, Henry Garlick, 130
Silvers, 54
Slade, Aaron, Jr., 172
Slade, Benjamin, 170, 172
Slade, Clark, 96
Slade, Mary Knight, 172
Smith, Caroline, 152
Smith, Don Carlos, 135
Smith, Emma, xiv, 16
Smith, George A., 182, 183
Smith, Hyrum
   arrest of, 111–13
   goes to Collusive, 23, 24
   goes to Kirtland, 32
   holds prayer meeting, 24
   imprisonment of, 123–24

Smith, Hyrum (*continued*)
    and marriage of Newel and Lydia Knight, 78–81
    martyrdom of, xv, 145–47, 152–53, 175, 189
    settles in Commerce, 123
    speaks in Far West, 101
    visits Colesville Saints, 19
    warned against Freemasons, 28
Smith, John, 187
Smith, Joseph, Jr.
    and apostasy in Nauvoo, 138–39
    arrest of, 111–13
    arrives in Far West, 102–3
    arrives in Independence, 41
    attends funeral of Polly Peck Knight, 39
    birth and early years of, 8
    casts evil spirit from Newel, xiv, 14
    character of, 5, 11–12
    Collinsville trial of, 11–14
    and conversion of Lydia Knight, 84–85
    and healing of James Knight, 129–30
    heals Lydia Knight, 127–28
    helps Newel finish mill, 100
    history of, xii, xvii–xviii, 1–2
    illness of, 125–26n8
    imprisonment of, 123–24
    and Kirtland Temple, 89
    Knight family's relationship with, xiii–xiv
    letter to Colesville Saints, 17–19, 26–28
    and marriage of Newel and Lydia Knight, 78–81, 86

Smith, Joseph, Jr. (*continued*)
    martyrdom of, xv, 145–47, 152–53, 175, 189
    Newel visits, 16, 124
    and organization of Church, 10–11, 42
    persecution of, 9–10, 13
    and problems with Hyrum Page, 21–22
    resettles in Independence, 37
    and Restoration, 7
    revelation given to, 29–30
    settles in Commerce, 123
    speaks with Colonel Searcy, 68–69
    successor to, 148
    threats against, 108
    and translation of Book of Mormon, 10
    visits Colesville Saints, 19–20
Smith, Joseph, Sr., 32, 90–91
Smith, Lucy Mack, 33n76
Stowell, Josiah, 12
Stringham, Esther Knight, 4, 7, 39n91
Stringham, Harriet, 125, 126
Stringham, William, 7

T

Thompson, Jonathan, 12
Thompson, R. B., 135
tongues, gift of, 84–85

W

Wellis, Ira T., 64–65
West (hired hand), 115
Whitmer, Christian, 50, 55
Whitmer, David, 19

INDEX

Whitmer, John, 16, 17–19, 26–28
Whitney, Newel K., 51, 53
Wight, Lyman, 63
Wilder, Doctor, 125, 126
Williams, Frederick G., 89
Willis, Ira, 167
Wilsons Store, 55
Worcester, Missouri, 118, 122–23

Y

Young, Brigham
   and beginning of Mormon exodus, 166

Young, Brigham (*continued*)
   in Council Bluffs, 190
   leaves Far West, 117–18
   and Mormon Battalion, 190, 191
   and mountain expedition, 192, 193, 204, 205, 207–8
   in Mount Pisgah, 184, 186
   and Nauvoo Temple, 152, 158–59
   requests Knight house for printing press, 103
Younger, Charles, 99

Z

Zion's Camp, 2, 66, 75

ABOUT THE EDITORS

Michael Hubbard MacKay is an associate professor in the Department of Church History and Doctrine at Brigham Young University. He is lead historian and editor of *Documents, Volume 1* in Documents series of *The Joseph Smith Papers* and the author or coauthor of several books, including *From Darkness unto Light: Joseph Smith's Translation and Publication of the Book of Mormon*; *Joseph Smith's Seer Stones*; and *Sacred Space: Exploring the Birthplace of Mormonism*. He is also the editor of several anthologies, including *Producing Ancient Scripture*.

William G. Hartley was a research historian for BYU's Joseph Fielding Smith Institute for Church History. He received bachelor's and master's degrees from Brigham Young University and completed doctoral course work at Washington State University. Hartley was a leading authority on Church history, having worked at the Church History Department and on the Joseph Smith Papers Project. His books have focused on family history research and histories of specific families and nineteen-century Latter-day Saint history. He and his wife, Linda, have six children.